JOHN TOD

John Tod as a young man. (Courtesy BCARS, PDP117)

JOHN TOD
REBEL IN THE RANKS

Robert C. Belyk

Horsdal & Schubart

Horsdal & Schubart Publishers Ltd.
Victoria, BC, Canada

Cover: "The Parting of the Brigades, 1826 (Yellowhead Pass)." HBC's 1938 calendar illustration by Walter J. Phillips. Courtesy of the Hudson's Bay Archives, Provincial Archives of Manitoba. (HBCA Reference, P-402 (N9034).

This book is set in Classic Garamond Book Text.

Printed and bound in Canada by Kromar Printing Limited, Winnipeg.

Canadian Cataloguing in Publication Data

Belyk, Robert C., 1944-
    John Tod

Includes bibliographical references and index.
ISBN 0-920663-42-7

1. Tod, John, 1794-1882. 2. Fur traders—British Columbia—Biography. 3. Victoria (B.C.)—Biography. 4. Vancouver Island (B.C.). Legislative Council—Biography. I. Title

FC3822.1.T62B44 1995   971.1'02'092   C95-910857-2
F1088.T62B44 1995

Contents

To the memory of
my mother,
Etta May Belyk

PREFACE

My interest in fur trader John Tod began five years ago when I was preparing a collection of British Columbia ghost stories. Tod's house, which was begun in 1850, was said to be haunted, and I wanted to include this tale in my book. As I read and reread the newspaper accounts of the haunting, it seemed that the master of Tod House had led an extraordinary life. He had been among the first Europeans to be posted by the Hudson's Bay Company to the territory that became British Columbia. The difficulty that faced me, however, was that much of Tod's biography in the press was ambiguous and contradictory. I wondered, what was the real story about John Tod? After completing the ghost book, I began to research the life of the Hudson's Bay Company fur trader, a task that would occupy me for more than four years.

The relationship between biographer and subject — even a subject dead more than a century — is always somewhat unsettling. I have spent many hours with Tod, and only his family and closest friends could rightly claim to have known him better. As the reader will discover, Tod had many faults, but there was also much to redeem him. Now that *Rebel in the Ranks* is finished I feel I'm losing an old friend, for Tod's image is no longer as vivid as it was during the preparation of the manuscript.

Writing a biography about the early Europeans who settled this land is not easy. Pioneer societies were not the best guardians of their history — there was always so much else to do. Moreover, few of the new arrivals saw themselves as contributors to history, with the result that their all-important journals, letters, and diaries have not been preserved. It is therefore fortunate that so many of John Tod's letters to his friend and longtime correspondent, Edward Ermatinger, have survived, and that the one-time Hudson's Bay officer was a conscientious preserver of fur-trade history. As a prolific letter writer, Ermatinger corresponded with not only Tod, but many other important figures of the fur trade. Today, many of these valuable documents are retained by the British Columbia Archives in Victoria.

That Tod lived long enough to be recognized as something of a relic encouraged others to also seek out and record his story. For that reason, I am grateful to early historian H. H. Bancroft and Victoria journalist Gilbert M. Sproat. Both men were aware of the trader's importance to British Columbia's early settlement and each made an effort to preserve Tod's history.

Finally, that great 19th-century corporate entity, the Hudson's Bay Company under the direction of Governor George Simpson, can be credited with saving many parts of Tod's story. A former clerk himself, Simpson built his frontier empire upon paper, and the letters between the governor and field officers such as Tod make interesting reading. It is through these and other sources that our picture of Tod emerges.

My approach to the material presented here should be mentioned. Although by current standards Tod had an indifferent education, his portrait in these pages is of a man of uncommon wit and intelligence whose writings offer a unique view of the fur trade. Yet it will be noted that while Tod was a master of the pithy phrase, his letters at times appear almost incomprehensible. The reason is his cavalier attitude toward punctuation. In his letters, the period is seldom used, while the comma is applied indiscriminately. Thus, to render Tod's quotes understandable, it has sometimes been necessary to change his punctuation.

It is impossible to thank everyone who contributed to the completion of this book. I would like to single out, however, David Mattison and Brian Young of the B.C. Archives and Records Service for their patient assistance in what must have appeared as my never-ending search for the most obscure documents. The work of the late B.C. archivist, Madge Wolfenden, whose research on Tod and his family made my own task so much easier, is also to be acknowledged. I would also like to thank Ann Morton and her staff at the Hudson's Bay Company Archives in Winnipeg, as well as the staffs of the National Archives and the National Library in Ottawa, for their many hours of help.

Closer to home, I'd wish to thank Ada Con and the staff of the Terry Fox Library in Port Coquitlam for their help in obtaining several microfilm sources. I owe special thanks also to Charlie Richmond, whose knowledge of the Fort McLeod area gave me some idea of the conditions that the Hudson's Bay employees faced there, John Adams of the British Columbia Heritage Properties Branch for his cooperation during this project and Brenda Loney who kindly opened her home to me and my wife.

My thanks to sister-in-law Sheri for her comments regarding the first three draft chapters, particularly because, as a busy writer with a family, she faced many other time demands. A simple thanks seems inadequate for my wife, Diane, who has had to endure my four-year obsession with Tod. As my first editor and critic she has always offered the wisest counsel. And also, thanks to publisher and editor Marlyn Horsdal who has now worked her magic on two of my manuscripts.

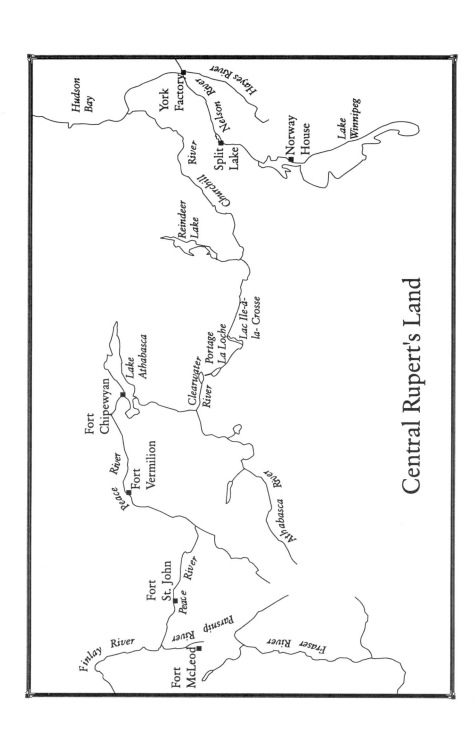

Central Rupert's Land

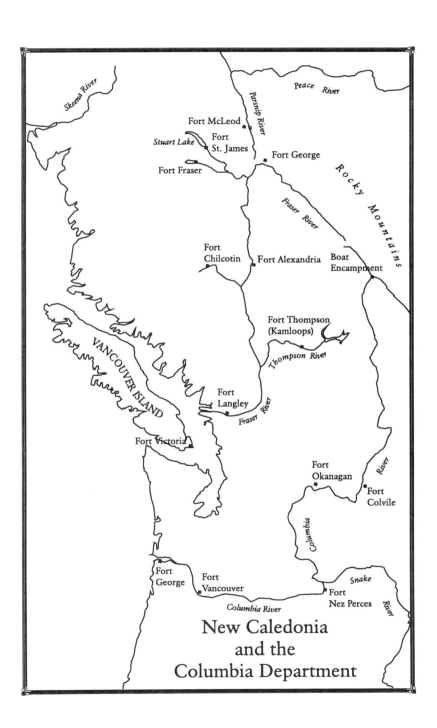

Skeena River

Peace River

Parsnip River

Fort McLeod

Stuart Lake

Fort
St. James

Fort George

Fort Fraser

Rocky Mountains

Fraser River

Fort
Chilcotin

Fort Alexandria

Boat
Encampment

Fort Thompson
(Kamloops)

Thompson River

VANCOUVER ISLAND

Fort
Langley

Fraser River

Fort Victoria

Fort
Okanagan

River

Fort
Colvile

Columbia

Fort
George

Fort
Vancouver

Snake

Fort
Nez Perces

River

Columbia River

New Caledonia
and the
Columbia Department

Introduction

Hudson's Bay Company fur trader John Tod never fit the romantic image of the rugged frontiersman. Even in the freshness of youth, Tod was something of a misfit. He had a large nose, oversized mouth and unruly hair, untamed by brush or comb. By 19th-century standards he was unusually tall, standing almost five feet, ten inches, with a lank frame and long limbs making him appear gawky. It was as if the parts did not fit entirely together. When he was in motion, which was often, Tod seemed oddly disconnected from the world around him. According to his friend, Victoria newspaper editor Gilbert Malcolm Sproat, "Tod always seemed to be somewhat separated from his environment, at any rate not half attached to it."[1]

Strangely, Tod was able to turn his awkwardness to advantage. When he spoke, his wildly moving arms and thumping fists were as much a part of his presentation as what he said. The American historian Hubert Howe Bancroft, who interviewed Tod not long before the latter's death in 1882, came away much impressed by the old trader. In his characteristically florid style, Bancroft later wrote about the eccentric occupant of Tod House:

> Had the mouth been small, the mighty brain would have burst; as it was, the stream of communication once set flowing, and every limb and fibre of the body talked, the blazing eyes,

the electrified hair, and the well-poised tongue all dancing attendance. ... Tod could no more tell his story seated in a chair than he could fly to Jupiter while chained to the rock of Gibraltar; arms, legs, and vertebrae were all brought into requisition, while high-hued information, bombed with oaths, burst from his breast like lava from Etna.[2]

Bancroft paints an engaging portrait of Tod, but there is a hint of something darker. He was capable of using his wild energy to overwhelm and intimidate those who opposed him. During an argument, he rarely backed down and usually demanded the last word. He was also vain, self-centred, jealous of those who possessed power and deeply antagonistic toward authority. Yet it is this independence of spirit that is so fascinating. Despite rising to the rank of chief trader, Tod remained an outsider. He was an individual unhappy with his lot, but bound, by almost feudal ties, to his employer, the Hudson's Bay Company.

Tod probably would not have regarded himself as a soldier, but indeed, within British Imperial policy that was the role he and his fellow employees played. With its military forces spread thin, the government relied on mercantile companies to raise its flag over its more remote territories. In the far northern reaches of the New World, the Hudson's Bay Company was Britain's physical presence — an army which occupied a vast hinterland in the name of the British Crown. In exchange for its services, the Company extracted the furs of beaver, marten, mink, otter and bear.

Yet it is a mistake to assume that the interests of Company and state were identical. The Hudson's Bay was not at war with nor did it wish to conquer the indigenous peoples of North America. It depended on them as partners in commerce. Relations between the Europeans and Indians were occasionally uneasy, for the gap that separated the cultures was great, but bloodshed on a major scale was relatively rare because both sides in the barter for furs felt that they had something to gain. Given the hardships of aboriginal life, the goods of European manufacture became important for survival. For the Company, despite many attempts to diversify beyond its dependence on furs, the sale of pelts remained its chief source of profit. The picture of an uneasy but effective European-Indian partnership would dissolve only with the demise of the Company's power in the west.

Looking back almost two centuries, one may ask why so many young Scottish youth chose to join the ranks of the Hudson's Bay

Company? There are many answers, of course. Certainly the idea of foreign adventure was a factor, for the untamed wilderness of North America with its "savage" Indians must have seemed exotic, indeed. More important, though, for the Scottish lower and middle classes, the fur trade was the only means up the economic ladder. Despite what some historians have claimed, by 19th-century standards, the Hudson's Bay paid its officers and servants well. But the money was well earned, for as John Tod quickly discovered, existence at the edge of the northern frontier tested the extent of human endurance.

* * * * *

As a social being, Tod was influenced by events within the vast sweep of history. The western world, during the last decade of the 18th century, was experiencing much social upheaval. In America, the 13 colonies had thrown off the colonial yoke, while in France the forces of revolution had sent the much-hated Louis XVI to the guillotine. In Britain, a revolution of a different sort was under way: the old cottage or "putting-out" system of manufacture was being replaced by factories. The resultant shift of population from the towns and villages of rural England to cities had a profound effect on Britain's social structure. By 1790, the Industrial Revolution had moved beyond the northern counties of England into the Lowlands of Scotland.

In the Highlands, though, it was not industry but agriculture that was in the midst of cataclysmic change. From 1750 on, there had been steady growth in the population along the western coast, which, in turn, put pressure upon the limited resources of Scotland's agricultural land. In an area where poor farming methods were combined with unpredictable weather and ineffective transportation, the lot of the average crofter was becoming increasingly desperate. In 1782-83, 1806-7 and 1811, famine was widespread throughout the western Highlands. As early as the middle of the 18th century, Scotland had actually become a net importer of grain.

For Scotland's large landowning families, economic reality was eroding their position of privilege — they were receiving little rent from their struggling tenants. Gradually, they began turning their land to more profitable enterprises. Large-scale sheep rearing was introduced to the Highlands as early as 1760; however, it was the Napoleonic Wars beginning in 1799 that eventually sealed the fate of the croft system. With the large British navy and army providing a ready market for cheaply produced mutton, Scottish landowners moved to evict tenants and replace crofters with sheep, and those resisting the coming of sheep often suffered the full force of the law.

Although small plots had been worked by the same families for centuries, crofters had no legal right to tenancy beyond the terms of their fixed lease. In some cases, they had not even that protection — they were driven from the land without notice. The changes in the Scottish countryside were, in many cases, dramatic. Between 1801 and 1831, the population of the Highland parish of Kildonan decreased by 80%. On the island of Harris in the Hebrides alone, seven townships were cleared at once. In a single blow, a 40-mile stretch of coastline was emptied.

Not all of Scotland's noble families ignored the suffering of their displaced tenants. One such aristocrat was Thomas Douglas, Earl of Selkirk. As one of Scotland's great landowners, Selkirk saw no benefit in ending the Highland clearances. "Ever since the introduction of sheep-farming into the Highlands," he wrote in 1805, "there has been a very unequal struggle between the former possessors of the land and the graziers. It would be difficult, perhaps, to quote an instance where tenantry have been able to offer a rent equal to that which their competitors would have given."[3] Instead, he favoured mass emigration of dispossessed Highlanders to the British colonies in North America, and by 1810 he had established two small settlements, at Baldoon in Upper Canada and on Prince Edward Island. Although not a complete success, the venture encouraged Selkirk to consider more ambitious plans. He was aware that control of much of the northern interior of North America was in the hands of one great commercial concern: the old and ailing Hudson's Bay Company.

Established in London in 1670 by England's Charles II for the purpose of exploiting the natural resources of the vast wilderness of Rupert's Land, the Hudson's Bay prospered for many years. However, because the original charter was vague about where Rupert's Land began and ended, competing traders were expanding their activities into the largely unexplored northern territories. The Hudson's Bay's chief rival was the North West Company, a loose association of inland fur traders — the "wintering partners" as they were known — and their Montreal agents who, after 1795, began to seriously threaten the London company's existence.

It is difficult at first to understand why the Hudson's Bay was facing such trouble, for the older company had a significant advantage over its Montreal-based rival. Through their great depot at York Factory on Hudson Bay, in the heart of the fur country, the Company had a shorter route by sea to the London fur market. By contrast, the North West Company had to employ brigades of voyagers paddling swift birchbark canoes along a dozen rivers and lakes to reach the rich Athabasca fur grounds from Montreal. The overland distance was nearly half a continent. As historian Chester Martin notes: "No fewer than 60 large lakes, 130 portages where canoes and goods were both taken from the water, and 200 smaller *décharges* where goods alone had to be carried, were to be counted in the voyage from St. Anne on the Ottawa to the Athabasca."[4]

The Nor'Westers did their best to improve their transportation routes. Sailing ships were built to ferry goods across Lakes Huron, Michigan and Erie, locks were constructed at Sault Ste. Marie and a road was planned between York (later Toronto) and Penetanguishene. But no matter what improvements the Canadians made, they could not overcome the Hudson's Bay's geographical edge. William McGillivray, a North West Company senior partner, calculated the Bay's transportation costs at about half those of his company.

This handicap, however, eventually gave the Nor'Westers an advantage. From the beginning of the fur trade, the servants of the London-based company had never established an extensive system of inland posts, waiting instead for the Indians to bring the furs to their major depots around Hudson Bay. The Nor'Westers, on the other hand, were pushing back the continental frontier in search of furs. They gained control of the vast Athabasca district, the rich inland heart of British North America.

In 1814, the Hudson's Bay Company's London Committee moved to meet the Nor'Wester threat by authorizing the establishment of a chain of its own forts in the Athabasca. Two years later, Hudson's Bay Chief Factor John Clarke established Fort Wedderburn on Lake Athabasca. It was soon evident that the Company was ill-prepared for the aggressive tactics of their North West opponents. Unlike the Canadians, the men of the London company had known only the relative comfort of the posts around Hudson Bay and not the harsh environment of the Athabasca.

The Nor'Westers' mastery of the forest instilled a pride unmatched by the employees of the bureaucratic Hudson's Bay and soon the exploits of the men who warred against the Hudson's Bay became the stuff of North West legend. Two such romanticized figures were Samuel Black and Peter Skene Ogden. In fact, both men were little more than common bullies whose activities in any other region of the British Empire might have earned them a hangman's rope. In this lawless northern wilderness, however, the two were heroes to their North West compatriots.

While Black and Ogden were the most famous marauders, many other Nor'Westers kept up the harassment of the Hudson's Bay men. Indeed, so successfully were they able to dominate the fur trade that by the beginning of the 19th century, the Canadians were exporting over three times the cash value of furs to London as their rival. The difficulties faced by the Hudson's Bay were reflected in the performance of Company stock. During the 1790s, Hudson's Bay dividends averaged eight per cent, but by the first few years of the next century, returns fell to four per cent and, after 1808, no dividends were paid at all. By this time, Company share prices were being discounted as much as 40%.

In 1810, Selkirk's associate Andrew Wedderburn was elected to the Hudson's Bay Company's governing Committee. In this role Wedderburn was influential in determining the new direction of the Company. The Committee — which did not include Selkirk, although he was a major player behind the scenes — at last turned its attention to making the Hudson's Bay Company once more a profitable enterprise. Almost immediately, Wedderburn proposed a retrenchment program to cut Company losses. The vast Hudson's Bay territories would be divided into two administrative districts, the Northern and Southern Departments, each under the control of a superintendent. In order to make the operations more efficient, Hudson's Bay chief factors, the highest ranking field positions, would participate in a profit-sharing scheme. However, there was more to Wedderburn's ideas than cost cutting. Acting upon the advice of a turncoat North West Company clerk, Colin Robertson, Wedderburn was prepared to resort to the aggressive tactics that worked so well for the Hudson's Bay Company's enemy.

One of the most controversial items to come before the Committee was Selkirk's plan to establish a colony at Red River. As in earlier Selkirk settlement schemes, the Red River was to be a colony for dispossessed crofters, but in this case the undertaking would be on a grand scale. Stretching from Lake Winnipegosis in the north to the headwaters of the Red River in the south, from the Winnipeg River in the east to beyond the present eastern boundary of Saskatchewan in the west, the 116,000 square miles of the original grant was actually larger than the entire island of Britain, and five times the size of Scotland.

The intention, according to a promotional circular, was to reduce the Company's dependence on European provisions then said to be eating up dividends normally paid to shareholders. The agreement between Selkirk and the Hudson's Bay seemed to be to the advantage of both parties. As well as selling the Company the surplus of its fields, the colony was to supply 200 men a year, and in turn, the Company was to provide the isolated settlement with transportation and supplies from the outside world. As far as the Hudson's Bay was concerned, however, Red River was of strategic importance in its on-going war with the North West Company. The terms of the agreement would make the immigrants dependent on the Hudson's Bay and hostile to those working against the interest of the London company. With the colony located on the canoe routes inland, the crofters controlled the rivers vital to trade in the northwest.

In case the Montreal concern had difficulty understanding the close ties between the Company and the colony, Miles Macdonell, the ex-army officer Selkirk chose as governor of the colony, was also given a commission as an officer of the Hudson's Bay Company. The North West Company objected to the scheme, warning of dire consequences should it go ahead, but neither Selkirk nor the governing Committee of the Company listened.

In 1811, the Hudson's Bay and Selkirk jointly recruited over 100 clerks and labourers in Scotland and Ireland for service with both the colony and the Company. Owing to a late start, however, the men were forced to winter over at York Factory. They did not reach the site of what was to become the Red River colony until the following spring. Later that same year, the first settlers arrived and the stage was set for the long battle between the Nor'Westers and its agents, on the one hand, and the Company and the colony, on the other.

While conflict occurred throughout the vast northern wilderness, the Red River colony became the focus of the worst violence, for both organizations could call upon a reserve of civilian soldiers — corporate militias owing their fidelity to one or the other great power of the fur trade. Long before Selkirk considered establishing a colony at Red River, the Metis, descendants of the unions between French fur traders and Cree Indians, had settled the area. For years, these people laboured for the Nor'Westers, and the North West Company held their allegiance. For the Metis, whose flourishing culture resembled neither its French nor Indian antecedents, the new immigrants were also a threat, a fact which did not escape the notice of North West fur traders who rallied them against the settlers.

Skirmishes between the warring camps continued intermittently until 1816, the year of the infamous "Massacre at Seven Oaks." In the late spring, a small army of Metis on horseback confronted colonial Governor Robert Semple and 20 of his men on foot. When the battle was over, the governor and 19 of his compatriots were dead.* The Metis, under the command of Cuthbert Grant, claimed only one casualty. Charges and counter-charges would continue for years, but what gradually became certain was that Selkirk's dream of a great crofter colony in the heart of North America was effectively over. The colony would continue to grow slowly, only because many employees retired there, taking their Indian wives. Unlike the people of Scotland or the Canadian colonies, the inhabitants of Red River were racially tolerant. By 1824, only 20% of the inhabitants at Red River were crofters; the remainder were Indians, mixed-blood settlers or retired Company servants.

Although the battle had gone to their opponents, the real winner at Seven Oaks was the Hudson's Bay Company. Selkirk, who blamed the North West Company for the murder of his men, took on his opponents in the courts, and the Canadians, who could not match the aristocrat's financial resources, were eventually driven by legal costs to the edge of bankruptcy. Exhausted, the Nor'Westers agreed to amalgamation with the London company in 1821. With the end of its rival, the Hudson's Bay Company expanded and consolidated its position in the hinterland of North America.

The period between 1821 and 1846 was the golden era of the Hudson's Bay. For the first time in its history, the Company had effective control of the vast, fur-producing territories of North America, an area of 3,000,000 square miles. One important reason for Hudson's Bay Company's success after 1821 was the London Committee's choice of George Simpson as overseas governor. More bookkeeper than brigadier, Simpson did much to turn the money-losing fur trade into a profitable investment for the London stockholders. Simpson had just the right personality for the job, possessing, in the words of historian E. E. Rich, "a strange mixture of obsequiousness and assertiveness which made him acceptable to

---

* Among historians, the exact number of dead has been the subject of some dispute.

his masters and to his followers alike."[5] Under the governor's stewardship, the Company reduced costs, while at the same time, it expanded activity in the west.

John Tod's insights into the characters of the major players within the fur trade, including Simpson himself, have been frequently quoted by Hudson's Bay historians, but this is only part of the story, for there is also a personal dimension. In this unfolding 19th-century drama, Tod was actor as well as audience.

Chapter One

THE NE'ER-DAE-WELL IS BACK

Although the exact date has been lost to history, John Tod was born sometime in October 1794, in Dumbartonshire, Scotland. His first home was a small cottage on the shore of the long, narrow lake named Lomond, but he was not there long. When he was still young, his family moved a few miles farther south to a house on the banks of the Leven River, a seven-mile stream joining the southern end of Loch Lomond with the Clyde River at the town of Dumbarton. The relocation probably meant his father was closer to work — the elder Tod was a senior clerk in a small cloth-printing factory. During the late 18th century, many textile concerns located in the Vale of Leven. The Leven River was an excellent source of lime-free water necessary for bleaching cloth, and the Levenbank area near the village of Balloch was the site of a number of "print-fields," where dye patterns were added to fabric produced in factories nearby.

The Todd family — John probably adopted the "Tod" spelling of his surname later to distinguish himself from other John Todds serving with the Hudson's Bay — was an early beneficiary of the increasing industrialization of the Scottish Lowlands after 1780. Although Tod would later claim to be ashamed of his parents' poverty, the family was by no means destitute. Despite the number of children — John was the eldest of nine — the Todds were reasonably well off by the measure of the day and his childhood was

1

materially comfortable. Given the father's position, the Todds would be among the more important families in the village. Thomas, Tod's youngest brother, even had the advantage of a university education, which a generation earlier was something usually attained only by the upper classes.

Tod's education, though, was more limited. Like other Lowland boys, young John attended a parish school. Elementary education in Scotland was neither free nor universal, but the cost was not excessive. By the turn of the 19th century, educators said, with some pride, "even day-labourers give their children a good education."[1] Yet, what was meant by a "good education" remained open to debate. Critics pointed out that access to schools did not necessarily mean the gaining of a high quality education. Often classrooms were without such essentials as maps or globes and, sometimes, even blackboards.

Moreover, the system itself was incapable of accommodating students such as Tod who were bright, but also challenging. Parish schools, certainly, were not places fostering the free exchange of ideas. Learning was strictly rote, with much of the school day devoted to the memorization of Bible verse and Latin text. These subjects held little interest for Tod — he preferred arithmetic, English language and natural history — and it was not long before he quit class to embark on what he later claimed was his own program of self-study. In old age, Tod recalled few happy memories of his early schooling.

Tod's problems also went beyond the classroom. As was the case with most Lowlanders, Tod's parents were Presbyterians, pious Christians who strictly kept the Lord's Day. While these early followers of the 16th-century French reformer, John Calvin, had begun as dissenters against Catholicism, there was little room for dissent within the sect itself. The tenets of the church were a strict rejection of the pomp and ceremony of Rome, and this bleak vision of the world has long maintained its particular appeal in Scotland. Concerning his own childhood experiences in rural Scotland early in this century, author Angus MacVicar wrote: "Why was everything about our Presbyterian form of worship so stern and black? On the one hand we sang hymns which told to 'let all with heart and voice before his throne rejoice'. On the other hand people came to church and sat in their pews with sombre clothes and grave faces as if they considered joy a mortal sin."[2] In his reminiscences of childhood, Tod wrote little about his own experiences, but from his later letters it is clear that he thought much about the nature of religion, and that he rejected not only the dogma that was the foundation of his parents' faith, but even Christianity itself.

In the Scotland of Tod's childhood, the religious world was tightly integrated with village life. The Scottish family was a structure almost as rigid as the church. With Tod's father away from home for long hours, his mother was the symbol of authority — a role she relished. She was a dour woman whose vitriolic tongue was used to keep everyone at a safe distance, and early on, Tod's rebellious nature meant he was often at odds with her. Once during a lightning storm, when the other children were hiding under their bed covers, he was observed sitting on a rock out in the open, clapping his hands with every crack of thunder. When the storm had passed, Tod overheard his mother telling a neighbour, "That boy has been different from all the others since the hour he was born, and I know not what will become of him. I fear little good."[3]

When he reached working age, Tod was expected to follow in his father's footsteps and take up a career within Scotland's expanding textile industry. After his 16th birthday, his father took him to a cotton goods warehouse in Glasgow where he was given a job as an assistant clerk. Since Glasgow was some miles away, it was necessary for him to move in with his grandparents who lived in the city. For someone as clever as young Tod, the work offered little challenge, so when the company porter became ill he volunteered to take on the man's duties as well as his own. Naively, he believed the additional workload would lead to an increase in salary, but his employer thought otherwise. Instead, the boy was doing two jobs for the same salary. Tod's long-simmering resentment came to a boil one day when his employer told him to deliver some packages — a job the young clerk felt was beneath his position with the company. When Tod resisted, he was fired.

After his dismissal, Tod returned from Glasgow to his parents' home in the Vale of Leven. When he arrived, Tod's mother met him at the door. "So," she said pointing a warning finger, "the ne'er-dae-well is back."[4] In tears, he ran to the print factory where he received a few reassuring words from his father. The next months he spent at home were particularly difficult for him because he had to endure not only the slights of his brothers and sisters, but also the scorn of the neighbours. In the Calvinist burghs of the Lowlands, idleness for whatever reason was neither condoned nor tolerated. It was a great relief, therefore, when he received a letter in 1811 from an uncle in

3

Glasgow informing him that a Mr. McDonald was looking for men to apprentice as clerks for Lord Selkirk's agricultural colony.

Back in Glasgow, Tod met with McDonald,* who was an agent for Thomas Douglas, fifth Earl of Selkirk. Selkirk, Tod discovered, intended to establish an agricultural colony at a place called Red River, which was deep in the Indian territories of North America. At the time of his enlistment, Tod was ignorant of the epic struggle then taking place on the other side of the Atlantic but he hardly cared what dangers he might face on the job. McDonald, for his part, was not particularly helpful, telling Tod only that he might be required to shoot bears. The wages for an apprentice clerk were small indeed — £20 a year with a five-pound increase yearly — but so eager was he to escape his mother's iron rule that he readily accepted the terms of the five-year contract. Besides, he knew that by the time he finished his apprenticeship, he would earn £100 a year, a far better income than he would receive as a clerk in Scotland.

Archibald McDonald, painted by G.A.B. Colthurst. (COURTESY BCARS, PDP40)

* This was probably Archibald McDonald, Selkirk's young protégé, who is known to have been recruiting employees for service at the Red River colony. McDonald later went on have a distinguished career with the Hudson's Bay and to become one of Tod's longtime friends.

Not long after his interview, Tod and a dozen or so other young men, also recruited as clerks, boarded a little ship at Glasgow. They were ferried to the small port of Stornoway, on the island of Lewis off the western coast of Scotland, where they were supposed to leave by Hudson's Bay ship for York Factory.

Before Tod left home, his father presented him with a few pounds in cash together with three books — the Bible, a collection of poems by Burns, and Buchan's *Domestic Medicine.* The money would be of little use in the Hudson's Bay territories known collectively as "Indian Country," but the three volumes would serve him well during the years of hardship ahead. The gifts were his connection to a past separated by distance as well as time, the reminders of people and places almost forgotten. Only twice during his lifetime would Tod return to Scotland.

Once at Stornoway, the boys were billeted in homes around the town. While waiting there, Tod first heard about the North West Company. Townspeople told stories of how the Montreal-based firm had tried to sabotage the Hudson's Bay Company's campaign in Norway where it had hoped to pick up a few recruits. The Nor'Westers had not confined their activities to Norway — in Scotland too, agents for the Canadians had been busy undermining the Hudson's Bay's recruitment efforts. While Tod had not strictly been hired by the Hudson's Bay, there was no doubt that the Canadians regarded Lord Selkirk's men, also, as their enemies.

Earlier that year, a letter had appeared in the *Inverness Journal* warning of the dangers faced by the new recruits. "Mr. Editor, it is my firm belief that many of them will perish before the Spring from excessive cold and from want of food."[5] It was signed, "A Highlander," but the letter was found to be the work of a North West Company partner, Simon McGillivray, who made sure it received wide circulation in the burghs of western Scotland where the Hudson's Bay Company got many of its servants.

The *Edward and Ann*, the ship taking them to the Company territory in Rupert's Land, was delayed — the vessel had battled headwinds all the way from Gravesend — and did not arrive until 17 July 1811. There were already passengers on board, for Selkirk had sent agents to Ireland to recruit labourers for his new colony. The Stornoway recruits were taken on board almost immediately, but the ship remained at anchor. Miles Macdonell, the governor-designate of Red River, who was on board, was supposed to pick up livestock destined for his colony, but there were problems — agents for the North West Company were again causing trouble. A customs official by the name of Reid, a relative of a North West Company partner, Alexander McKenzie, made the task difficult by demanding unnecessary paperwork.

While it was crucial that the vessel take on its cargo and depart before winter set in on Hudson Bay, Macdonell was incapable of taking decisive action. A man of poor judgment and weak character, he had been an unfortunate choice for the important and demanding role of governor of the new colony. The ex-army captain was not equal to the challenge.

After Tod and his companions arrived on board the ship, the Company foolishly tried to save money by giving them a steady diet of oatmeal porridge served without milk. After three days of this food, the recruits were becoming increasingly restless, and one man, by the name of Hamilton, even complained to Captain Thomas Gull. The skipper was hardly sympathetic. "Do you know what you can do?" he bellowed. "You can jump overboard if you don't like your fare."[6] That was all the encouragement Hamilton needed. He stripped off his coat and boots and plunged over the side. Although the ship was anchored far off shore, more men joined him, and soon all were putting distance between themselves and the ship. Seeing the commotion in the water, many fishermen on shore set out in their dinghies toward the men splashing in the water.

After he overcame his initial surprise, Gull ordered lifeboats lowered over the ship's side, but both armadas reached the swimmers about the same time. The result was an awkward tug-of-war between sailors and fishermen, with the men in the water caught in the middle. Since it was usually the Stornoway boats that won these contests, most of the escapees gained their freedom. To round up the deserters, the humiliated Macdonell had to seek the help of the marines stationed aboard a navy ship anchored at Stornoway. There were, nonetheless, many who escaped during the time the Hudson's Bay ship remained in the harbour. According to John McLeod, one of Tod's fellow apprentice clerks, of the two dozen or so men who signed on with him on the island of Lewis, only four actually sailed.

The *Edward and Ann* finally weighed anchor on 26 July 1811, with 104 passengers, but without some of her cargo, including the prize cattle Selkirk had purchased for the colony. The desertions were obviously a concern for Macdonell, but what was potentially even worse, the ship would be in danger of being caught in the pack ice that would soon close Hudson Strait. Because the route was much farther north than York Factory, the ship's destination, the passage was blocked long before ice formed at the south end of the bay. For Tod and the others below deck whose concerns were more immediate, however, there was some good news. Once the anchor had been weighed the quality of food improved and only rarely were the recruits served the dreaded oatmeal.

The voyage was difficult and, for Macdonell, it must have seemed that fate was against him. Since he had left the Thames in late spring, little had gone right and now the *Edward and Ann* was again battling strong headwinds. For Tod, who had few responsibilities, life on board was comfortable enough. He had little interest in the day-to-day operation of the ship, but there were many young men his own age with whom he could pass the time. When the *Edward and Ann* reached Hudson Strait, Tod saw the first fields of floating ice. A solid white mass was already beginning to cut off the channel between Baffin Island and the continent. As the ship sailed on, the channel became increasingly narrow, and when no clear opening remained, the vessel stuck fast in the unbroken plain of white sea ice.

After it was clear that their situation was desperate, Tod and several others landed on the ice pack to hunt for game, but all they saw was a large white bird a crew member identified as an Arctic falcon. Tod fired but missed, making no contribution to the ship's stew pot. Had the ice continued to close in the *Edward and Ann* would have been crushed like an egg shell, but fortunately, several days later, a new channel appeared and the ship sailed once again into open waters.

The *Edward and Ann* did not reach York Factory until 24 September. No ship had previously arrived so late in the season and no voyage from Stornoway had taken longer — a record 61 days. After disembarking, Tod had his first close look at a Hudson's Bay fort. York Factory, the flagship of Company posts, was impressive. The buildings — Tod estimated 30 or 40 in total — were enclosed within a high, oblong stockade with galleries running along a few feet below the top of the timbered walls. There were also bastions with cannons around the perimeter and a look-out tower extending high above the stockade. These elaborate precautions were taken, not because of the danger of hostile local tribes, but rather, Tod was told, against raids by the Nor'Westers. The Hudson's Bay Company, he discovered, had a healthy respect for its rival.

Some buildings at the fort, Tod noted, were tilted at odd angles, a condition he correctly ascribed to the swampiness of the terrain. The post had been built on marshland at the mouth of the Hayes River and the frost heaves played havoc with the structures. Adding to the damage were the spring floods on the Hayes River. While its location was convenient for inland trade, York Factory was not a comfortable post.

Selkirk's original plan had been for Macdonell's party to arrive at York Factory early enough in the autumn months to make the 600-mile journey southward to Assiniboia. He had intended the young recruits to put in next year's crop before the worst weather set in but, instead, they would have to winter over at York. William Auld, a Lowland Scot appointed superintendent of the Company's northern posts the previous year, was unsympathetic to the plight of the crofters and hostile to Selkirk's settlement scheme. He was, as Colin Robertson later wrote to Selkirk, "one of the greatest enemies your Lordship ever had."[7] As might have been expected, Tod and his fellow apprentice clerks experienced an unfriendly reception at York Factory. The recruits were told to take their meals in the kitchen — an arrangement many of the apprentice gentlemen regarded as a personal slight. Auld claimed that he did not have enough winter supplies for Macdonell and his party, so the Red River colonists were sent 23 miles up the Nelson River to establish camp. The site, Macdonell had been told, was near a caribou winter migration trail, but few animals passed by that year. The men spent a cold and uncomfortable winter huddled in the rude huts they had constructed.

By a stroke of good fortune, Tod did not accompany the others to Nelson Encampment. He and another apprentice clerk were selected by Auld to serve the Company at an outpost at the mouth of the Severn River, about 200 miles to the east of York Factory. As a result they avoided the hardships faced by the others, including an outbreak of scurvy that killed one recruit.* Before they could begin their trek, Auld required Tod and his companion, John Brackenridge, to learn something of wilderness survival. The plan was that the two were to camp a few miles up the Hayes River from York Factory, where they were expected to construct a wigwam.

---

* The difficult conditions at Nelson Encampment combined with Miles Macdonell's weak leadership eventually contributed to a mutiny that was not put down until the spring, when Auld starved the participants into submission.

Building such a shelter, however, presented a problem — the dwelling was usually covered with birchbark, but birch did not grow in this area. Tod and his colleague therefore had to cover their small lodge with animal skins which they had brought. In the centre of the cone-shaped structure they built a fireplace, around which were placed tree boughs, bearskin rugs and blankets. The two recruits were expected to live off the land, which here, at least, was not difficult. Ptarmigan were so plentiful that it was possible to snare them in nets. After about a month in the bush, they were recalled to York Factory to begin their journey to Fort Severn.

By now the Hudson Bay winter had set in, and Tod had shed his European dress in favour of the clothes of the country — a cloth coat under which was worn a vest lined with flannel, buckskin breeches, cloth leggings, three pairs of socks and moose moccasins covering his feet. Bay men had found years earlier that Indian foot gear was superior to European-style boots because it did not constrict the flow of blood to the feet. Over his shoulders, he hung a pair of mittens tied together with a long piece of cord. Some form of hand protection was, of course, essential, for unprotected skin would be damaged by the cold within three or four minutes. Around his waist, Tod wore a crimson sash after the fashion of the voyagers. From his belt hung another essential piece of equipment, the fire bag containing flint and steel. There was also enough room in the bag for a pipe and tobacco: one of the few pleasures to which a Bay employee could look forward. The only familiar clothing he retained was a plaid shawl under his coat. The coat itself was the set piece of the uniform: for European employees it never varied from a particular shade of blue, which was, at the time, the Hudson's Bay Company colour. Positions were loosely denoted by the ornamentation each man wore: the lower ranks were attired in more decoration, the higher ranks, less.

On their trip to Fort Severn, the two recruits were to be accompanied by two Hudson's Bay Company servants. One was an old Orcadian who had been with the company a long time. (Since the beginning of the 18th century, the Orkney Islands had been fertile recruiting grounds for the lower ranks of the Hudson's Bay Company and by 1799, over three-quarters of all overseas employees were Orcadians. The Company's London Committee believed Orcadians were well-suited to the wilderness of North America. This barren, windswept archipelago off Scotland's northern coast was, like Hudson Bay itself, an inhospitable environment, and the Orcadians had a reputation for enduring the worst conditions without complaint. Their supposed quiet, compliant nature eventually brought them into disfavour with Andrew Colvile and the other London Committee members who considered them too docile to deal effectively with the aggressive Nor'Westers.) The other escort was a former English sailor named Joe Hall. For Tod, who was not experienced in the use of snowshoes, the 15-day trek was arduous and made worse by Hall who would go on ahead, leaving Tod and Brackenridge to lag helplessly behind.

Although an important supply depot for inland trade, Fort Severn was considered by Hudson's Bay men to be more or less a commercial backwater. However, without the pressures of some of the more important posts, it was a good place to begin training new recruits. Soon after his arrival, Tod was learning the business of the fur trade. His experience as a clerk in the Glasgow cloth warehouse stood him in good stead with his new employers, for his duties included keeping post accounts. In charge of Fort Severn was James Swain, Sr., and assisting him was James Wilson, a quiet-spoken officer from Kirkwall in the Orkney Islands. Tod and his fellow recruit had not been at the Severn outpost long before tragedy struck. One evening late in January 1812, Swain had to go to the second floor of a storage shed. The trader took a lamp with him, but in climbing the stairs, he lost his balance and struck his head on the edge of a barrel. Following the accident, Tod and the injured man's son took turns keeping what was obviously expected to be the death watch on Swain. One night, about three days after the accident, Tod was sitting in Swain's room when James Wilson came in. He said nothing but stood watching the unconscious figure of his friend prostrate in the bed. Tod saw an expression of sorrow suddenly cross Wilson's face. Then without a word, he disappeared through the door.

A short time later the stillness of the evening was broken by the crack of a gun. At the time, Tod thought little about the noise because it was common practice to set firearm traps, for wolves and other predators occasionally venturing too close to the fort at night. Not until the following morning was the actual source of the sound discovered. A servant noticed that the door to one of the sheds was ajar and there, on the floor, was the body of Wilson. There was little doubt what had happened: after leaving Swain's bedside, the assistant trader had taken his gun, gone to the shed and shot himself in the head.

To their undoubted astonishment, Tod and Brackenridge found themselves in charge of the Severn post. Fortunately, Captain George Taylor, the skipper of a Hudson's Bay Company trading schooner, was also at the fort and able to provide some assistance. The first task was to see to Wilson's burial — not an easy job owing to the frozen soil. The labour was made more difficult because of the way Wilson had died — none of the servants at the fort could be induced to lend a hand. Most of them were Metis whose culture was uncomfortable with suicide. Eventually, however, a grave was clawed in the frozen soil and the man given a proper burial. As Tod recalled, it was a long time before the incident was forgotten. In the days following Wilson's death, these normally courageous mixed-blood servants were afraid even to go out at night alone.

Ironically, if, as it appeared, Wilson's suicide was the result of despair over the condition of his friend, he acted rashly, for after two weeks during which Swain remained critically ill, the trader suddenly showed signs of improvement. It was some months, though, before he recovered completely. In his report, submitted later, Swain concluded sadly that in Wilson, "the Service has lost ... a most valuable Officer and a most trustworthy and diligent Man."[8]

* * * * *

Tod's first winter at Fort Severn was a harsh lesson in survival, for although winters in Scotland were cold and bleak, nothing in the Lowlands had prepared him for the desolation he found on Hudson Bay. At home there were at least rolling hills to break the white winter expanse, but here the landscape was low and almost feature-less. Occasionally, in the protection of a river bank, a few scrub pines stubbornly clung to life, or once in a while a swamp willow braved the worst of winter in the open, but there was little else.

Fort Severn had a few domestic animals, including a cow that provided milk for Swain's large family. The livestock were the result of the London Committee's on-going efforts to make the Company's posts less dependent on provisions shipped from Europe, but the plan had not been properly thought out, for after the brief Hudson Bay summer, natural forage was buried under many feet of snow. Surprisingly though, the cow seemed to thrive on a diet of finely chopped fish. It had expensive tastes, for the meals took many hours to prepare.

Less trouble than the cow were two other farm animals, an English horse and a pig. Neither was particular about what it ate —

during the winter, both dined on goose bones and other leftovers. Although goose was the dietary staple of those living around Hudson Bay — animals and humans alike — fish was regarded as a welcome change. Smaller fish obtained during the winter months were allowed to freeze without being gutted, but larger species such as salmon or trout had to be dried and then smoked over an open fire. Despite the cold — winters here were less severe than at York Factory, but temperatures rarely rose above 40 degrees below zero on the Fahrenheit scale — the flesh of deer and other animals would not keep unless it was cut into small pieces and repeatedly dipped into water. Freezing meat this way was time consuming, so most Company forts in the region relied on salted goose as their winter staple.

While Tod was at Fort Severn, his childhood interest in natural history was reawakened. During the winter, he would find frogs frozen hard in the muskeg, dig the little creatures out still frozen and then take them to the warmth of his fire. Amazingly, once subjected to warming, they would suddenly come alive. Yet when he repeated the process — re-freezing then thawing the frog — the amphibian would not revive again. Lacking the sophisticated nomenclature of the naturalist, Tod was nonetheless a keen observer of the world around him and his experiences on Hudson Bay gave him insight into the interrelationship among polar bears, foxes and seals in the subarctic food chain. Male polar bears (females go inland to give birth to their cubs), he noted, spend the winter in a search for seal breathing holes in the ice. "When the bear finds a seal hole, down he goes beside the orifice in the frozen surface, keeps concealed, watching all the time for the appearance of the seal."[9] Since arctic foxes were also familiar with the bears' behaviour they kept themselves well hidden. When the bear was successful, the foxes also signalled their pleasure by scampering around, but always at a safe distance. After the bear took its fill, the foxes were free to scavenge the remains. Thus unintentionally, Tod observed, the great, white northern predator hunts for more than itself.

By mid June, spring had come to Hudson Bay and Tod stored away most of his winter gear. Animals that had been absent from the barren white landscape were now plentiful. Squirrels climbed the few budding trees, beavers left their lodges to cavort in the open water and, overhead, the great bald eagle circled lazily. Yet the warmer weather was not altogether pleasant. Although the veterans were less affected by the pests, the recruits were bothered by swarms of insects suddenly materializing in the late spring air. After the thaw, the "land" around the bay became two-thirds water. Solid ground was no more than hundreds of low and muddy islands poking above the surface of the salty marsh. A little farther inland, the marshlands gave way to hundreds of shallow lakes separated by low clumps of land that made travel difficult, for the canoes had to be hauled out of the water, the goods unloaded, and everything carried over the soggy terrain until they came to the next lake.

In 1812, soon after spring break-up, the fur brigade arrived from Trout Lake post, about 200 miles farther up the Severn River. At Fort Severn, the boatloads of pelts were exchanged for a new supply of trade goods to be taken back upriver. One of those arriving at Severn that spring was James Monkman, an assistant trader. Before they had been seriously challenged by the Nor'Westers, the Hudson's Bay men had been content to remain in their forts around Hudson Bay while Indian trappers brought the pelts to them, but their rivals had forced them out of complacency. By 1811, the Hudson's Bay had already established a few forts farther inland. Trout Lake was one such post and Tod was ordered to accompany Monkman back upriver to act as his assistant.

It took 15 days of hard paddling up the Severn and Fawn rivers to reach Trout Lake. The first post there had been built by the North West Company before the turn of the century, but now the Hudson's Bay was attempting to reassert its authority over the territory. Tod never recorded his assessment of the place, but other Hudson's Bay men did not think highly of the Trout Lake posting. Apprentice clerk Francis Ermatinger, who was there 11 years after Tod, described it as a "Dam [sic] hole ... where I must be starved (unless fed at my own expense) in a Pig stye."[10] For Tod, though, Trout Lake was a chance to gain much needed experience and, once there, he began to learn about the fur trade in earnest. Monkman, a former sailor with the Hudson's Bay Company who had taken a job as assistant trader, was a knowledgeable teacher. One of Tod's most important tasks was to learn the local Indian language and this he accomplished with the help of Monkman's mixed-blood wife and children.

The language spoken in the area was an Indian dialect know as Swampy Cree. Surprisingly, he found it easier to master than Latin, perhaps because Monkman's pretty young daughter gave him lessons. Tod's knowledge of the Cree language would serve him well in the future, for it was understood throughout Hudson's

Bay Company territory as far west as the Rocky Mountains. During his time at Trout Lake, Tod learned much about the inhabitants of the North.

One day an Indian trapper presented Tod with a gift — a young beaver which had been taken alive. Beavers usually make excellent pets and this animal was no exception. It was not long before the young creature had become very attached to the Monkman children. As a result, however, the trader's living quarters suffered badly, for if by chance the beaver was shut in a room away from the children, it would begin gnawing through the door to reach its playmates. This particular beaver had one unusual trait: an abiding hatred for the Cree people who came to Trout Lake to trade. After arriving at the post, Indians would squat on the floor in the trading room, placing their backs against the wall and their belongings on the floor beside them. Seeing its enemies occupied in conversation, this beaver would sneak into the room, make its way silently toward them, and pick up one of the objects the visitors had laid on the floor — a knife, pipe, tobacco or almost anything else — with its front paws and press it under its chin. Then the thief would waddle to the door and, once outside, with a flick of its powerful tail send the article flying into the bush. The beaver would repeat the process until it had disposed of all the visitors' objects on the floor. Tod saw the irony of the situation — while it was true the Cree were responsible for the slaughter of thousands of its kind, the greater enemy was the Europeans who bought the pelts from the Indians. As clever as the animal was, it of course failed to understand this.

It was not long before Tod was venturing farther away from Trout Lake to barter for furs. As his apprenticeship progressed he was becoming more proficient in the art of trading, although he could not yet be given the responsibilities of a full-fledged clerk. In 1813 Monkman was transferred to Red River, and clerk Adam Snodie was given charge of Trout Lake. Snodie was a man with a mission — the Company wanted to open one of the last unexploited areas in Rupert's Land and he was ordered to establish a post at Paint Lake, 400 miles to the west. Tod would later claim that the territory had never before been visited by Europeans but a generation earlier, Montreal traders had explored the region. The Indians who inhabited the area, the Cranes, were a known cause for concern.*

* The identity of the native people Tod and other Hudson Bay officers have called the Cranes is difficult to determine. They were probably one of the subdivisions of the Woodland Cree Indians.

According to reports from other Indians, the Cranes were exceedingly violent. The Company also faced another problem — they could spare no experienced clerk to lead the expedition. Unable to go himself, Snodie was forced to put Tod in charge. Before Tod left, however, the senior trader made it clear that the designation was little more than honorary — the real head of the expedition would be an ancient Orcadian servant named Archie whose official title was interpreter and boat foreman.

In military fashion, the Hudson's Bay Company made a clear distinction between the ranks. The men were divided into two classes, officers and servants, and the gulf between them was great. Officers were regarded as gentlemen and accorded certain privileges of rank, including a separate mess at the larger posts. The clerks were the lowest rank of the officer class and were usually responsible for the day-to-day operation of most Company posts. Apprentices such as Tod were in a kind of gray area — they were neither servants nor full-fledged officers.

The servants were the equivalent of enlisted soldiers and were, in turn, divided into a number of sub-classifications ranging from common labourers, on the lowest rung, to interpreters and postmasters, at the top. As was the case in the military, members of the lower ranks were seldom admitted to the officer class. The separation between the two classes often worked considerable hardship on the clerks stationed at the more remote posts. Even without a fellow officer nearby, a clerk could not cross the boundary between the ranks to fraternize with the more numerous servants. For many men, the loneliness endured in the isolated posts was as severe a hardship as the harsh weather or shortage of food.

While the officers received much of the glory, Tod had discovered it was experienced servants such as Archie who kept the wheels of the Hudson's Bay Company organization turning. In a difficult situation, Snodie had logically turned to a seasoned veteran rather than the inexperienced apprentice. Also assigned to the expedition were three other Orcadians and an Indian guide.

The small party had been gone about two days when they met a lone Indian. The stranger began to speak with their guide who then refused to go any farther. Later it was learned the guide had been told by the stranger that if he proceeded into the territory, he would be killed. That night he stole silently away, leaving Tod and his companions alone. Fortunately, Archie's experience saved the expedition from disaster and the men managed to make their way through hundreds of miles of swamp and muskeg to the area where they were supposed to establish a post. By the time they reached the shores of Paint Lake, it was almost the middle of October, and winter was not far away. The key to survival was an adequate supply of fish and game nearby, for they had taken only enough supplies to reach their destination — according to Company policy the men were expected to live off the land. But soon after their arrival the lake began to freeze over, and it was necessary to begin work immediately on the wooden huts that would be home.

It was not long before they realized how wrong their choice for the post's location had been, for while fur-bearing animals were plentiful there was little suitable game in the area. Some fish were caught by nets set in a hole in the ice, but the catch was always small, both in size and number; no more than half a dozen small carp were ever taken at once. In the end, it was unpalatable animals such as muskrat, fox, mink, wolverines, otter and marten that served as their daily fare and even these scrawny predators could not always be killed in large enough numbers to satisfy their appetites.

The harsh conditions of that winter revealed to Tod a basic insight into human nature. Individuals, he observed, complain loudest when there was still something to eat; let there be nothing and their spirits suddenly picked up and they redoubled their efforts toward refilling the empty larder. Because he was, officially at least, in charge of the expedition, Tod felt it necessary to bear his own hunger stoically, but given the sparseness of the menu, silence was difficult to maintain. He passed the long winter days cleaning his flintlock rifle or reading the three books his father had given him before he left Scotland. He found reading to be a great bulwark against the loneliness of the wilderness, and the Bible, particularly, became both a subject of study and a source of comfort.

With snow on the ground, the hunting expeditions that Archie sent out were usually unsuccessful — most of their food was obtained in traps. One day in the early spring Tod was out by himself checking the trap line when he came upon caribou prints in the snow. He examined the marks carefully — the edges were still soft for the snow had not had time to freeze. He followed the tracks for many miles but he never overtook the animals. When he returned to the post with only a mink for dinner, Tod did not mention his find to his companions — the disappointment would have made their situation seem even worse than it was. Eventually, however, a few caribou were shot and life became somewhat easier.

16

When the ice on Paint Lake melted, Tod and his companions made preparations for their return to Trout Lake. Although the expedition had not been successful — the Cranes were still at war with a neighbouring tribe and were in no mood to trade with the Europeans — the furs they had trapped more than covered expenses. Further, the information they obtained about the Paint Lake area would serve the Hudson's Bay Company well in later years. It had been a difficult winter, but not without reward — Tod had learned much about wilderness survival, knowledge that would be invaluable in his career.

Chapter Two

THE HEROES OF THE OPPOSITION

T od stayed at the Trout Lake post for the remainder of his five-
year apprenticeship. Although it was due mostly to the
experience of Archie and the other servants who accompanied him,
his success at Paint Lake did not go unnoticed. He had gained a
reputation for displaying courage and initiative, qualities highly
regarded by Governor William Williams. In 1816, Tod finished his
apprenticeship and was transferred to Fort Severn on Hudson Bay.

Tod was, of course, familiar with Fort Severn; he had served there
five years earlier. Now, as a qualified clerk, he was given charge of
the facility. There were other changes as well. John Brackenridge,
the recruit who had accompanied him to Fort Severn in 1811, was
no longer with the Company. The attrition rate for apprentice clerks
was high — the harsh climate and difficult working condition
resulted in the resignation of many young recruits. Leaving the fur
trade was not always easy, however, for the Hudson's Bay
demanded that its employees give a year's advance notice. As Tod
discovered later, when it wished to keep a valued employee the
Company could and did make leaving very difficult.

For the Europeans living along the shores of Hudson Bay, the
short summer passed quickly, and it was not long before preparations were under way for the coming winter. Autumn was the season
of the great goose kill at Fort Severn, as it was September when the
birds passed over the fort on their annual migration south to the

Mississippi Delta. The goose hunt was important to the Cree, who took enough for their own needs and bartered the surplus birds at the fort for supplies. But because the Hudson's Bay was unwilling to rely entirely on the Indians for its winter provisions, the Company also sent its own employees to take part in the kill. Tod participated in the slaughter on at least one occasion. Before the flyover began, blinds were constructed along the marshy shores of Hudson Bay and crude decoys were deployed while he and his companions waited in ambush. As the flock passed overhead, the birds suddenly spotted the decoys and flew down to investigate. When the birds were in range, the riflemen opened fire.

The entire operation was well organized. Each Company shooter had a number of assistants to reload his rifle and retrieve the fallen birds. There was no sport in the shoot, for the flyover was brief and it was necessary to kill as many geese as quickly as possible. Before the last goose passed, perhaps ten thousand or more birds were shot, but these, according to Tod, represented only the smallest fraction of the birds that flew south. Once salted, many of the geese would be shipped on to York Factory where they would be distributed to the posts around Hudson Bay.*

The intermittent warfare between the Nor'Westers and Hudson's Bay men continued during Tod's three years at Fort Severn. In 1815, Chief Factor John Clarke led a brigade of about 50 men into Athabasca territory. The purpose of this force was to intimidate not only the Nor'Westers, but also the Indians who had long traded with the enemy. The scheme backfired, however, for it was impossible to kill enough game to keep such a large force supplied. The men had brought few supplies with them — in keeping with Hudson's Bay policy, trade goods took the place of provisions in brigade canoes.

Sadly for Clarke and his company, the Nor'Westers remained masters of Athabasca, and under the leadership of wintering partner William McIntosh, they successfully discouraged local Indians from trading with the Hudson's Bay. Before winter finally came to an end, 16 of Clarke's men had died from starvation. The terrible consequences of the Athabasca expedition caused the London Committee to briefly rethink its policy regarding the carrying of provisions, but it was not long before the lesson was

---

* Severn's location on the birds' flight path meant that the post was a major provisioner for other Company forts.

forgotten. As the Company expanded westward, many of the newly established posts were denied sufficient provisions to carry them through the first few difficult months, with the result that men continued to die needlessly.

The tragic Athabasca incident did not curtail the Hudson's Bay's activities there. The territory was far too rich in furs to abandon. Nevertheless, Hudson's Bay men were often on the losing end of encounters with the daring and resourceful Canadians. The Company faced still more problems. A year after the Athabasca disaster, the London Committee received news of the Massacre of Seven Oaks, which ended Selkirk's dream of a prosperous crofter colony in North America.

In 1818, Tod was transferred to Island Lake, a fort about 250 miles inland from York Factory, where he was put in charge of the district. Like Fort Severn, Island Lake was far from Athabasca country, the front line of the conflict, but now at least he had more to occupy his time. While there he began a relationship with Catherine Birston, the mixed-blood daughter of Magnus Birston, the assistant trader at the Island Lake post. In that year, Catherine gave birth to a boy whom the couple named James.

During the early years, the Company had opposed marriages between Hudson's Bay Company men and Indian women, but by the beginning of the 19th century, the London Committee had finally bowed to the inevitable and tacitly recognized these relationships. While the so-called "country marriages" were not formally constituted, a code governing the conduct of Company employees had nonetheless emerged. A trader was not bound legally to his country wife, and could (and often did) move on to new relationships, but he was expected to maintain his former family, at least until his earlier spouse was under the "protection" of another man.

At Island Lake Tod met Edward Ermatinger, a new recruit who would become his lifelong friend. Edward's brother Francis, or Frank as he was usually called, was also an apprentice clerk with the Company. Unlike most recruits, the two were not natives of Scotland — Edward was born on the island of Elba in 1797, and Frank a year later in Lisbon. Their father, a commissariat officer with the British forces in Europe during the War of the First Coalition, had been born in Canada. Little is known of the boys' Italian mother, who died shortly after giving birth to Frank. Edward and Frank were educated in Britain and, through their father's connections, were taken on by the Hudson's Bay Company in London in 1818.

Later that year, the two brothers arrived at York Factory aboard the Company ship *Prince of Wales*. Frank was assigned to Fort Severn while Edward was sent inland to Island Lake. There, the elder Ermatinger learned the fur trade under the direction of district master Tod. He had an aptitude for accounting, a skill highly valued by the Company, and was a diligent and conscientious worker.

During their years in Britain, the two boys had been raised as gentlemen, and Edward, particularly, was a good classical scholar. Tod, whose own formal education was limited, was thoroughly impressed by the learning of his apprentice. The many cold winter nights that were passed around the post's fireplace gave Tod a glimpse into a world he had not previously known. Although he was never able to emulate the behaviour of the upper classes, so important to 19th-century social acceptance — his coarse manners revealed his rural upbringing — Tod, for the rest of his life, was fascinated with books and gradually attained a good self education. His later letters to Edward reflected his general interests in the arts and sciences.

Edward was also an accomplished musician and a good teacher. Soon Tod was accompanying his friend's violin on an ancient flute Edward had given him. Music would henceforth be an important part of Tod's life, and even years later, he would recall wistfully the many Sunday evenings at Island Lake the two devoted to the performance of hymns.

In the fall of 1819, Tod and Edward journeyed with the brigade to York Factory where they met a party of Swiss and German colonists, former mercenaries and their families whom Selkirk had recruited for Red River. At a dance held in one of the post's large storage sheds, Tod witnessed for the first time couples performing the graceful waltz. As Edward, in the company of other musicians, played his violin, Tod watched the young girls in their peasant dresses whirling around the floor in perfect time to the music. It is not difficult to imagine the effect of this night upon a young man from a small Scottish village. He carried the memory into old age.

The next evening, Edward and Tod, as yet no expert on the woodwind, and one of the immigrant musicians, practised together in the fort's guard room. Edward played not only the violin but the flute with great skill, and composed his own music. Before the trio parted, the musician gave Tod a bound book of German waltzes, a rare gift considering the transportation costs to Hudson's Bay territory. About a third of the book contained only lined pages, later used by Edward to write his own musical scores. When he and Tod eventually separated, Tod took his book with him and treasured it the remainder of his life. Although they spent less than two years together at Island Lake, they had formed an enduring friendship, and despite the distances between them, the two corresponded regularly.

Elsewhere in Hudson's Bay territory, the music was less harmonious, for the battle between the London and Montreal companies continued. In 1817, the Nor'Westers had deceitfully lured Chief Factor John Clarke away from Fort Wedderburn, and then seized it. A North West partner, Archibald Norman McLeod, took about 50 Hudson's Bay employees prisoner at Fort Wedderburn, releasing them only when they swore not to return to the territory for at least two years. The following year, the Hudson's Bay Company sent former Nor'Wester Colin Robertson to reoccupy Fort Wedderburn. Robertson completed his assignment without incident but made the mistake of attending unarmed the burial of one of his men who had died in an accident. He was captured by a party of Nor'Westers that included Samuel Black. Robertson eventually escaped and made his way to a Hudson's Bay Company fort, but it would not be his last encounter with his former associates of the North West Company. The Nor'Westers also seized a number of other northern forts in the vicinity of Lesser Slave and Reindeer lakes and threatened others as far south as the Saskatchewan River. Not until 21 June 1819, could the Hudson's Bay Company claim victory over their adversaries, when the new overseas governor, William Williams, captured 11 Nor'Westers near the mouth of the Saskatchewan River. Some of the prisoners escaped, including wintering partner Benjamin Frobisher who eventually paid a price for his freedom: he starved to death on the barren shores of Cedar Lake.

Tod had no part in the capture of the Nor'Westers, but a number of the prisoners, including Angus Shaw, Duncan Cameron and John George McTavish, were held under his supervision at Rock Depot on the Hayes River. The three were taken to York Factory where they were shipped to Britain for trial. Once there, however, they were soon released for lack of a prosecutor. The British government was reluctant to become involved in what they regarded as an intercompany squabble, preferring instead to shift the dispute to the Canadian courts. The Hudson's Bay, however, had little faith in colonial judges, believing them biased toward its Montreal adversaries.

While the Hudson's Bay had failed to achieve victory in the courts, it had nonetheless succeeded in disrupting North West operations in Athabasca. The Nor'Westers, who usually got the better of these encounters, were outraged by the capture of their comrades, and it was rumoured in London that the Montrealers intended to reciprocate by capturing Governor Williams himself. By issuing warrants of dubious legality, both companies had tried to use the law to justify the taking of prisoners, and it was said the Nor'Westers planned to take the governor east to the Canadian colonies for trial.

The London Committee's choice of Williams as governor had more to do with his skills in the art of war than his experience in business. A former sea captain with the British East India Company, the new governor was regarded as a man of outstanding courage and authority — qualities needed in the ongoing battle with the Nor'Westers. Yet curiously, Williams's military success only gave the London Committee more cause for concern. The directors had begun to consider the idea of settling matters with the North West Company and it seemed clear that provocative action on their part would only make matters worse.

In the spring of 1820, the Nor'Westers almost succeeded in their plan; only chance prevented Williams from falling into the hands of about 60 Nor'Westers near the mouth of the Saskatchewan River, where the governor had earlier captured Frobisher and his men. So worried were the Company's directors that they sent a deputy from London empowered to act in Williams's place should the governor be captured. The new second-in-command was George Simpson.

Despite Simpson's eventual importance within the fur trade little is known of his early life. The illegitimate child of a minister's son, he was born in Scotland, probably in 1786 or 1787. When he was in his early 20s he was given a job in his uncle's sugar brokerage where he came to the notice of Hudson's Bay Company principal Andrew Wedderburn Colvile. In 1820, Simpson was hired by the London Committee and sent to Norway House where he met with Williams. Later that year, Simpson took Colin Robertson's place in Athabasca when the latter had fallen again into the hands of the Nor'Westers.

In the same year, Tod relocated his district headquarters to Oxford House on the Hayes River. The move reflected the Hudson's Bay's increasing preoccupation with the western trade: while the Island Lake post had been important in the Company's expansion south of Hudson Bay, Oxford House was crucial, not for

23

the number of pelts collected there, but for its strategic location on the route between Lake Winnipeg and York Factory. At Oxford House, Tod would have overseen the movement of the Athabasca fur brigades through his territory. It would not be long, however, before events in London overshadowed field strategy.

In November 1820, Nor'Westers Angus Bethune and John McLoughlin sailed for England from New York. The reason for their London visit eventually became clear: the Montreal company was engaged in negotiations with their rival. While the Nor'Westers had won most of the battles, they had lost the war. The business arrangement between the wintering partners and the Montreal agents meant that all profits were divided annually among the principals. Because the North West Company had no financial resources to carry them through lean times, the partners teetered on the edge of insolvency. The Hudson's Bay victory, however, was not a rout, and the terms it offered were generous enough. After the takeover most senior Nor'Westers were given management positions within the Hudson's Bay, as either chief factors or chief traders. However, some of the most aggressive opponents of the Hudson's Bay, including Samuel Black and Peter Skene Ogden, were excluded from the new organization. Black's bravery in the service of the Canadians was not forgotten by his former colleagues. In 1821 they presented him with a ring inscribed: "To the most worthy of the worthy Northwesters."[1]

Meetings held later at Fort William, the North West Company's principal post, and at Norway House, the Hudson's Bay Company's main inland depot, determined the structure of the reorganized fur trade in British North America. Administratively, the Hudson's Bay territory east of the Rocky Mountains was divided into two immense departments: the Northern under the governorship of George Simpson, and the Southern under William Williams. The power of the overseas governors was not absolute — each department had its own council made up of chief factors who, in theory at least, exercised considerable authority over the general operation of the fur trade.

The upper ranks were to benefit from a profit-sharing scheme. The idea was not revolutionary, for both companies had had profit-sharing arrangements with their senior employees in the past. But now, with the Hudson's Bay holding the North American fur trade as a virtual monopoly, the value of the scheme was potentially far greater. In the agreement of 21 March 1821, 40% net annual earnings of the fur trade were divided into shares and allotted to commissioned officers — the chief factors and chief traders. The former received two shares each; the latter, one. The difficulty for clerks such as Tod was that a commissioned position became available only on the retirement or death of one of the 25 chief factors or 28 chief traders, and a clerk could wait years before his name appeared on the promotion list.

While the potential for profits was great, the reorganized company faced many problems. A primary concern for the new governor was that the men from both sides still harboured long-standing grudges. According to Tod's memoirs, one of Simpson's first tasks as governor was to close the division in the ranks. To this end, York Factory became the site of the most memorable dinner party in the history of the fur trade. Tod's memoirs provide the only surviving account of this occasion, and doubtless the truth has been embroidered. Like many of his fur-trade contemporaries, Tod was a story teller, and this tale was repeated many times to appreciative audiences on the front porch of his retirement home. Yet it is a mistake to dismiss these stories out of hand, for in many cases his facts are surprisingly accurate. Given that Tod's memoirs were recorded late in life, he had a remarkable memory for names, dates and places.

Simpson organized the dinner at York Factory during the summer of 1821. All the officers from both sides were invited. Tod was at York Factory when the dinner guests pulled their canoes up on the river bank near the fort. Defeat had not broken the spirit of the Nor'Westers, he observed, "they were by [no] means, apparently, humbled or in the least subdued, but strode haughtily around York Factory as if it were their own post, Fort William."[2] Tod, who had not been on the front lines of the battle, was generous in his praise for those whom he called "the heroes of the opposition."[3] Many of those present, however, were not as forgiving. Indeed, so tense was the atmosphere, it seemed more likely that a renewed battle between the longtime adversaries would be the high point of the evening.

When at last the dinner bell rang, those assembled began making their way into the large mess hall. Tod selected a chair in an isolated corner of the hall and watched the seating. If the demeanour of the guests was a proper indication, the banquet would be as joyous as a funeral: silently, and with the greatest solemnity, the crowd filed into York's great hall. Not surprisingly, given the individualism of the fur trader, formal dress ranged from the costume of a Cree warrior to clothes which would not have seemed out of place at a London dinner. None was more gloriously attired than Colin Robertson, the former Nor'Wester who had been the strategist behind the Hudson's Bay victory over his old employers. A flamboyant figure at ordinary times, Robertson outdid himself on the evening that was to be the high point of his career. The collar of his coat was trimmed with the fur of no less than three rare, long-haired, winter marten. Elsewhere on his jacket, he had used the same fur as trim — pelts which would have fetched a high price at the London auction houses. Robertson's splendid attire had the desired effect — in a room full of experts on the value of fur, all eyes were upon him.

As the first arrivals reached the tables, there was sudden confusion: no one was sure where they should be seated. So great was the enmity between the camps that a successful outcome to this union seemed impossible. The milling mass reminded Tod of a biblical tale about an "incongruous animal seen by the King of Babylon in one of his dreams, one part iron, another of clay, though joined together they would not amalgamate."[4] Although forced into close proximity, each group intended to keep to itself.

However, in the midst of the crowd was Governor George Simpson who, with the utmost tact, began breaking down the wall separating the parties. Simpson, in later years never high in Tod's estimation, was obviously the right person for this difficult job. "Had that old bluff 'salt' Governor Williams been at the helm in place of his more skilful successor," Tod noted, "it is hard to say what turn of affairs might have taken at that particular juncture. The rough sailor was known to have a peculiar relish at all times for a good hard fight, more especially when there seemed certain prospect of one of the parties being 'well licked,' which he used to say was the most legitimate way to end disputes."[5] Simpson, on the other hand, reached his ends through diplomacy, and the vanquished were treated with dignity and courtesy.

Long-standing feuds between many of the men meant that considerable care had to be given to determine where each one of the more than 70 guests was to sit. Still, several mistakes were made and it seemed likely old scores would be settled on the spot. Seated at the same table as Tod was Hudson's Bay trader John Clarke who had been responsible for the ill-fated Athabasca brigade in 1816. Clarke was perhaps typical of the odd assortment of individuals who seemed drawn to the North American frontier. Of him, Tod wrote:

"with neckerchief and shirt collar always up to his ears, and his head above the level of ordinary men ... he would occasionally soar into the regions of imagination too far beyond the mental reach of his hearers, his flight thus forcibly exemplifying the oft repeated remark that 'there is but one step from the sublime to the ridiculous'."[6]

A better soldier than trader, Clarke had been employed by American traders before working for the Hudson's Bay. One of his fiercest opponents in Athabasca was the Nor'Wester William McIntosh who was now seated across the table from him. McIntosh had been responsible for the deaths of Clarke's men during the Athabasca expedition, and both had once engaged in a gun fight across a blazing campfire. While neither man was injured, the animosity between them was deep.

Yet, as disastrous as this seating arrangement was, there were other combinations potentially more explosive. Elsewhere at Tod's table, a Nor'Wester Tod called "Blind McDonnel" had been placed opposite Bay man Alexander Kennedy. Eight years earlier, the two traders had battled each other with swords, and time had not dulled their hatred. Each still bore the marks of that encounter. "I shall never forget the look of scorn and utter defiance with which they regarded each other the moment their eyes met," Tod wrote. "[McDonnel's] nostrils actually seemed to expand, he snorted, squirted, and spat, not on the table, but between his legs and was as restless in his chair as if he had been seated on a hillock of ants; the other looked equally defiant, but less uneasy and, upon the whole, more cool."[7] Aware of the two enemies now facing each other across the table, Tod was grateful that neither man carried weapons, but at the slightest provocation, McDonnel and Kennedy could have snatched up knives and forks from the table and pressed them into service.

Indeed, bloodshed might have been the outcome of the incident had it not been for the old Nor'Wester, Simon McGillivray, who was sitting at the head of the table. McGillivray, one of the North West Company's most respected generals, had frequently planned North West strategy against the London company. Earlier, he had often spoken about the legitimacy of the North West cause and the ".nulity" of the original Hudson's Bay Company charter. Now though, McGillivray was aware the battles were over and it was time to put aside the past. Observing the little drama taking place down the table, he sent a message which was, as Tod noted, "couched in the most gracious terms"[8] requesting his former colleague,

McDonnel, to take wine with him. Given McGillivray's stature within the North West Company, the suggestion would have seemed like an order, but nonetheless the message had to be repeated several times before McDonnel took his eyes off Kennedy long enough to accept a place near the head of the table.

There were many other awkward moments during the evening. Hudson's Bay clerk Robert McVicar was forgiving enough to drink with one of the Nor'Westers who had recently held him captive as a prisoner of war in an evil-smelling cellar. So terrible was the sulphurous odour permeating his cell, McVicar joked he had been given a foretaste of hell. Gradually though, the wine had an effect, and the old grudges, if not entirely forgotten, seemed now less important. As had been Simpson's intention, the animosities were dissolving within Bacchus's pleasant mellow haze. In the end, those who had arrived as proud and arrogant Nor'Westers left as men of the Hudson's Bay. By any measure, the evening had been an outstanding success.

* * * * *

The Hudson's Bay, which for years prior to 1821 had had difficulty attracting new recruits to the wilds of British North America, suddenly had too many employees. As the London Committee recognized, it was in the best interests of the stockholders to pare down its ranks as quickly as possible. The task was daunting, for the number of redundancies included not only Hudson's Bay clerks and servants but Nor'Westers as well. George Simpson estimated at the time of the merger there were twice as many employees as were currently needed. Between 1821 and 1825, many who had been valued more as soldiers than as traders were retired or dismissed.

Interestingly though, not all of the casualties of the Company's new peacetime policies were from the lower ranks. Governor Williams, who had been the London Committee's often praised "gallant" and "manly" warrior before 1821, was recalled as head of the Southern Department in 1826 after he had failed to bring operating costs into line. An old soldier, Williams quietly faded away while George Simpson's star burned ever brighter.

Simpson, the former clerk from a London sugar brokerage, was now governor of an overseas empire larger than most of the European continent. Although the job was difficult, Simpson was equal to the challenge, and for the next 40 years, the "Little Emperor" was to leave his mark on the history of the west.

George Simpson, governor of the Hudson's Bay Company. (COURTESY NAC, C114188)

As a result of the reorganization, Tod lost his position as district master of Island Lake in 1822. He was succeeded by John Work, a young clerk from Donegal, Ireland. Work had recently been in charge of Fort Severn and had formed a warm friendship with Frank Ermatinger. In later years, Tod too would come to know Work and the younger of the Ermatinger brothers well.

For a short time, Tod was the master of the Company's post at Sandy Lake, but in the summer of 1823, he was again transferred — this time to York Factory where he was put in charge of the fort's fur sheds. Since most of the animal skins were scraped of flesh and dried before they were transported to York Factory, Tod did not have to prepare the pelts for shipment to London. In the fur shed, however, he had to tend the kettles that were used to reduce kitchen wastes to soap and candle wax. This was a particularly unpleasant job — the fires under the kettles made the room stiflingly hot, while the noxious odours arose — but at least he was still in the Hudson's Bay's service. Over 200 servants and clerks were discharged in 1823 alone, and those fortunate enough to secure new contracts did so at reduced wages. The Ermatinger brothers also kept their jobs, but Edward was moved from Island Lake to the Hudson's Bay post at Lac La Pluie in 1822. Frank remained at Fort Severn.

For Hudson's Bay servants and officers who had long struggled against the North West Company, victory had a bitter taste indeed. Although personally he did not hold a grudge, Tod noted the irony when Chief Factor John George McTavish was appointed superintendent of York Factory. Only a year earlier, McTavish had been one of the Nor'Westers held by Tod at Rock Depot. Now Tod was clerk to the man who recently had been his prisoner.

Chapter Three

THE VOYAGE WAS A TERRIBLE ONE

Tod had not been impressed by William Williams's military-like organization of the Hudson's Bay Company's operations in North America. Throughout his career Tod had difficulty dealing with authoritarian figures and the governor was no exception. Yet with Williams, power was at least unambiguous, and the boundaries of authority clear. Tod knew where he stood with his straight-talking superior and was thus able to avoid difficulties, but his relationship with Williams's successor, George Simpson, was a different matter.

From the standpoint of stockholders, the London Committee made an excellent choice when it picked Simpson to be governor, because his talent for administration was the quality the hard-pressed Company needed. Under Simpson's stewardship it prospered, but the governor also had his dark side — even given the standards of the time, his sexism and bigotry were legendary. A man of singular coldness, he was able to dismiss the Indian and mixed-blood women who shared his bed as nothing more than "bits of brown." With a favourable balance sheet, the London Committee rarely questioned Simpson's handling of the fur trade, but there remained much unrest among the clerks who were responsible for the day-to-day operation of the trading posts. As John McLean, a former chief trader who served under the governor observed, "His caprice, his favouritism, his disregard of merit in granting promotion ... could not have a favourable effect on the Company's interests."[1] A vain and vindictive man, Simpson demanded deference and absolute compliance from his subordinates. On what amounted to a whim, Simpson could disrupt the lives of entire families as employees were transferred half a continent away.

Tod's difficulties with his superior began when he was managing the fur sheds at York Factory, where the governor had his headquarters. While the job was a step down from his responsibilities prior to amalgamation, Tod had made many friends among the young clerks at York Factory. He was not, however, destined to remain there long, for his quick temper soon led to trouble.

As was the usual practice among the Company's senior officers, Simpson had a personal servant, a young man named Tom Taylor. The relationship between the two men was more than servant and master — Taylor's sister Margaret was the governor's current country wife. The young man's authority thus was far greater than his humble station implied; according to Tod, Taylor's close relationship with Simpson earned him the nickname, "the Governor's Tom," and even chief factors trod warily around him. Tod, however, who saw himself as a leader among Company clerks, was not to be bullied by a steward, no matter how well-connected.

From early on Tod had problems with Taylor, but matters came to a head one morning when the clerk met an incoming brigade to tally its furs. On this occasion the canoes arrived in the very early morning, before he had a chance to have breakfast. After completing the time-consuming task, Tod and the brigade officer retired to the mess hall for breakfast. Since the hour for breakfast had long since passed, Tod went to the servants' room and ordered breakfast for two. Taylor, who happened to be there at the time, and who, as personal servant to the governor was also in charge of the other mess stewards, overheard the conversation. He came to Tod and accused him of missing breakfast because he had slept in. Angered by what he regarded as the man's impertinence, Tod grabbed Taylor by the throat and struck him hard.

The blow had the desired effect — soon hot meals appeared before the two officers. Taking advantage of his apparent easy victory, Tod warned the servant that the next time he forgot his station it would cost him his tongue, but his triumph was short-lived. Taylor quickly reported the incident to his master, and a few minutes later the servant returned with the governor. Angrily, Simpson demanded to know whether it was true that Tod had threatened to cut out the man's tongue. Although Tod had felt justified in his actions — while Simpson did not condone physical violence, Hudson's Bay servants frequently received the back of the hand from officers — his self-control began to fail in the presence of his superior. As Tod spoke he raised his voice and began to strike his fist nervously into the palm of his hand. Simpson, who apparently interpreted Tod's behaviour as a physical threat, stepped back suddenly, tripping over a stool as he did so. Had Tod not caught him, Simpson would have fallen, but this served only to further incense the governor. As he retreated from the room, he shouted, "You shall hear from me, sir."[2]

Simpson was as good as his word. One day, about a month after the incident, Taylor came with a message that the governor wished to see Tod. The clerk was ushered into Simpson's private office, and informed that the governor and the governing Northern Council had decided that he should be transferred to New Caledonia. Although the council, which was made up of chief factors, had in theory considerable power, Simpson seemed to have no difficulty obtaining what he wanted, and there is little doubt that Tod's transfer was instigated by the governor.

Simpson's manner was cordial, but in fact he had exacted his punishment. A rich fur-producing region west of the Rocky Mountains, before 1821 New Caledonia had been a North West preserve, and no Hudson's Bay man had set foot in the territory. According to Tod, a transfer to New Caledonia was about as welcome as a trip to Botany Bay, the British penal colony in Australia. Rumours about an inhospitable climate and fierce Indians had been spread by the Nor'Westers and Hudson's Bay officers feared being sent there.

Whatever Tod's faults he was clearly not a toady — the kind of subordinate Simpson favoured. Yet the governor was also too shrewd to allow his personal feelings to interfere with the good of the Company. Tod was a good officer, and remote New Caledonia was considered an ideal place for trouble makers, for it was far away from Simpson. And Tod was not the only one — many other clerks whom Simpson disliked would eventually follow him beyond the Rockies.

Tod, though, was ready for his fate, and he grasped the surprised Simpson's hand and thanked him. New Caledonia, he said, was just the place he wished to be sent. "I did not care," he later claimed, "had they sent me to the North Pole."[3] While this ploy may have saved his dignity, the truth was that he knew little about New Caledonia (or Western Caledonia as it was still called by former Nor'Westers). As in other fur-producing territories in North America, the borders of the area were never clearly defined, but it was roughly bounded by the Coast Range in the west and the Rockies in the east, extending as far north as the 57th parallel and as far south as the Thompson River. Administratively, New Caledonia was part of the Columbia Department, which included much of present-day Washington and Oregon as well as the northern Rocky Mountain states.

Tod had not been reassured by the reports he had heard from former Nor'Westers who had come from New Caledonia, but he was not entirely sure these stories could be believed. It was difficult to accept that any territory could be as bad as the boastful new colleagues claimed. Besides, as his friends pointed out, his transfer was in theory a promotion. Amalgamation had meant that the Company had a surplus of clerks, and many junior officers were either dismissed or given jobs with little real responsibility. At least in the far west, he would be in charge of a trading post again.

Simpson's reasons for banishing Tod may not have been entirely personal. The governor correctly suspected that his clerk was all too fond of what Simpson called a "Glass of Grog."[4] Given the difficult life of the fur trader, a man's reliance on alcohol was not surprising, for spirits were easy to obtain. The Hudson's Bay had long been in the liquor trade and had over the years supplied large quantities to the Indians. During the days of rivalry with the North West Company, the London Committee regarded the practice as an unavoidable evil — if the Hudson's Bay had not supplied the natives there was little doubt that the competition would. After amalgamation, Simpson came under increasing pressure from London to reduce the Company's trade in alcohol. Although he did not entirely favour prohibition — an ample supply of trading-post rum on Company shelves also meant that the lower ranks willingly turned their wages back to the Hudson's Bay — Simpson succeeded in dramatically reducing its use.

When alcohol became a problem, the governor strongly believed that New Caledonia was the place to send hard-drinking officers. The high mountains, unnavigable rivers, and rugged forests meant that the cost of imported goods, including alcohol, was great. In 1832, nine years after Tod had been transferred west, Simpson confidently noted that the trader "has had no opportunity of indulging ... since he went to New Caledonia."[5] While this was not entirely true, liquor was certainly more tightly controlled in New Caledonia than elsewhere. But this was probably an excuse. It is most likely that Simpson's principal reason for transferring Tod was that he simply disliked him.

* * * * *

Early on the morning of 19 July 1823, Tod slipped into his place on board a York boat as it pushed off from shore. The vessel had none of the grace of the birchbark canoes that had so long dominated the fur trade — the flat-bottomed craft was ponderously slow and awkward to handle. Still, the Hudson's Bay was gradually replacing its canoes with York boats in the territories east of the Rockies, because these vessels could carry much more cargo than the birchbark canoe. As far as Simpson was concerned the romance associated with the canoe counted for little, for the governor's watchword was "oeconomy."*

Tod, who had been put in charge of a four-boat brigade, was making the journey without Catherine Birston, his country wife or their son, James. Catherine evidently had no desire to share his fate

A York boat, successor to the freight canoe. (COURTESY NAC, PA145192)

* While others travelled in York boats, Simpson himself continued to rely on a canoe for his personal use. The governor, who delighted in speed, found any other craft too slow.

in New Caledonia, and his parting from her was almost certainly acrimonious. Years after their separation Tod continued to regard Catherine with the kind of passion usually reserved for an unfaithful lover. This may have not been too surprising for not long after his transfer west, he wrote to his friend Edward Ermatinger that she was "under the protection of another."[6]

Tod's charge of the Athabasca brigade was only temporary. The boats had been gone less than a week when they were overtaken by a express canoe under the command of Chief Factor John Stuart, the 44-year-old explorer and trader who had become a legend within the North West Company. In 1808 he had been with Simon Fraser during his journey down the wild river that eventually bore the latter's name, and in 1809, two years before Tod began his career in the fur trade, Stuart was already superintendent of New Caledonia. The Hudson's Bay victory in 1821 made little difference to him, for the governor and Northern Council appointed Stuart to his old job in New Caledonia.

Yet, while Stuart was one of the great legends of the fur trade, he was overshadowed by another officer accompanying him — Samuel Black, the Nor'Wester who had once terrorized the Athabasca. Only days earlier, Black had been taken on by the Hudson's Bay at a salary equivalent to that of a chief trader. While the London Committee was generally thought to have been responsible for hiring the former Nor'Wester, in fact it had been Simpson's idea. "I feel highly flattered that so much attention has been paid to my recommendation,"[7] Simpson wrote Andrew Colvile on 8 September 1823. Not surprisingly, the move was unpopular among those Hudson's Bay officers who had suffered at Black's hands, but since the decision had been made by the London Committee there was nothing that could be done.

Black, moreover, was not the only excluded Nor'Wester to benefit from Simpson's new employment policy — Peter Skene Ogden, Black's old friend, was also taken on at the same time and sent to the difficult Snake River territory. Simpson was even willing to forgive Cuthbert Grant, the mixed-blood leader who was behind the infamous Massacre at Seven Oaks. Simpson awarded him property and gave him the title, "Warden of the Plains." Grant's new-found respectability provoked an angry response from the residents of Red River — soon after he had received his honour he was assaulted in a settlement store. There was nothing personal in Simpson's motives: from a business standpoint each man was less dangerous within the Company than without. As the nucleus of a separate new enterprise in the west, disgruntled North Westers could have offered the Hudson's Bay serious competition.

When Black arrived at York Factory on 12 July 1823, Simpson offered him a formidable task — the exploration of the Finlay River to its source. For the governor, the possibility that the largely unexploited northern region of New Caledonia held a vast treasure of furs could not be ignored. The terrain where the Finlay rose was said to be difficult and the Indians of the area hostile, but Black was eager to oblige, for this was the kind of challenge on which he thrived. Simpson, however, did not trust Black and the governor wished to make sure the former Nor'Wester's orders were not open to misinterpretation. The delay in completing the letters that defined Black's terms of reference and gave him the authority to draw on supplies at Hudson's Bay trading posts in the Peace River district meant that he missed the departure of the Athabasca brigade.

In order to overtake the boats, Black left with Chief Factor John Stuart aboard the latter's express canoe. While such vessels were usually fast, Stuart was loaded down with not only cargo for New Caledonia, but also Black's supplies for the Finlay expedition. Three officers — Stuart, Black and Donald McKenzie, Jr., a clerk and former army officer who in 1818 had begun a second career with the Hudson's Bay — as well as a boat foreman, Patrick Cunningham, and a crew of eight were wedged in between the cargo. With its gunwales almost to the water line, the canoe had only a marginal advantage over the York boats it had recently overtaken. The overloaded vessel was always in danger of swamping, and even a moderate wind forced it to the protection of the river bank with the result that much time was lost.

Before the vessels continued on, Tod switched places with Black who took charge of the Athabasca brigade as far as Rocky Mountain House where he was to winter before beginning the exploration of the Finlay. Stuart, now with Tod on board, was bound for New Caledonia. "The voyage was a terrible one," the clerk recalled in his memoirs.[8] Because the canoe was so overloaded, the men on board had to endure the terrible pain of legs cramped in one position for hours at a time. Further, because New Caledonia, from the time of Simon Fraser's early exploration, had been a North West stronghold, the Canadians stationed there were isolated from the warfare that had taken place in Athabasca and Red River, and could not understand why their representatives had negotiated a deal with their rivals. Stuart made no secret of the fact that he regarded the men of the London Company as inferior to their Montreal counterparts. This attitude led to much tension between the chief factor and his two Hudson's Bay clerks. The animosity was not one-sided — the men of the London Company were not without their own feelings of resentment. While the victory had been theirs, now their company seemingly had delivered them into the hands of the enemy.

By the time the canoe reached the Split Lake post on 31 July, it had started to rain, and Stuart decided to spend the night in the relative comfort of the fort. As they were prepared to leave the next day, a stiff wind began to blow and Stuart was reluctant to test his overloaded boat in the choppy water of the lake; it had been further loaded down with five bags of pemmican to sustain them during the next leg of the journey. As he waited for a change in the weather, Stuart came across a battered little canoe on the shore of the lake, which he decided to put to use. If the load could be shared between both boats, he would not have to wait for dead calm before testing the lake.

The remainder of the day was spent readying the canoe and the following morning the winds had moderated enough for them to resume their journey. Tod, with Donald McKenzie and Patrick Cunningham, took turns paddling the vessel, but they had not gone far when the wind increased again, and both boats had to head for shore where they stayed most of the day. When they set out again the smaller craft began to leak badly, which made it difficult to paddle. Stuart in his own boat had to proceed slowly so that the little vessel could keep up. After two days it was clear that the little canoe, far from aiding them, was only a hindrance, and on 4 August they abandoned it after transferring the cargo back to the larger one. The following day Stuart purchased a small canoe from a party of Cree camped on the lake shore. Tod, Cunningham and the chief factor himself took turns paddling the vessel, but with a heavy load progress was slow, and on 7 August it too was abandoned.

Three days later Stuart and his party finally reached the western shore of Split Lake where they entered the eastern end of the Burntwood River. While the going was easy along the Burntwood, their crossing of Frog Portage was difficult, for the land was marshy. Although it was the height of the short northern summer, the weather remained wet, but Stuart pushed on despite the frequent downpours. A further difficulty arose because the route they were taking was new. The guide was unfamiliar with the trail, and took a wrong turn that added an extra day and a half to the journey. Their dwindling provisions were of increasing concern to Stuart; the pemmican they had brought with them from Split Lake was now almost gone.

On 15 August they reached Fort du Traite on the north bank of the English River near the outlet of the Deer River, where the northern and southern routes from York Factory converged. While they were portaging around the rapids near the post, the birchbark skin of the canoe was ripped from one gunwale to the other simply as a result of carrying it. Although the canoes were extremely fragile, a small tear could usually be fixed in an hour. In this case, though, the damage was more serious, and Stuart was forced to delay half a day while the split was mended. When the cedar frame itself was damaged, repairs took even longer. At the rapids near Fort du Traite, Stuart found a note from his friend, clerk George McDougall, who was in charge of a four-canoe brigade bound for New Caledonia. McDougall's boats had passed along the same route little more than a week earlier.

Although Tod found the scenery pleasant at first, the cramped conditions in the canoe as well as the exhausting overland passages did not permit him to enjoy a country that was entirely new to him. The terrain took on a dreary sameness that eventually blurred into grey shadows, and years later he could recall few images of his first momentous crossing of the continent. On 16 August they reached the small Hudson's Bay outpost at Rapid River, which they found deserted "except for a few starving Chipeweans [*sic*]."[9] Since 1821, the Company had closed or relocated many posts, and the men from the fort had been moved some miles away to the shores of Lac La Ronge. On 22 August they reached the narrows separating Sagwenew Lake and Lac Ile-à-la-Crosse.

As they approached Portage La Loche on the evening of 26 August the canoe was again halted by strong winds. The next day the weather remained poor — the wind continued and the sky had clouded over. Not until the following day did they carry their boats ashore at Portage La Loche. As Tod, McKenzie and the others made camp, Stuart left to cross the portage himself. He had hoped to find McDougall and the brigade camped along the trail, but his slow progress almost certainly meant that the canoes had already left. As he walked on the rain began to fall heavily, turning the portage trail to mud. It was not until late that night that he reached the banks of the Clearwater River, but there was no sign of McDougall. He did, however, come across an Indian lodge, and the natives agreed to help Stuart transport his canoe and cargo over the portage.

The next day Stuart and his men were overtaken by two chief factors, Edward Smith and James Keith, and clerk Colin Campbell. The three had left York Factory on their way to Fort Chipewyan a week after Stuart. As they prepared to leave the portage on 31 August Stuart paid off his Indian packers with a plain cotton shirt each. Earlier, he had picked up several pieces of dried meat, which he traded for tobacco, and although not enough to sustain his company for long, the provisions were welcome indeed.

After leaving Portage La Loche the two canoes continued east along the Clearwater River as far as Fort of the Forks where they joined the north-flowing Athabasca River. As the days passed, the cramped conditions added to the discomfort of everyone aboard Stuart's canoe. Once under way it was impossible to change positions, for the craft was so delicately balanced that even a slight shift in weight could overturn it.

On 3 September the voyagers paddled across the shallow east end of Lake Athabasca to Fort Chipewyan, which had been built on a small rocky peninsula jutting out into the water. Chipewyan was one of the Company's most important interior forts, and a storehouse for the Athabasca fur trade. Stuart was pleased to find his friend, clerk George McDougall, and the New Caledonia brigade at the post waiting for him. While they had arrived from Norway House without major incident, the four canoes McDougall had brought along "were bad beyond description."[10] Stuart managed to replace the two worst vessels with boats in somewhat better condition. The remaining two canoes were repaired as well as possible. The post was an important meat station where brigades usually received ample provisions for their journey to the next supply post, but Fort Chipewyan was apparently running short, for Stuart obtained only one bag of pemmican to take them along the Peace River.

After giving his men several days of light duty Stuart set out again on 6 September with McDougall and the New Caledonia brigade. Before leaving Lake Athabasca, though, the brigade stopped by Old Fort Chipewyan on the south shore, which was still used as a fishing station, where Stuart and his men picked up 33 sled dogs to take back to New Caledonia. The dogs were an extra burden, but with the addition of the New Caledonia boats, the crowding in Stuart's boat was lessened; Tod and McKenzie were given command of a canoe each. Stuart, McDougall and one of the boat foremen, La Vallet, had charge of the other vessels.

Although the ferocity of the Peace did not rival some of the rivers Tod would face later, there were nevertheless many gravel shoals along its nearly one thousand mile course, and a moment of carelessness could result in disaster. Not long after they reached the Peace River, Tod's canoe was holed by a rock, and two boat foremen, Paul Brown and Daniel Ross, fell back to repair the damage while the clerk went on ahead with the brigade. The canoes were delicate and difficult to manage at the best of times, but worse, none of them were in perfect shape. Another problem was that this was the end of the dry season and the river was low. Later that day Brown and Ross caught up as the others waterproofed their vessels with pitch, a necessary precaution for ahead of them was the Boyer Rapids. "Gumming," as the task was called was important because a leaky boat was difficult to manoeuvre in a swift-flowing river. A canoe not properly maintained was a potentially lethal instrument.

After passing through this stretch of white water without incident, the five canoes camped near the outlet of the Jackfish River. The following day Tod's canoe was damaged again and he had to fall back for repairs. McKenzie in his own boat waited behind in case his fellow clerk needed help. It was not until the following day that the two canoes caught up with Stuart and the brigade. Tod had been given the canoe with the least experienced crew, a situation for which Stuart made little allowance. As his journal indicates, the chief factor had little patience with his new Hudson's Bay officers. However, on 14 September, the problem was with the old Nor'Wester George McDougall's canoe — his boat was holed twice, a fact which Stuart passed off quickly in his journal. McDougall was probably not popular with the clerks who had served on the other side — he had started out his career with the Hudson's Bay in 1815, but had defected to the Nor'Westers the following year.

By the middle of September the scrub brush along the bank, the groves of cottonwood and poplar lining the surrounding hills, and the birch crowding many of the small islands in the river, had taken on the warm colours of autumn. While the days were pleasant, the summer was over and the heat from the evening campfire was welcome. By the time they reached Fort Vermilion, the old North West Company fort near the mouth of the Boyer River, the bag of pemmican they had received at Fort Chipewyan was almost gone, and they obtained a small supply of meat and potatoes from the officer in charge. The brigade's progress continued to be hampered by the poor condition of the canoes.

On 22 September, there was a favourable wind and Stuart rigged a sail, but instead of increasing his speed, the billowing oilcloth suspended from a paddle seemed only to slow him down. Early the following day McDougall's boat was damaged as it passed through a stretch of white water. As his men repaired the gash the others prepared breakfast, and later that day they finished the last of the provisions. With Fort St. John, the nearest post, still many miles upstream, it appeared that hunger would be their companion for days to come. Fortunately, the following day the brigade came across a hunter standing over a freshly killed moose. Stuart managed to trade a quantity of tobacco for meat, and after setting up camp later that evening on Upper Canoe Wood Island the officers and servants enjoyed a hearty supper.

Toward evening on 30 September, the canoes reached Fort St. John where they found the clerk, "Mr. Guy Hughs, [sic] an Interpreter and two men all well."[11] At the fort they obtained a ration of dried provisions for the remainder of the journey to New Caledonia. For some reason, however, they did not get the potato allotment they had expected — a disappointing turn of events, for the tuber had become a Peace River staple. Early frost in the Peace River country was not unknown, and some years the crop was small.

Although his men were obviously tired, Stuart did not allow an additional rest day. It was apparent that by the time he reached the Rocky Mountains the short autumn would be coming to an end. At dawn the next morning the five canoes pushed farther along the Peace. When they passed a small island on 2 October they were confronted by a dam made up of rotting logs, tree roots, and branches partially blocking the channel. As Stuart's canoe passed near the tangle, the current became stronger and his crew had difficulty pressing the craft forward. Had they failed to paddle free, the undertow would almost certainly have carried them back beneath the tangle of debris. Fortunately, the paddlers managed to reach open water, and that evening they camped at the mouth of the Beaver River.

On the following day, Stuart's canoe became separated from the others when he took the wrong channel and found himself hemmed in on the north by high cliffs. Squeezed in by the rocks the river seemed to boil as it pressed against the canoe, but the vessel and its occupants eventually reached the main channel unharmed. Despite his wrong course Stuart remained far ahead of his companions, and as night approached he had his men prepare a great bonfire to act as a beacon for the other boats. After the others had landed at the camp and settled around the fire, they were suddenly aware of the sound of barking dogs in the distance. The animals were Stuart's — during an earlier stop one of the servants had neglected to return them to the canoe. Although they had run along the shore some miles, the cliff had prevented them from catching up, and the distressed animals howled all night, much to the annoyance of everyone.

In the morning Stuart sent his canoe back for the dogs, but when the current carried the boat against a canyon wall, the frame and skin were shattered, which required extensive repairs. Adding to their difficulty, there was little birchbark available to mend the vessel's fabric. While the other four boats went on ahead, Stuart and his men continued repairs on the canoe, but the job was not completed until late afternoon. That night he camped near the mouth of the Grand River and the following day he and his men overtook the brigade.

As they neared the upper reaches of the Peace, the river that had earlier been as much as a quarter of a mile wide was now no more than a few hundred feet across. The swift-flowing water was contained by a steep canyon that towered above them. To Tod's amazement the rock face was studded with countless millions of small marine creatures. These little animals that had once thrived under an ancient sea could now be seen by the river travellers, and it was possible to bring the canoe right up to where the stone shells were visible in the canyon wall. While Tod was later impressed by the beauty of the Rockies, his encounter with these ancient creatures was the highlight of his journey. That the age of the fossils contradicted the biblical account of Creation — which claimed the planet was no more than a few thousand years old — may have been the first step in Tod's rejection of his religious roots. Although it would be many years before he formally broke with the religion of his childhood, he would increasingly question the Calvinist belief in the literal truths of the Old Testament.

On 5 October the brigade pulled ashore on the north side of the river. Ahead, their way was blocked by the worst stretch of white water on the river. Although only 12 miles long, the trail leading along the narrow pass behind Portage Mountain was one of the worst crossings of the entire journey. As they began their trek the path was swampy in places — muddy portages were always the most difficult, for under the weight of their burdens, the men would sink deep into the ooze — but later, the trail began to rise steeply, and the going became even more gruelling. Fortunately, on his way to York Factory during the spring Stuart had arranged with the Rocky Mountain Indians to meet him at that spot to trade. (Because of the long-standing hostilities between these people and the Beaver nation, the Rocky Mountain Indians were unwilling to go to Fort St. John, which was deep in the heart of enemy territory, to trade.) On the trail were between 60 and 80 natives, with their pelts. After the trading was completed the Indians helped move the canoes and cargo across the portage.

Even with additional assistance, the task was not easy, for the route Stuart had taken in the spring was now overgrown with scrub. The Indians had begun to chop away the tangle of brush, but there was still much to do, and after setting up camp the Hudson's Bay men continued the job. After five days of difficult labour, Guilbeau, one of the voyagers, deserted. With few men in New Caledonia, the Hudson's Bay could not afford the loss of any of its employees, and Stuart wasted much time in a fruitless search. Tod was assigned to watch the east end of the trail and McDougall the west, in the event Guilbeau should attempt to flee the portage, but neither man saw any sign of the deserter.

That evening as was the custom, Stuart and his officers joined the elders at the Indian camp where they sat around a great campfire, smoked pipes and talked. The particular dialect of the Cree that Tod had learned from Monkman's daughter at Trout Lake served as a common language among the Indians living as far west as the Rockies. Stuart, who did not speak Cree, was at a disadvantage, and after a few hours he bade his host good night and made his way to his own camp farther along the trail.

During the night, the barking of the dogs in camp convinced the chief factor that Guilbeau was hiding in the bush not far away. A search of the woods the following day, however, revealed no sign of the voyager, and to Tod it seemed increasingly likely that the missing man had sought the protection of the Indians camped on the portage. He approached Stuart and volunteered to search the village, but the chief factor, who placed little value on the abilities of Hudson's Bay officers, made it clear that he did not believe the clerk capable of catching a voyager. As a further rebuke Stuart sent instead the turncoat McDougall. Later, when his friend returned empty-handed, Stuart grudgingly sent Tod, and after an hour, during which the clerk played cat-and-mouse through the Indian encampment with the deserter, he finally captured the man. The natives, who had watched the chase from the sidelines, were displeased — it was considered a breach of aboriginal law to kill a camp guest. Eventually, however, they allowed Tod to take the servant back after he assured them that no harm would come to Guilbeau.

When Tod returned with Guilbeau secured by a rope tied around his neck, Stuart was incredulous. The chief factor would not believe his clerk had been able to capture a North West voyager himself, and demanded to know which Indians had caught the deserter. Tod had by now become tired of the Nor'Wester's insults and, aware that Stuart could not speak Cree, suggested the chief factor return to the Indian camp and ask the natives himself.

On 14 October the last of the cargo was transported to the west end of the portage. The crossing had taken nine days and nine bags of pemmican, half a bag more than Stuart had expected — due, he believed, to the carelessness of one of his voyagers who had been responsible for it and had allowed the others to freely sample its contents. "I inflicted corporal punishment as an example to the others," Stuart noted in his journal.[12] The canoes cleared the portage at last at noon on 15 October. After the strains and mishaps of the crossing all the boats remained in poor shape, but Stuart's craft was particularly leaky. The following morning Stuart sent the other canoes ahead while his own vessel was unloaded and regummed. Late that morning he caught up to the others who were pulled up on the river bank. Earlier, one of the men had spotted a caribou near the water and by good fortune he had managed to shoot it. Their first meal of the day turned unexpectedly into a feast. Unfortunately, during the chase Tod's canoe had been caught up on a shoal, but the damage was minor and repairs were soon completed.

As they continued west the weather remained clear and they made good time as far as Finlay Rapids, only a mile from where the Parsnip and Finlay rivers converged to form the Peace. The river at this point was too dangerous to bring even partially unloaded canoes through using lines from shore — the preferred method, since the boats did not have to be hauled overland. Although the portage was short, much time had to be spent removing the cargo and then carrying everything around the rapids. The sky had now clouded over and rain had begun, which added to the difficulty of transport. Before they pushed off the following morning all the canoes had to be gummed again. It was only a short paddle to the junction of the Finlay and Parsnip rivers, but Tod and McKenzie took the wrong channel. Stuart had called out to them but they were too far ahead to hear, and it was some time before both clerks realized their mistake and turned back. Tod's boat had been damaged enough to require regumming, and he remained behind while the other canoes continued south along the Parsnip River.

Tod rejoined the others late the following day, 21 October. With the Parsnip so low it was easy to damage the fragile vessels, and as a result much time had to be spent maintaining them. After supper that night McDougall's men, using torches, set about recalking their vessel. As they usually did, the boats started out at daybreak, and only later did they come ashore on one of the small islands in the Parsnip to have breakfast and allow the dogs exercise. By the time they were ready to leave, all of the animals had returned to the canoes except "Sergant," a dog belonging to Stuart's canoe. Whether he was motivated by compassion or simply Sergant's value as a sled dog is not clear, but while the other four canoes went ahead Stuart continued a futile search for the lost animal. Only when he finally returned downstream to the previous night's camp did he find the missing dog. The search for Sergant had taken three hours, but later that day Stuart caught up with Tod, McKenzie and La Vallet, the boat foreman, near the spot where the Nation River emptied into the Parsnip. All four boats were in such poor shape that it had been necessary to gum them again, and it was not until late that evening that they found McDougall's camp many miles upstream.

On 24 October Stuart and his party received bad news from New Caledonia. The canoes had stopped near where the Little River joins the Parsnip when Chief Trader William Brown from Fort Kilmaurs on Babine Lake arrived, and told Stuart that two Company servants, Joseph Bagnoit and Belone Duplante, had been murdered at Fort George. While it was probably not until some time later, when he had interviewed James Murray Yale, the clerk at Fort George, that he got the full story, Stuart did not discount the seriousness of the situation. "No greater misfortune could have befallen the Department," he noted in his Journal.[13]

At this spot the brigade left the Parsnip to follow the Little River to its source at McLeod Lake, but they had not gone far when

McKenzie's canoe struck a shoal. Although the cargo was saved the vessel was badly damaged, and despite the oilcloth wraps the contents were soaked. While the others went ahead, McKenzie and his men remained behind waiting for help to be sent from Fort McLeod. The weather was now against them — all day the men in the four remaining boats faced either downpours of rain or flurries of snow — but for Stuart, the end of the journey revealed a final piece of ill luck. As the brigade crossed McLeod Lake the chief factor saw all that remained of his headquarters. "The whole of the buildings of my snug little Fort," he wrote disconsolately, "were carried away in the summer by uncommon high flood and the people are now encamped in huts between the site of the Old Fort and the Little River."[14]

James Murray Yale. (COURTESY BCARS, 28791)

Chapter Four

THAT INHOSPITABLE STEPMOTHER, NEW CALEDONIA

I n the spring of 1823, Fort George had been under the command
of James Murray Yale, a veteran Hudson's Bay clerk who was
assisted by Joseph, his Indian interpreter, and two labourers, Joseph
Bagnoit and Belone Duplante. The men were constructing a new
building at the fort and two young Indians were also hired to help.
Bagnoit and Duplante seemed to get along well with their new assistants — the four employees slept, ate and worked together.

Yale had been ordered by Stuart to remain at Fort George;
however, he decided to make an excursion to the Hudson's Bay
Company posts at Fraser and Stuart lakes, about 400 miles, with
Joseph acting as guide. The purpose of the trip was supposedly to
borrow a cross-cut saw, but this was only an excuse for Yale to see
his friends at the other posts.

Yale may have disobeyed Stuart's orders simply to spite his
superior, for the clerk had little liking for North West Company
officers. Although born in Lower Canada in 1796, he had joined the
London Company in 1815. A short time later he was sent to Fort
Wedderburn in Athabasca, the scene of some of the fiercest fighting
between the two companies. In 1817 Yale was captured at Fort
Chipewyan, and spent five months as a North West Company
prisoner at Great Slave Lake. Among his Hudson's Bay companions,
Yale's bravery was well known. In his memoirs, Tod, who was
seldom free with his praise, described Yale as "a small man in

stature, but courageous, and having as the Indians say, a big heart."[1] Yale's transfer in 1821 to New Caledonia placed him under the command of the former Nor'Wester, John Stuart, which for a front-line Hudson's Bay soldier must have been galling indeed. Yet it was equally true that the clerk could not have imagined the consequences of his small act of rebellion. Before leaving for Stuart Lake he had no hint of what would happen.

When Yale and Joseph returned they came upon a grisly scene — in the servants' sleeping quarters were the bodies of the two labourers, Bagnoit and Duplante. Both men had been stabbed and their heads severed. From the condition of the remains it was evident that neither servant had been dead long. That at least two murderers were involved was probable, for remaining on the floor beside the bodies were two bloody hatchets. Since there were few signs of a struggle it was likely that both men were killed while they slept.

The Indians living near the fort were aware of what had happened, and before Yale's return one of the local chiefs had posted a guard to ensure nothing was stolen from the fort. After checking the stock Yale knew that the motive had not been robbery, for little was missing. The likely suspects were the two young Indian carpenters, for both men had fled the fort, but since only he and Joseph were left at Fort George, Yale decided not pursue them. Instead he remained at the fort, awaiting the return of Stuart from York Factory.

After he reached Fort McLeod Stuart dispatched Tod, McKenzie, McDougall and ten Canadiens to reinforce Fort George. Tod, who was in charge of two canoes, was delayed along the way, which aroused the ire of the chief factor. The tensions resulting from the Fort George murders had increased the already considerable friction between the Hudson's Bay and North West Company officers, and Stuart had little confidence in the loyalty of Yale and his colleagues. Stuart regarded Yale's insubordination as a threat to his authority, and he was determined the clerk should be harshly dealt with as an example to other Hudson's Bay officers. Yale was thus charged with negligence resulting in the deaths of two men, but in keeping with the Company's military organization, as an officer, before he could be dismissed, he was entitled to a hearing before the governor and council. The investigation of the charges was undertaken by Simpson, but because of the slow communication it was more than a year before the governor presented his report to the chief factors.

* * * * *

Fort George had been built by the North West Company wintering partner, Simon Fraser, as the base camp for his historic exploration of the Fraser River. Like Fort St. James on Stuart Lake, Fort George was protected by a high palisade — from early on the relations between the Europeans and the Carrier people, who lived not only in the territory around Fort George but in much of northern New Caledonia, were often tense. Simon Fraser had warned the Carriers in 1806 that the murder of Europeans would be met with reprisals. Stuart, however, was now in a difficult position, for it was certain that the few men guarding the fort were no match for the Carriers. He briefly considered bringing a number of the fearsome Beaver Indians in from the Peace River to protect Fort George, but later events made this move impossible. During the winter the Carriers continued to bring furs to the fort, but the Hudson's Bay men remained suspicious of their trading partners. Recalling another European marooned on an island within a sea of hostile natives, Tod later described the experience as a "sort of Robinson Crusoe existence."[2]

Adding to the feeling of helplessness and frustration among the Europeans was their dependence on the Carriers for provisions. A poor salmon harvest that fall had meant that supplies were difficult to obtain. While Yale remained in charge of the post, McDougall spent much of his time visiting neighbouring villages in search of food. The shortage of fish had produced a seller's market, and although the Company had not been opposed to arriving at hard bargains with the Indians during times of plenty, the Europeans complained bitterly when the situation was reversed. "In no part of Indian Country are the whites a match for those natives who Know the advantages they possess," Stuart wrote angrily.[3] While Stuart was not entirely disappointed with the Fort George returns, it was clear that his men were more eager to trade their goods for fish than for furs.

Although in later years Tod and Yale became friends, an incident that year strained their relationship. Soon after Tod arrived, Yale suddenly turned on his companion, Joseph, and began to strike him, claiming he was also one of the killers. The charge was obviously false — the murders apparently had not been planned and Joseph had been with Yale many miles away from the fort at the time — but the clerk was not acting rationally. Worse for Joseph, Tod, far from restraining Yale, joined in on the assault. Tod later claimed that he acted only to protect his fellow clerk who was in poor physical condition as a result of an inadequate diet, but this was almost surely an excuse. Since their return, Joseph had remained with Yale and would thus have shared the clerk's meagre rations. Neither man was likely to have been robust.

Word of the beating would never have reached Stuart had it not been for the letter Tod had written to Chief Trader William Brown at Fort Kilmaurs, which was sent via McLeod Lake. Although it was a private correspondence the chief factor intercepted it and read its contents. Since the letter has not survived it is not certain exactly what Tod wrote, but it seems clear that the clerk presented a humorous account of his recent journey across the continent, and that Stuart as brigade leader received the full measure of Tod's sharp wit. What was ultimately more damning, though, was that he boasted of the beating that he and Yale had meted out to Joseph.

Stuart did not reply to Tod's letter until after his interview with Yale at Fraser Lake early in February. Obviously aware that he was in serious difficulty, Yale shifted some of the blame for Joseph's beating to Tod whom he claimed had joined in unbidden. On 16 February 1824, Stuart wrote Tod, "your unwarranted assault on the Interpreter ... a man though an Indian has served the Company for an equal length of time and equally faithful as you ... and one who on this side [of] the Mountains, is so much more a consequence to the Company than yourself — that if not in consideration of your former Services, I would, as an example to others dismiss You from the Company's Service at once."[4] Instead, Stuart suspended Tod without pay "until cleared from the stigma under which Through you, the whole of the Company's Servants must appear in the eyes of the Indians."[5]

Once Tod received the letter, it did not take him long to reply to Stuart's denouncement. On 1 March he wrote the chief factor at Fort McLeod:

> With regard to Your intention of stopping my Salary, you may keep it and do what you please with it — I am informed, you were ungenerous enough to open a private letter addressed to Mr. Brown — In this Country especially in this part of it, you can act with impunity [on] any piece of injustice your tyranny may Suggest, but it would not be well for you to do so in a Civilized Country.[6]

Later in the letter Tod dismissed the assault charge as frivolous and challenged Stuart to stand with him before the governor and council at York Factory.

While Stuart occupied the moral high ground in the affair, he was undoubtedly aware that the council would have regarded Tod's behaviour as no more than a misdemeanour. The chief factor's intention, however, was probably not to punish Tod, but to break the solidarity of those Hudson's Bay officers who had rallied behind the embattled Yale. In his letter Stuart implied that Yale had put much of the blame for the assault on Tod.

After Tod reached Fort McLeod on 5 April, he would have received a more complete account of what Yale had alleged, and some weeks later he submitted another letter to the chief factor. By now his tone had changed, for he maintained that he had engaged in the beating because he believed that the Indian was one of the murderers. Further, he wrote "you must be well aware that from Mr. Yale and from him alone I could receive my information."[7] Since Tod was now at Fort McLeod, the matter could have been handled through a face-to-face meeting between the two men, but there is little doubt that Stuart wanted the clerk's own handwritten statement so that it could be used against Yale later at the meeting of the Northern Council.

Given Tod's cooperation, Stuart was willing to accept that the clerk had been misled by his colleague at Fort George. "It might teach you how far to place faith in any thing he [Yale] might afterwards tell you," the chief factor advised.[8] Generously, Stuart not only reinstated Tod, but cleared the stain on his record as if nothing had happened. "I am ... more pleased at the motive that led to it [the beating] than disatisfied [sic] at the deed itself however unjustifiable," he noted.[9]

Yale, however, was not so easily forgiven. With the charges still hanging over his head, he was moved in the spring to Fort Alexandria, a few hundred miles farther south on the Fraser, where he awaited the Northern Council's decision.

Some months after the deaths of Bagnoit and Duplante, another tragic incident took place in the neighbouring Peace River district. In early November a band of Beaver Indians killed five Company men at Fort St. John. Although the Hudson's Bay's plan to close the post was at the root of Indian discontent, the murders may have been sparked by Samuel Black who, before he began his expedition to the Finlay River, had spent some time at Fort St. John. The explorer's relationship with a local Indian woman had apparently angered the Beavers living nearby. When the Indians struck, Black was not at the post, which left the unfortunate clerk, Guy

Hughes, and his men to take the full force of Indian anger. The mood of the Hudson's Bay men on both sides of the Rockies was increasingly desperate.

* * * * *

One of the anecdotes Tod included in his memoirs concerned his return journey from Fort George in April 1824. Despite his suspension he had been given the responsibility for transporting the winter fur returns by sled to Fort McLeod. Tod's companion on the trail was a servant, a longtime resident of New Caledonia who was particularly noted for the fine elk-skin coat he owned. As it happened, the sled run was more difficult than either traveller had anticipated, and they had not taken enough provisions. To make matters worse, they ran head on into a fierce snowstorm that further slowed their progress. Halfway to Fort McLeod the men and dogs ran out of rations.

On their third night out, tired and hungry, Tod and his companion prepared for sleep. As was his practice the servant bedded down in his warm, ankle-length coat. Before falling asleep himself, Tod noticed that instead of taking its usual place by the fire, one of the dogs settled behind the man's back. Although such loyalty in a sled dog was unusual, Tod thought little of the animal's behaviour. Exhausted, he soon fell asleep.

The next morning as was his habit, Tod rose first to tend the fire. In the half light of a late winter dawn, his companion coughed and stirred slowly. Then suddenly the man sat up and began frantically to search the area where he had been sleeping. Tod soon discovered the reason for the servant's behaviour — his much-prized elk-skin coat was missing.

Puzzled, Tod examined the area around where his companion had slept. On the ground were a few gnawed shreds of what looked like coat. It was clear to Tod what had happened. As the servant slept, his faithful dog — the animal that had preferred his company to the warmth of the fire — had chewed his coat off his back. Angry, the man took a stick and was about to beat the animal when Tod intervened. After all, Tod admitted later, the thought of his companion's coat in the stew pot had also crossed his own mind once or twice.

After several more days on the trail, the hungry travellers finally reached Fort McLeod. The old man's magnificent coat, though, was only a memory.

* * * * *

Due to the uncertain mood of the Indians, the Fort George post was abandoned in the spring of 1824, and the officers and servants who had wintered over were dispersed throughout the territory. Tod remained at Fort McLeod where he acted as Stuart's clerk. The McLeod Lake establishment had been built in 1805 by the North West explorer Simon Fraser, and was the first trading post opened in New Caledonia. Beyond its historical importance, however, there was little else to recommend it. "A more dreary situation can scarcely be imagined, surrounded by towering mountains that almost exclude the light of day, and snow storms not seldom occurring, so violent and long continued as to bury the establishment," wrote Chief Trader John McLean, who passed that way in 1833. "I believe there are few situations in the country that present such local disadvantages."[10] Simpson, too, during his trip to New Caledonia in 1828, was no more flattering, declaring flatly that "McLeods Lake is the most wretched place in Indian Country."[11]

Like others who were used to the predictably cold climate of Hudson Bay, Tod did not easily adjust to the changeability of the McLeod Lake weather. Although the winter temperature at the post was usually well below freezing, the occasional Chinook brought a rapid rise in the thermometer. Given the dreariness of his daily routine, Tod eventually found that the unpredictability of the weather at least broke the monotony.

Fort Mcleod, CA. 1900. (FROM MORICE, The History of the Northern Interior of British Columbia)

The post at McLeod Lake was destroyed by the flood of 1823, and a detailed description of the reconstructed Fort McLeod was not recorded, but it probably resembled other small Hudson's Bay establishments in New Caledonia. Without a stockade and with only a small complement of regular employees, the fort was not easily defended. However, since the Sekani who lived in the area of the fort were favourably regarded by Hudson's Bay traders, elaborate defences were considered unnecessary.

In most Hudson's Bay posts, the living quarters for the officer in charge and the storerooms were built across a courtyard from the great hall where trading took place. At smaller posts like Fort McLeod, the mess hall was used for trading. Servants' quarters were usually separate from the other buildings that lined the courtyard. Commonly, these accommodations were not provided by the Company, but built by the lower ranks during their free time. Although in larger establishments servants and officers messed separately, the personnel at Fort McLeod probably ate together. Fort McLeod's isolation meant that goods and furnishings of European manufacture would have been difficult to obtain. Even in important depots such as Fort Vancouver, which was completed in 1825, the dwellings of the clerks and servants were spartan. The clerk's country-made bed frame, table and chairs were provided by the Hudson's Bay. Mattresses were frequently no more than a pile of a dozen blankets, or a quilt made from the feathers of local game birds. The company also supplied a limited number of tin plates and cups for the use of its employees, but towels and blankets were regarded as personal property and had to be purchased. Commissioned officers often received better quality supplies, including china and glassware, but it is doubtful that Chief Factor Stuart, at Fort McLeod in remote New Caledonia, could claim such luxuries.

For all employees living at Fort McLeod, obtaining enough to eat was often a challenge. In the vast Hudson's Bay empire, Company employees were expected to live off the land, but in New Caledonia this was particularly difficult, for there were no great herds of buffalo in the far west as there were on the plains. Also, although wild ducks and geese were plentiful in some places, the Company did not bring in salt to preserve them — it was too costly.

Almost everywhere in New Caledonia, Indians depended upon salmon for existence, and the size of the yearly run often meant the difference between starvation and survival. Not surprisingly, the natives wasted little of the fish. Even the seemingly inedible parts were used — a great delicacy among the Indians was an oil obtained from the heads of salmon.

While the Europeans were equally dependent on salmon, the pink-fleshed fish was never popular on Hudson's Bay dinner tables. According to Chief Trader Joseph McGillivray, with few exceptions "there is nothing more offensive to the olfactory organs than an 18 or 24 [month-old] salmon — its effluvia when roasting is quite intolerable."[12]

In a report to the Company, McGillivray provided a description of the preparation of the fish and its effect on the Indians:

> The salmon when cured loses 4/5th of its weight, becomes crisp, and of reddish appearance, rendered blackish by the incessant smoke which must be daily kept up to prevent flies from settling on it. Fish thus cured forms their constant diet without any condiment, and what is a fact, that it actually files the teeth to the very gums. I have observed many young men about 25 years of age who had their teeth worn away, and at 40 they have positively none. The same effect operates on the whites — its ravages are not so perceptible as we come to these countries at an advanced period in Life.[13]

Yet the fish often produced other difficulties for the Hudson's Bay men. Unlike the Indians, the Europeans may have lacked natural immunity to the bacteria that survived the preservation process, and intestinal upsets among Hudson's Bay employees were common. One of Tod's anecdotes concerned his friend Yale, who before the 1821 amalgamation had been posted to the Peace River district, where salmon imported from New Caledonia was also a staple. There he faced the infamous Nor'Wester, William McIntosh, who tried to poison him. According to Tod, it was only because Yale's stomach had become so hardened, "by long acquaintance with the rough fare of that inhospitable stepmother, New Caledonia, that the diabolic attempt altogether failed."[14]

Sometimes, though, the effects were more serious. The death of a servant prompted D. E. Cameron, the clerk at Fort Kilmaurs on Babine Lake, to write to Chief Trader Donald Manson in 1845: "Poor Couturier expired on the night of the 4th. ... He began to fall off ... from the effect, I firmly believe, which salmon has on some constitutions, as in the cases of J. B. Desmarais and Thibeault last year."[15] Tod's objection to salmon had more to do with the monotony of his meals: with so little variety in his diet, he sometimes craved other foods. Like other Hudson's Bay traders, Tod seemed little interested in including the roots and leaves eaten by the Indians in their diet — the Europeans regarded these plants as inferior fare. He did attempt a small garden, but in a part of the territory where frosts were common even in summer, vegetables often did not survive until harvest.

At Fort McLeod, Tod faced an added problem, for even salmon were not easily obtained at the post. Although the fish travelled hundreds of miles inland to spawn, their range did not quite reach McLeod Lake. In autumn, dried salmon had to be hauled from Stuart Lake to Fort McLeod, an overland distance of more than 80 miles. The trek over the mountains was difficult — Simpson recalled it was one of the most tiring sections of his journey west in 1828.

Tod, in his memoirs, does not provide a portrait of his day-to-day existence at McLeod Lake. Through much of the year, though, it is clear that he was away from his post in search of game. It was not only a way to pass the time, but if he were successful, it meant an increase in provisions. The pelts of beaver and other animals he trapped or shot also added to his post's yearly fur returns. The difficulty was that in the mountains around McLeod Lake animals were scarce, with the result that he often came back empty-handed.

Another food source was the small freshwater whitefish that was plentiful in local streams. It was difficult to catch, though, for it passed easily through the nets of European manufacture. The only successful fishing method was using a woven basket called a *vorveau*, but the secrets of its construction were known only to a few Indians. For his supply, Tod was thus forced to rely on native fishermen. In some of the lakes and streams he was able to fish using a rod and line, but the trout were often difficult to catch. From April to June, during the spring run-off, and again in early autumn, the fish did not readily take a hook.

Another food source was the only domestic animal raised by the Indians. This was the giddee, a breed of dog characterized by its small size, sharp nose, small ears and curved tail. In his reminiscences of New Caledonia, Tod implied that dog flesh was eaten by the traders only as a last resort — when it was impossible to obtain anything else — but in truth, the canine had long had an honoured place in outpost cuisine. As early as 1808, Simon Fraser noted that among his voyagers dog was always a favourite meal. North West officers likely acquired their taste for the animal from the lower ranks. After 1821, on festive occasions the giddee became the main course for many a Hudson's Bay dinner.*

* * * * *

Under the Nor'Westers the Columbia district, which included New Caledonia, had operated at a loss, and once in charge Simpson attempted to alter the territory's balance sheet. To this end, the governor instituted rigorous economies, and thus, despite a surplus of personnel elsewhere in Company territory, New Caledonia remained habitually understaffed. There were only 36 servants and eight officers in the entire territory in 1822, the year before Tod made his journey west.

John Stuart remained in charge of New Caledonia less than a year before being transferred to the Saskatchewan district. Appointed in his place was William Connolly, also a former Nor'Wester. Born at Lachine in Lower Canada in 1787, he joined the North West Company in 1801. In 1818 he became a wintering partner and was transferred to Cumberland House on the Saskatchewan River. More a diplomat than a soldier, Connolly worked out an agreement with his opposite number in the Hudson's Bay, Thomas Swain, by which neither side would poach the other's furs. After amalgamation, Connolly was appointed a chief trader, and in 1825, after assuming control of New Caledonia, was promoted to chief factor. Unlike the imperious Stuart, Connolly made no distinction between Hudson's Bay men and Nor'Westers. Indeed, his letters to his superiors reflect his concern for the welfare of all his employees.

Unfortunately, Connolly established his new headquarters at Fort St. James on Stuart Lake while Tod remained at Fort McLeod. Without its role of district headquarters and supply depot, the post was reduced to a fur-trade backwater. "In consequence of the recent changes in this department my situation has become more lonesome," Tod wrote Edward Ermatinger in 1826. "I am not now as formerly assailed with the landing of noisy brigades and canoes,

* Tod's inaccuracies on this subject may have sprung from his wish not to offend Victorian-era sensibilities. Tod had written his account of New Caledonia for the American historian H. H. Bancroft, knowing that some of his stories would be included in the latter's books. It was obvious that some readers would have found the fur traders' preference for canine flesh less than acceptable.

men, women, and dogs clamouring for potatoes and fish — which though certainly attended with some moments of uneasiness yet afforded me many hours of pleasure."[16] Although the returns at McLeod Lake were considerable, he was sometimes the only employee at the post, and he was much affected by his isolation. Not even the Sekani people who usually lived near McLeod Lake visited him in the winter — in late autumn, most moved away to their winter camp grounds where firewood was more plentiful.

Fort McLeod, for Tod, had one advantage: it came with its own small library left over from a former occupant of the post. In a territory where transportation was both difficult and costly, these books were a valuable asset. Tod still carried the three volumes given to him by his father; the collection of Burns's poems remained a particular favourite, and his letters to Edward often included a line or two from the Scottish bard.

Tod also passed the time with another familiar pleasure — music. By the beginning of 1826, the ancient flute he had received from Edward at Island Lake had fallen into disrepair, and he wrote his friend to ask for a new instrument. Later, Tod would increasingly rely on Edward to manage his dealings with the outside world. About the time he received his new flute, Tod also acquired a fiddle, sent by either Edward or his brother Frank. Tod had played Edward's instrument before, but he had much to learn, and the woods around McLeod Lake must have echoed with the occasional sour note.

In the isolated frontier posts, sheet music was also a rare and valuable commodity. When Tod left Island Lake, he had taken with him the music book given him by the Swiss settler in 1819. Since Edward had used the extra ruled pages for some of his own musical scores, Tod's departure meant that he was without some of his own pieces. In one of his letters Edward asked for their return, but Tod was unwilling to part with them. "It is a pity you did not forward the music paper as I would have copied the pieces you mention," he replied. "I would tear out the original and send them to you, but that I regard them as the productions of a particular friend and cannot, therefore think of parting with [them]."[17]

During his time at Fort McLeod, Tod entered into a relationship with a native woman. Given his isolation, his new companion was probably a local woman, a Sekani from McLeod Lake. In 1826, he wrote to Edward that "my fellow labourer in the vineyard is possessed of an excellent ear for music and never fails to accompany me on the flute with her voice when I take up the instrument."[18] The relationship was of some duration, and Tod fathered at least one daughter. In 1829 he replied to Ermatinger's inquiry, "she still continues the only companion of my solitude — without her, or some other substitute, life, in such a wretched place as this, would be altogether insupportable."[19]

Tod probably did not exaggerate her importance, for in the harsh conditions at McLeod Lake, a woman familiar with the country would have been invaluable. "Connubial alliances," Simpson had argued, "are the best security we can have of the goodwill of the natives."[20] Before his marriage to his cousin Frances in 1830, the governor had enjoyed many such alliances.

* * * * *

To exploit the potential of the Company's new territories, Simpson began to establish new forts in the far western hinterland. The largest of these was Fort Vancouver, near the mouth of the Columbia River. Although the trail was difficult, Simpson concluded the route westward was better than packing the furs east over the Rockies to York Factory. At Fort Vancouver, Company ships could take on their cargo and transport it directly to England — a significant savings.

The increased demand for clerks in the west meant that many of Tod's longtime friends also made the reluctant journey to new posts across the Rockies. In 1825 the Ermatinger brothers were sent to the Columbia Department — Frank was posted to Fort Thompson while Edward was assigned to Fort Vancouver. Although Fort Vancouver, the Columbia Department headquarters, was comfortable compared with Fort McLeod, Edward considered himself badly treated by the Company and contemplated quitting the fur trade altogether. Edward's presence in the far west did not give Tod much pleasure. The bleakness of his New Caledonian existence had already laid his spirit low, and the possibility of Edward's departure further added to his general depression. "Is it possible we have parted never to meet again?" he wrote despondently. "I hope not. But hope (that never failing sheet anchor of some) I am almost fairly tired of."[21]

Another in Tod's circle of friends, John Work, was now at Spokane House. Work had accompanied Peter Skene Ogden in his expedition to the Snake River country in 1823. The young Irish clerk was well known for his romantic adventures, and his divorce of his country wife, apparently as a result of her infidelity, was an unexpected turn about. "In the affair ... [Work] was far from exhibiting that example of Christian forgiveness as did the Levite sojournying [sic] on the side of Mount Ephraim," Tod gossiped to Edward in 1826.[22]

Also assigned to the Columbia Department was Peter Skene Ogden's old friend, Samuel Black, who had recently returned from his exploration of the Finlay River. For Black and his clerk Donald Manson the journey had been incredibly difficult for the terrain was rugged. Before they reached Thutade Lake, the headwaters of the Finlay, many of their Indian packers had deserted, and Black, Manson and the few remaining men had to struggle on alone. Although he had failed to find a river outlet to the northern Pacific Coast, Black had shown Simpson that he could follow orders. As a reward for his effort he was promoted officially to the rank of chief trader and given command of Fort Nez Percés in the Columbia territory where he remained for five years.

Meanwhile, in 1825 the charges Chief Factor Stuart had preferred against James Murray Yale were finally dismissed. In July the council of the Northern Department met and concluded that there was no evidence to suggest that the tragic "accident" was the fault of the young clerk, and "That the said J. M. Yale be not discharged from the service."[23] The decision to exonerate Yale was based on a report prepared by George Simpson. In it, the governor supplied a motive for the crime: one of the native workers had once been the lover of Yale's country wife. When either Bagnoit or Duplante discovered the pair together, he threatened to reveal what he had seen to Yale, and the two Hudson's Bay men were murdered to keep them silent. While the Company was eager to apprehend the fugitives, both men had made good their escape. In 1825, one of the accused was reported to have crossed the Rocky Mountains where he died at the hands of the Cree. Of the other, a Carrier by the name of Zulthnolly, nothing had been heard.

In late February 1826, Tod received an assistant, a young Hudson's Bay officer named James Douglas. Although Douglas later seemed to go out of his way to assist his longtime acquaintance, Tod never completely trusted the ambitious younger man. Of Afro-European parentage, Douglas was born in British Guiana in 1803. He attended school in Lanark, Scotland, and in 1819, while still in Britain, joined the North West Company. He was sent to the Ile-à-la-Crosse district and remained there until long after the 1821 amalgamation. In 1825, he was transferred to New Caledonia.

Later, Douglas would be closely associated with the transformation of New Caledonia from a vast, fur-producing wilderness to the booming gold colony of British Columbia, but in 1826 such changes were still a long way off. He remained with Tod only a few months before being transferred to Fort St. James as one of Chief Factor Connolly's clerks. There, he married Connolly's 15-year-old daughter, Amelia, on 27 April 1828. The marriage was not regarded with favour by everyone, for the chief factor had promised his daughter to James Murray Yale. This change in plans soured relations between Yale and Connolly.

On a broader front, relations between the Carrier Indians and the Hudson's Bay men also remained strained. Despite years of searching, the Europeans had been unable to capture the fugitive Zulth-nolly who had been hidden by members of his tribe. In April 1828, five years after the Fort George murders, another killing occurred at Babine Lake when a servant, Duncan Livingston, was shot to death. Only after the deaths of the two Indians accused of Livingston's murder did tensions ease somewhat.

Three months later there was another serious incident, this time at Fort St. James. The principal actor in the affair was James Douglas, who had remained at Fort St. James after his marriage. During one of Connolly's visits to Fort Vancouver, his son-in-law was left in

Fort St. James, CA. 1900. (FROM MORICE, The History of the Northern Interior of British Columbia)

charge of the depot. On Stuart Lake, not far from the post, there was a large encampment of Carrier Indians, one of whose chiefs was Kwah, a warrior who had considerable power and influence among his people.

On a day when Kwah was away from his lodge, Douglas received intelligence that Zulth-nolly, the man accused of the murder of the two Fort George servants in 1823, was hiding in the village. Believing that the settlement of this old debt would further his career, Douglas wasted no time — he and his men began a search of the Indian camp. Eventually, after an exhaustive search, Zulth-nolly was found hiding in one of the lodges. Douglas and his men took the fugitive outside and beat him to death on the spot. After returning to the fort, Douglas quickly dashed off a dispatch to Connolly who was still at Fort Vancouver:

> When I wrote you last I little apprehended that I would have occasion to address you again before your arrival here, but the accomplishment of a much desired event renders it now particularly necessary ... I allude to ... the death of Zulth-nolly, whom we dispatched on the first of this month in the Indian Village of this place, without confusion or accident happening to any other individual ... the Indian named was one of the murderers of Fort George Who had hitherto Contrived to escape the punishment his crime so deservedly merited.[24]

When Kwah returned to camp and discovered that the fugitive had been murdered he was angry, for Zulth-nolly had been under the protection of the people of Stuart Lake. Douglas, who could hear the drums and commotion in the village from the fort, expected trouble. Kwah, though, did not act immediately, but waited several days until the clerk and his men had grown complacent. Then after the main gate had been left open and unguarded, Kwah made his move. He and his followers simply entered the fort and, almost without a struggle, captured everyone at the post. The humiliated Douglas was forced to pay indemnity in the form of trade goods to the family of the deceased.

Kwah's capture of Fort St. James was a considerable embarrassment to Douglas, and in later years the story, in various versions, received wide circulation among his friends and enemies alike. Tod, who was less than a hundred miles away and would have heard first-hand accounts, included a version of the incident in his memoirs. After his rise to power, Douglas never mentioned the incident publicly.

Less than a month after the trouble at Fort St. James, Tod had a visit from George Simpson, who had arrived on an inspection trip of the Company's western posts. The two large canoes that carried Simpson and his entourage, including a piper to provide an afternoon's entertainment for the governor and his party, reached Fort Chipewyan on Lake Athabasca in August. There they took on several passengers: a clerk, William McGillivray, and his family who were destined for a new posting in the west. Also with the governor were Chief Trader Archibald McDonald, who had been given charge of a new Company post, Fort Langley, which had been built near the mouth of the Fraser River, and Dr. Richard J. Hamlyn, who was now posted to Fort Vancouver as medical officer.

On 11 September 1828, Simpson and his party reached McLeod Lake where Tod and his two assistants, Joseph Letendre and Louis Gagnon, were taken by surprise. The three were facing a difficult time — last year's supply of salmon had been exhausted and there was little to eat. Simpson, in a later dispatch to London, declared what he had observed at Fort McLeod: "Its compliment [sic] of people ... we found starving, having had nothing to eat for several weeks but berries, and whose countenances were so pale and emaciated that it was with difficulty I recognized them."[25] The sight of his emaciated clerk clearly disturbed the usually imperturbable Simpson, and Tod shrewdly pressed his condition to advantage. Given the sacrifices he had made in the Company's service, Tod believed he should have been considered for promotion — he had spent 17 years working for the Hudson's Bay.

It did not take him long, however, to squander the good will he had earned with the governor. According to Tod, during the visit he caught one of the governor's guides making off with a highly prized sack of seed potatoes. The clerk immediately struck the man, knocking him down.* As a result, Tod was quickly brought up on charges before Simpson, who imposed a small fine. Tod cited some technicality and refused to pay, and the charges were quietly dropped.

* The cause of the dispute, however, may have been more than potatoes. According to the journal of one of Simpson's travelling companions, Chief Trader Archibald McDonald, the blow was apparently the result of the guide's particular and unwelcome interest in Tod's country wife.

Before he left McLeod Lake, the governor gave Tod little hope for promotion. In a letter to Edward a few months later, Tod put on a brave front by declaring, "my disappointment was the less, as I never entertained sanguine expectations."[26] In fact, life at Fort McLeod was getting more difficult. Like many longtime residents of the frontier, Tod had begun to suffer the long-term effects of such a harsh existence. He had occasional bouts of "a severe pain that attends me in the hip when I walk, stand, or even sit in the position required to write."[27] He believed the condition, which was later diagnosed as sciatica, to be the result of cramping his legs within the limited space of a canoe, but it was more likely brought on by his inadequate diet.

After their brief visit with Tod, the governor and his entourage reached Stuart Lake on 17 September 1828. Simpson, of course, had been made aware of the recent difficulties at Fort St. James, and for this reason he intended his arrival at Stuart Lake to be a show of Company force. As described by Archibald McDonald in his journal, it was an impressive sight:

> The day, as yet, being fine, the flag was put up; the piper in full Highland costume; and every arrangement was made to arrive ... in the most imposing manner we could, for the sake of the Indians. Accordingly, when within about a thousand yards of the establishment, descending a gentle hill, a gun was fired, the bugle sounded, and soon after the piper commenced the celebrated march of the clans. ... The guide, with the British ensign, led the van, followed by the band; then the Governor, on horseback, supported behind by Doctor Hamlyn and myself on our chargers, two deep; twenty men, with their burdens, next formed the line; then one loaded horse, and lastly, Mr. McGillivray (with his wife and light infantry) closed the rear.[28]

Chief Factor Connolly arrived from Fort Vancouver several hours after Simpson. A few days later, some leading Carrier chiefs were summoned to Fort St. James to meet the governor. After the Indians had arrived, Simpson began to harangue them about their recent conduct. Chief Trader McDonald, who attended the meeting, described the events in his journal:

> [Simpson] represented to them how helpless their condition would be at this moment were he and all his people to enter

upon hostilities against them. That a partial example had been already made of the guilty parties, but that the next time the Whites should be compelled to imbrue their hands in the blood of Indians, it would be a general sweep; that the innocent would go with the guilty, and that their fate would become deplorable indeed.[29]

During his speech, Simpson singled out Kwah for particular rebuke, noting his part in the incident at Fort St. James earlier that summer. Then, obviously on cue, Douglas rushed forward to intercede on the chief's behalf. After his lecture, Simpson showed his generosity by passing out rum and distributing a little tobacco. Then, as the piper played "Song of Peace," Kwah and the other chiefs were dismissed.

The governor obviously enjoyed the role of "potentate" of the Indian territories, but for those in charge of the isolated posts, his practices sometimes created on-going difficulties. Tod noted that the governor's habit of distributing gifts to some chiefs created envy in the hearts of those who failed to receive these Imperial favours. Expectations were also raised that post officers would likewise bestow gifts, with the result that many chiefs became dissatisfied.

Whether Kwah saw through this little charade or not is unclear, but many others, including Zulth-nolly's relatives, were not inclined to forgive Douglas. On 20 September, John McDonell, a clerk from the Fraser Lake post, was ambushed on his way to meet Simpson at Fort St. James. Although the assailant's gun "carried a couple balls within a few feet" of McDonell, the clerk escaped without injury.[30] On 9 December 1828, the Fort St. James journal recorded that while travelling near Fraser Lake, "Mr. Douglas relates a most atrocious attempt ... was made against his life."[31] While few of the details of the incident were ever recorded, Douglas was clearly disturbed.

Several weeks later the traders at Fort St. James conspired to get even. On New Year's Day, as was the custom, a celebration was held at the fort to which some of the local Indians were invited. What was unusual about this year's festivities, however, was that the Company was particularly generous with its rum. Also, while the officers frequently passed around the spirits, they took none themselves. The traders acted swiftly once all their guests had fallen unconscious. After the native women and the lower-ranking native men were carried outside the fort, the traders fell upon the remaining chiefs and beat them soundly. Of the Carrier leaders, only old Kwah and his nephew Tlœng were spared.

In the morning when the chiefs and elders awoke outside the fort, their bodies were bruised and battered. While he alone was not responsible for the beatings, Douglas remained the focus of Carrier anger. The following month Connolly was obliged to write to Simpson at Fort Vancouver, "Douglas' life is most exposed among these Carriers, he would face a hundred of them, but he does not much like the idea of being assassinated, with your permission he might next year be removed to the Columbia, wherever he may be placed he cannot fail of being essentially useful."[32]

On 30 January 1830, Douglas said goodbye to his father-in-law and set out for the safer surroundings of Fort Vancouver. For the young clerk, New Caledonia had been unkind, indeed. He had been humiliated at the hand of Kwah and driven off. As it turned out, though, the defeat was no impediment to his career, and by the time Tod renewed his acquaintance with Douglas some years later, the latter's fortunes had taken a remarkable turn.

*   *   *   *   *

For Tod, also, New Caledonia was a difficult posting. The transfer of the New Caledonia district headquarters and supply depot to Stuart Lake in 1824 meant that he had difficulty obtaining alcohol. While spirits were in short supply in New Caledonia, such luxuries were not entirely denied the higher ranks. It is doubtful, however, that much of the commissioned officers' brandy flowed to the clerks in the more isolated forts.

The Company continued to provide spirits to the Indians, but the amount was usually small and allotted only on special occasions. After Peter Warren Dease had replaced William Connolly as superintendent of New Caledonia in 1830, Tod wrote to his new superior: "Mr. Connolly — the officer in charge of the district — previous to his departure from here, made [the Sekani] very liberal promises of spirits and tobacco should their hunt, on his arrival in the fall, be found to equal his expectations."[33] Tod's claim is suspicious because, given Governor Simpson's obsession with economy, Chief Factor Connolly's "liberal promises" would have been extremely rash. It seems more likely that Tod was testing the new superintendent to see what comforts he could obtain for himself.

The spirits Tod did receive were clearly not enough to meet his wants. In a letter to Edward in 1829, he made oblique reference to his plight. "[It] has been said that a man's greatest enemies are those of his own household, and the truth of which I, in some digree [*sic*], still continue to experience. A craving appetite with so little to satisfy it is not only a disagreeable inmate, but certainly a very dangerous enemy."[34] Without even the uncertain comfort of a glass of grog, his existence was becoming unendurable.

Because of its isolation and the difficulty in obtaining provisions, Fort McLeod was one of the worst postings in all the Hudson's Bay territories. It was, nonetheless, a profitable operation and Tod had managed it well. While Simpson may have had no desire to promote a clerk whom he personally disliked, he was also aware of Tod's value to the Company. For this reason, the governor's letters to Tod offered much encouragement but few promises. Tod, though, was not taken in by easy praise. "I have rec[eive]d a flattering Letter from Gov[erno]r Simpson," he wrote Edward at the beginning of 1830, "but fine words have now no long have any effect on me. I require something more substantial to Keep me from despondency."[35] With little chance of advancement within the Hudson's Bay, Tod saw his future as increasingly bleak.

Chapter Five

JUST CAUSE TO COMPLAIN

Adding to Tod's misery at Fort McLeod was Edward's decision to leave the Hudson's Bay. The young clerk remained discontented with his lot at Fort Vancouver and, in autumn 1826, he gave Dr. John McLoughlin, the new chief factor of the Columbia Department, his resignation. However, separation was not always easy. As well as prior approval from the Northern Council, the Company demanded written notice one year in advance.

In 1827, McLoughlin gave Edward command of the York Express — the mail canoe that made the annual journey between the Columbia and Hudson Bay — apparently with the hope that the council would deal with the clerk's resignation while he was at York Factory. Although Edward was prepared to leave during its July meeting, the council failed to approve his resignation, and he returned to Fort Vancouver to wait another year. In 1828, Edward again accompanied the express east, and this time, the council approved his withdrawal from service. In August, he left York Factory by canoe for Montreal where he remained several months before taking passage for England.

Tod was not certain whether his friend would ever return to North America. At first he had not wished to see his friend leave Company service, but he changed his attitude once it was clear that Edward was indeed retiring. "I sincerely hope things are going on prosperously with You and that You may never have cause to regret leaving this worst of Countries," he wrote in 1829.[1] Edward's bold step only made Tod's plight at Fort McLeod seem even less enviable. Although dissatisfied with his treatment, Edward had at least enjoyed the comparative comforts of Fort Vancouver. Moreover, as a clerk at the western headquarters, he would have been more likely than Tod to receive promotion. Within the Hudson's Bay, field service counted for little — the clerks who received promotion were those placed close to powerful figures such as Chief Factor McLoughlin. Tod had no such patron. Frank Ermatinger had also supported his brother's decision to withdraw. Despite his complaints — he claimed he did not care for being "shuffled from one [post] to another like a pack of cards" — there is little doubt Frank enjoyed the excitement he found within Company service.[2] He had originally been sent to Fort Thompson but had spent much of his time elsewhere, for he was often called to fill in for sick or absent officers at other forts.

Like Frank Ermatinger, John Work spent much of his time on the move. Although Work was stationed at Fort Colvile on the Columbia between 1826 and 1830, he was often away from the post. Work's health had not been good — he had serious and recurring problems with his eyes, which at times badly affected his vision. In the winter of 1828, he came down with a bout of quinsy, or inflammation of the tonsils, from which he had hardly recovered when he was attacked by a young bull. These injuries were so severe that Tod noted in a letter to Edward, "he is never likely to get ... better."[3] (Tod turned out to be unduly pessimistic, for Work eventually recovered.)

Although they failed to see each other sometimes for years at a time, Tod and his circle, which included not only the Ermatinger brothers and John Work, but Chief Trader Archie McDonald and clerk Thomas Dears, maintained solid and long-lasting friendships. The thread that connected them was extremely thin — personal letters were a rare and much valued commodity in the Columbia Department. Mail to the world beyond the Rockies went out only once a year with the York Express. Incoming letters were sent via the Columbia Express in the fall. It was also possible to send mail east to Canada via the Hudson's Bay ships that called at Fort Vancouver, but this route saved little time, for the letters made the long and difficult voyage around the tip of South America to London before finally returning to North America. The slow mail undoubtedly increased Tod's feeling of isolation, for even the simplest of personal items, such as strings for his violin, had to be ordered far in advance.

* * * * *

While at Fort McLeod, Tod was sometimes given one or two assistants, French-speaking servants who earlier had been employed by the North West Company. Before amalgamation, the officers of the Hudson's Bay had a grudging admiration for these Canadiens, who were regarded as true masters of the forest. Yet, as Tod discovered, not all these servants fit the usual romantic image. One such disappointment was his assistant, Joseph Letendre, who proved to be a singularly inept adventurer.

Tod only once made the mistake of taking Letendre on a hunting and trapping expedition to the Rocky Mountains. "The Canadian was not used to seeing wild animals and was naturally timorous and nervous."[4] Tod cautioned him to keep control of himself regardless of what he faced. The two men had proceeded by canoe along the Parsnip River, setting beaver traps at places Tod believed the animals would visit. After a few days, they turned around and began heading back. This was an easy part of their journey and little paddling was needed as they were travelling with the current. Under a cobalt blue sky, the day was pleasantly warm, and Tod's mind was drawn to the richness of nature's colours — the greens of the mosses, the metallic sheen to the wet rocks in the river and, like silver wool, the lichens clinging to the trees along the banks. Indeed, so caught up was he in the beauty of his surroundings, he forgot the purpose of this expedition. As they reached a point where the river was split into two channels by a small island, Tod hardly noticed a thick patch of Oregon grape covering one of the banks. Suddenly he was brought back to consciousness by a swishing sound — the thick vegetation covering the bank began to rustle.

Seeing the bushes shaking, Letendre became very agitated. The more experienced Tod reached down to the floor of the canoe, picked up his double-barrelled shotgun, aimed at the bushes and squeezed the trigger. The pellet blast, as far as he could tell, had failed to find its mark, but as they watched, a black bear lumbered onto the bank and waded into the river, apparently intending to swim to the opposite side.

Bears have poor eyesight, and probably this one did not see Tod and Letendre until it was almost on top of them. Before the bear had time to strike, Tod fired the second barrel. By now the bear was so close there was little chance of missing with his weapon. Even with the full blast of the shotgun at its chest, the creature did not fall but retreated up the slope beyond the river bank.

After he found a place to land, Tod pulled the canoe onto shore and set off in the direction of the bear. Letendre, who was thoroughly frightened by what had happened, came more slowly. Tod followed the bloody trail until he found his quarry sitting by a flat rock, badly wounded but still alive. Without time to reload, he picked up a heavy tree branch and brought the rude club down as hard as he could on the animal's head. The piece of wood shattered and the bear swayed, but it was obvious that it would take more than a stick to kill the beast. When Letendre arrived, Tod shouted at him to get the long-handled axe from the canoe. Tod struck one blow with the flat side of the weapon, but still the animal would not go down. Only when he cleaved the bear's skull with the axe blade did it finally topple over dead.

Tod, who was exhausted and covered in blood, collapsed on the ground beside the bear, while Letendre ran to the river to get some water for his champion. The axe remained fast in the animal's skull. Nothing Tod could say would make Letendre remove the weapon, for he feared once the blade was removed, the creature would return to life.

More than a decade earlier, Archie McDonald, Lord Selkirk's recruiter, had told Tod that a clerk's job might be to hunt bears, but the task was more difficult than he could have imagined. It had been almost impossible to fell the animal. Indeed, when he later came to examine the bear's heart, he discovered the organ had been penetrated by a lead ball. The creature should have died almost immediately but it had continued on, carried only by its strength of will. Like his Sekani neighbours, who revered the bear, Tod gained a deep respect for this ruler of the forests.

While the immediate excitement was over, they had yet to check the beaver trap. The mechanisms were set below water, so that once caught, the animals would be held under and drowned. The jaws of one device, though, had not been set deep enough, and as they rounded a bend, they were surprised to see a beaver held fast but very much alive. As the canoe approached, the beaver began thrashing about, which was enough to cause the Canadien to become very excited. With its captors momentarily distracted, the beaver moved forward and sank its teeth into the side of the canoe below the water line. In seconds the boat began to fill with water, forcing the two trappers to paddle desperately for the river bank. While the two men repaired the boat, the beaver managed to escape — albeit at the cost of a foot.

Despite the loss of the animal in the trap, the expedition had been successful. Tod and Letendre had taken three other beaver. The bear, too, was a worthwhile prize, for not only was its flesh highly regarded by the traders, but the skins fetched a high price at the London market. After the difficulty with his faint-hearted companion, though, Tod generally hunted alone.

* * * * *

Tod's knowledge of animals of the forest was derived partly from his desire to improve his chances of securing game, and partly from his enjoyment of observing nature. One animal that caught Tod's interest was what the French-speaking servants called a *siffleur*, a relative of the prairie dog. He found it surprising that this member of the squirrel family was able to make hay. The little mammals would nibble off the tall grass near its base and then lay it neatly in a stack until the top layer was dry. Then they would turn the pile over to allow the grass underneath to dry. Once the process was complete the animals would take the hay into their burrows where they would use it for both food and bedding.

This mountain variety, like its prairie cousin, was very social, and Tod was intrigued by its habit of posting a sentry on a high outcropping near its community. When a fox, eagle or other predator was spotted, the sentinel would sound an alarm — a high-pitched whistle of particular length and frequency — warning its fellow villagers of the nature of the approaching danger. Tod noted, also, that some Indians seemed to have adopted a practice similar to that of the *siffleur*. When band members became aware of an enemy near at hand, they would let out a number of brief cries which warned their comrades. One long cry meant that while the enemy was close by, there was no immediate danger.

Tod, who had earlier studied the habits of the polar bear, found its southern kin — the black, brown and grizzly bears — equally fascinating. Unlike most bears, the grizzly was unable to use its claws for climbing, scaling only trees around which its forelegs could reach. The bears' habit of sucking their paws, he noted, was due to the fact that during hibernation the old pads are sloughed off. The process caused the paws to itch, which the animals tried to relieve by biting and sucking. When the bears first attempted to walk after the winter, their new pads were very tender. Tod observed that in the early spring the animals would often leave a faint trail of blood, leading him to believe there were other hunters in the area. Later he realized this was not the case.

He observed that the bears pick their dens not long before the beginning of winter, the male and female choosing separate locations. After entering, the animals seal up the opening with tree boughs, stones and mud. The female bear, while still in a state of hibernation, gives birth to her cubs in January. He noted correctly that, during hibernation, the animal could be roused and, during exceptional circumstances, may even leave its den during the winter. Tod's keen interest in the bears contributed to his concern for their preservation. Although bears were easier to kill while in hibernation, he did not kill mothers with cubs unless he required the animals for food.

Tod's nature lessons were not quickly forgotten — even years after his retirement, he was able to give his friend Gilbert Malcolm Sproat an accurate and detailed picture of the life cycle of the beaver. He noted that the beaver's practice of chopping down trees served two purposes: the trunk and limbs of trees such as the poplar provided building material for the dens and dams the animal constructed, while the tender tips were consumed as food. Fish bones found in the lodge led him to conclude wrongly that the beaver also ate flesh, but in fact unused lodges were sometimes the home of fish-eating animals, including the otter.

One place Tod often visited was Perch Lake, only about a dozen miles west of his post. During the spring run-off it was a single lake, but for most of the year it was actually two mountain pools joined by a short stream. There was little unusual about the spot, but during one visit Tod noticed something that caught his interest. He had been paddling along a second stream which linked Perch and McLeod lakes when he noticed beaver droppings of considerable size. The leavings were so large Tod found it difficult to believe the source was actually a beaver.

After he returned to Fort McLeod, Tod questioned the local Sekani about the fur-bearing animals at Perch Lake. According to the natives, there were only two beaver in the area, an old couple which had lived there for years. They were clever and had survived so long the female was now long past the age to produce offspring.

Tod was impressed by the Sekani tales, and took the capture of these animals as a personal challenge. Returning to the spot where he had earlier seen evidence of the beaver, he searched the area for two or three days, until at last he found what he was looking for — a wide trail leading from the river bank to a small pond some distance back in the woods. Near the pond he saw more beaver markings.

He prepared to set his trap at a spot near the beaver trail. Using the blade of his hunting knife as a spade, he cut a large earth plug which he carefully removed by slipping the paddle of his canoe underneath it. Into the opening he put a large steel trap, which was then attached by means of a chain to a nearby tree. After cautiously setting the jaws, he camouflaged the spot with some of the soil he had removed from the hole, all the while taking care not to touch the earth with his hands. Beaver were known to have an excellent sense of smell and the Perch Lake pair had a reputation for being even more cautious than their kin elsewhere. Although castor or beaver musk was often used to attract these animals, Tod thought it was useless in this case for these animals had long ago proved themselves too clever for the usual ruses.

The next morning, Tod discovered his trap had captured one of the elusive beavers — the animal's hind leg was firmly held by the device's steel jaws. In its efforts to escape, the creature had flattened the vegetation in a wide arc around the trap. Now it lay exhausted on the ground, and Tod quickly killed it with a few blows. As he had imagined, the animal was huge, so big in fact he could not lift the entire carcass into his canoe. The animal was black and when cured, the pelt was larger than a Hudson's Bay blanket. As he examined the body, he noted its two front paws were missing, perhaps the result of earlier encounters with steel traps.

Tod did not know what had happened to the beaver's companion — an animal said to be as large as the one he had killed — but its fate was of little concern to him. He had set out to prove himself more clever than the wily beaver and more cunning than his Indian neighbours, and his exploits became the stuff of Sekani legend. But when he came to recall the story later on, he was sorry for what he had done. In old age himself, Tod could only mourn the loss of that venerable creature he had so thoughtlessly sacrificed on the alter of youthful ego.

* * * * *

75

Like Tod's, life for the Indians of McLeod Lake was very difficult. In his memoirs, Tod related an incident concerning a old native fisherman, a Sekani by the name of Cheway who, during the mild months, lived with his family close to the fort. Cheway was the only person in the vicinity of Fort McLeod who could make the *vorveaux* used in freshwater fishery. Tod had thus to depend on the old man's largesse, for ownership of the baskets gave him a monopoly on the fishery. Tod grew accustomed to receiving a few fish from Cheway during the season, but one year he received none at all.

The whitefish were a relief from the monotony of the salmon, and without his usual supply, Tod spent more time away from the fort, hunting. On one such foray, not long before the spring thaw, Tod noticed a smudge of smoke against the distant trees. The clerk made his way toward the spot where the grey curl seemed to begin, and there to his surprise were Cheway and his family, many miles from the winter camp of the Sekani.

Cheway and his young wife were in grave condition; it was evident that they had not eaten for days. Their child was already dead — the little body lay huddled near the campfire. As Tod learned later, they had existed for days on nothing but boiled leather. When even that had been eaten they had prepared for death. It was then Tod had arrived.

Tod set out with Cheway and his wife; the woman was a little stronger and could go on her own, but he had to carry the fisherman on his back. When he could carry his burden no longer, Tod dug a large pit in the snow, placed Cheway and his wife in it, and covered them up until only their faces were exposed. Tod went on alone to Fort McLeod where he obtained a dog sled. Returning to the spot where he had buried them, he placed the old man and his wife on the sled and took them to the fort. During the next month, Tod nursed the couple back to health and, when they were at last well enough to leave, Cheway freely expressed his gratitude. From then on, whenever Cheway made a successful catch, Tod was given whitefish.

Whatever his difficulties in getting along with his superiors, he usually maintained a good working relationship with his trading partners, the Sekani. There were occasional difficulties, however, such as the case when Tod found himself caught between two feuding parties. One day he received a few Sekani who had come to barter furs. These Indians were not from McLeod Lake, but lived in the mountains some miles away. After Tod had acknowledged them, the Indians were invited into the mess hall to trade. Tod usually began by giving each man a small gift, and to obtain the twists of tobacco he would present, he had to walk to the storehouse across the compound. His guests were thus left alone. During his absence, a party of Beaver Indians arrived from the Peace River territory and came upon the Sekani in the mess hall. The Beaver were old and bitter enemies of the Sekani, and it seemed there would be bloodshed on the spot. In his memoirs, Tod provided a vivid description of his role in settling the dispute:

> On each side of the big mess hall, they were drawn up ready to use bows and arrows, guns [etc.] on one another. Hearing of this I rushed in bare armed, commencing to abuse them at an awful rate; swore and kicked; rushed at one side then at the other, seized their arms, and banged them about generally. One fellow was about driving a dagger into another. Seizing this I took it from him, and the mark of it remains in my hand to this day.[5]

Tod took their weapons and threw them into the fire. This decisive action defused the situation, and the confrontation ended without bloodshed.

While this tale may have grown more colourful in the telling, it is certainly true that Hudson's Bay traders feared being caught between two warring parties. The Company refrained from meddling in the affairs of the Indians. For example, in 1825, a feud between the Carrier and Chilcotin peoples had prevented the Hudson's Bay from establishing a new post in the latter's territories. Rather than be caught in the middle of the conflict, the Company decided that it was prudent to wait for hostilities to cease.

* * * * *

In 1829, Tod accompanied William Connolly and the New Caledonia brigade south to Fort Vancouver where he was to receive medical attention for his sciatica. At the post he was examined by Dr. McLoughlin who prescribed blistering, an extremely painful technique. Given that Tod had a chance to see his old friends John Work and Frank Ermatinger, the discomfort was endurable. "We all three lodged at the new Fort," Tod wrote Edward, "where we passed many pleasant days and nights together."[6]

77

While Tod was away, however, tragedy struck at McLeod Lake. Another clerk, William McGillivray, arrived at the post, with his family, to replace him. Unfamiliar with the territory, McGillivray sent his wife and infant son in the company of Tod's own daughter and another child to fish in a nearby river. This particular stream, Tod later noted, was very fast and dangerous, and McGillivray's plan had been reckless indeed. During the journey their canoe over-turned suddenly, spilling its passengers into the raging torrent, where "all, except mine, sunk to rise no more."[7] (Ironically, two years later, McGillivray himself was drowned in the Fraser River.) Tod's mention of the child who survived the canoe tragedy is the only indication that his union with the woman at McLeod Lake produced offspring. Whether the child survived to adulthood, however, is unknown.

Tod returned to Fort McLeod much improved, but it was not long before he was again discomfited. In the spring of 1831, he wrote Edward: "I have been of late mostly confined to bed, propped up with pillows and bolsters, like some old ruinous steeple 'nod[d]ing to the moon'."[8] The condition, apparently, was an abscess on the hip that put pressure on his sciatic nerve — possibly the result of overuse of the blistering compound McLoughlin had prescribed for him.

There were, of course, many Indian practitioners of folk medicine in New Caledonia, and not far from Fort McLeod lived an ancient shaman who had a considerable reputation among his people. One day, after happening to visit the post and observing Tod hobbling painfully about, the old man offered to treat him. Tod, like most Company officers, had little faith in such methods. He declined, saying he would use the potions given him by the white doctor. However, despite Tod's pronouncements, his own physician's prescriptions seemed to be less and less effective in alleviating his condition. Some months later, the ancient healer returned to Fort McLeod and saw that Tod was still bent over in pain. The shaman remarked disdainfully that he thought the great white doctor would have made Tod straight by now. Although Tod still had no faith in Indian medicine, he doubted that the old man could make his condition worse and he reluctantly agreed to put himself in the hands of the native healer.

The following day, the shaman arrived carrying a grease-stained leather bag. In it, wrapped up in leaves, were many small packages, each with its own distinct identifying mark. Tod noted the sack contained other bundles as well, larger ones that were covered by sheets of soft bark and held together by bird claws. The healer proceeded to examine his patient, after which he sorted through the parcels until he found one with the correct mark. He separated it from the others, and began to build a fire into which he placed several large stones. He waited until the flames had made the rocks red hot, and then he carefully placed them in an Indian bark kettle containing water.

After a few minutes the water had come to a full boil, and Tod was manoeuvred so that his buttock was over the steam. As the heat began to penetrate, the old man took a finely pointed flint and pressed it deep into Tod's flesh. Then he drew the sharp edge along so that a large wound was opened on the hip. As he withdrew this crude scalpel, blood began to pour out. At first the patient bore his treatment stoically but when the substance contained in the package was applied to the open wound, the pain became so severe Tod writhed in agony. Without heed his tormentor continued to apply the chalky powder.

At last the shaman was finished and Tod was given a quantity of the same medicine for later use. The substance was not a harmless placebo — according to Tod, "The power of this stuff could be felt by the hand even by holding it some distance away." The treatment had been difficult to bear, but it was effective. "The matter and blood that ran out of the wounds was something astonishing, but I began to feel better."[9] He was never troubled by the pain again, and although Tod offered considerable payment, the old man would take only the smallest fee for his services.

During his time in New Caledonia, Tod noted a few other plants that were commonly used as medicines by the Indians. The sticky buds of a native white wood tree were gathered in early spring and rendered down into a thick concentrate that was then mixed with deer fat to produce an ointment. When applied to minor cuts, scrapes and sores, it aided healing. Although Tod was not familiar with its name, the tree was probably the balsam fir, a plant known to many of the Indian peoples of New Caledonia. In one form or another, the evergreen was used to treat a variety of conditions including consumption and constipation.

To reduce a fever, the Indians relied on a syrup boiled down from a large, woody, parasitic fungus which clings to the outer bark of the pine tree. This large, cone-shaped primitive was obtained only with difficulty; its usual habitat was the higher reaches of the tree, well beyond the outstretched hands of the Indians who valued it so highly. It was usually necessary to cut down the host to obtain the prize — a fact which may have added to the potency of the medicine in the patient's mind.

A plant in common usage was the wild blackberry, the roots of which were pulled up and then brewed into a tea to stop diarrhoea. Another important remedy in the Indian medicine chest was a concoction made from, among other substances, bear fat and rendered spruce bark. As Tod noted, the smell of this potent mixture, which was used in the treatment of coughs, was very strong.

The medication Tod believed had cured his hip pain was probably made from a plant known as false Solomon's seal. The roots were ground up and applied to a wound to draw out infection. Among other tribes, the medicine was produced differently — the roots were also boiled and the resultant decoction used in the treatment of backaches.

While he was in New Caledonia, Tod witnessed what seemed to him to be miraculous cures. Some years after leaving Fort McLeod, he returned to New Caledonia where he spent a brief period at Fort Alexandria on the Fraser River. One day he saw a young Indian whom he judged to be in the final stage of syphilis: the fellow was so weak he had to be carried about on a stretcher. When Tod asked why he was making what seemed to be his last journey, the man's companions said they were taking him to a renowned Indian medicine man who lived some miles farther upriver. Tod thought little of the incident until several months later when he saw the same young man returning. No longer on a stretcher, he walked confidently on his own — apparently completely cured. In answer to Tod's questions, the man said he had been fed medicines made from Oregon grapes and soapberries, together with another unknown medicine on which he was not permitted to look (but which he recalled made him very sleepy).

At times the native doctors' healing arts even included surgery. Some New Caledonia natives had a particular fondness for gambling, and Tod had known one man whose addiction to the games of chance was so severe that he had lost everything including his family. When he had nothing else to give up, he took a gun, placed the barrel in his mouth and pulled the trigger. Even in suicide the man was not a success, for the attempt resulted only in severe head injuries: a portion of the victim's skull was blown away and both eyes were propelled out of their sockets. Soon the Indian practitioners were at work on the patient. His eyes were replaced in their sockets and the damaged portion of his skull was reconstructed. Tod noted that the man's recovery was almost complete, the only lasting trace of the injury being a slight slurring of speech.

During his early years at Fort McLeod, the clerk was surprised to discover that the Sekani creation myths were remarkably similar to the Christian creed. According to Tod, the Sekani believed that "... God made man out of clay, and woman from his ribs; they were put in a nice place, with fruit, one tree was not to be touched, and so on."[10] Like Christians, the Sekani also held that their misfortunes began when they ate of the forbidden fruit, for the result was that they were driven from their own temperate land and sent into the wilderness. The location of the Sekani's version of Eden was apparently westward. When he questioned them as to where their ancestors had come from, the Indians pointed in the direction of the Pacific Ocean. What surprised Tod was that some of the Sekani had had no contact with missionaries — he was only the second European to meet certain Indians inhabiting the more remote areas.*

There were many other legends indigenous to the Sekani people. They had, for example, a profound fear of a mythological animal said to destroy anyone sleeping on the ground. For that reason, the Sekani constructed scaffolds high in the branches of trees where they spent the night. Above the ground they were safe because the beast could not climb trees.

Although he had benefited from their medicine, Tod's attitude toward the Indians of New Caledonia was far from enlightened. He remained in intimate association with the Sekani at McLeod Lake, but he saw the Indians and their culture through the eyes of a 19th-century European. "I trust in God," he wrote Edward in 1826, "that in compassion for the miseries I have endured in this land of savages, that he will be pleased to spare us both to live and see that day, when we may participate in the pleasure of each others Company."[11]

As with many of his colleagues within the Hudson's Bay, Tod's knowledge of the culture of his aboriginal trading partners was

* The Sekani, however, were not as isolated as Tod supposed. A significant trade had long existed between the aboriginal peoples of the Pacific coast and the Indians of the interior. It seems likely that, together with the goods of European manufacture, Christian stories were passed inland.

superficial. "There is a marked difference between Indians who lived on fish, and those who lived on hunting; the former were mean, sneaking, thieving, and deceiving; would scarcely ever tell the truth," he noted in his memoirs. "The latter were noble, generous, would scorn the idea of theft; they could not be more insulted than if charged with theft."[12]

To illustrate his point, he related a story about the behaviour of the hunters and fishermen. In 1829, he and Chief Factor Connolly were with the fur brigade as it travelled south to Fort Vancouver. When they reached a patch of white water on the Columbia River where their half dozen or so boats had to be pulled up on shore and carried around the rapids, Connolly decided to hire a hunting party of Nez Percés Indians who happened to be camped nearby. The Nez Percés, who inhabited the interior of the Columbia territory, were, Tod believed, "the noblest band in the country."[13] For payment in tobacco, the Indians undertook the task immediately and soon the boats and their contents were transported over the portage.

However, when it came time for payment, Connolly suddenly became concerned that once the debt was discharged, the Nez Percés would turn around and attack the brigade.* He refused to make payment until the boats were loaded again and were thus less vulnerable. As the Hudson's Bay men stowed their cargo, the Indians waited on shore. Finally, when the task was finished, a servant was sent out with a bag of tobacco. By this time, the Indians had already mounted and were watching the proceedings on horse-back. Not willing to venture too close to the natives, the man began to spread the tobacco out in large handfuls on the rocks by the river. When the Nez Percés did not move forward to take their payment, the chief factor demanded to know what was wrong. The hunters said nothing, but remained on their horses and watched while the bag was emptied. Then, without a word, they suddenly turned and rode off, leaving the tobacco where it had been scattered.

Before the brigade was under way, though, another band appeared. These were one of the coastal peoples who had come inland to catch salmon as the fish headed up the Columbia to spawn. From a place of concealment, they had watched what had taken place, and when the Nez Percés withdrew, they moved in and

---

* Tod claimed that Connolly had become apprehensive after reading Washington Irving's adventure novel, *Astoria*, which was about conflict between Indians and Europeans. The book, however, was not published until 1836, seven years after this incident.

snatched up the tobacco. "*They* could not be insulted," Tod concluded.[14] Yet it was also true that, for the fishermen, pride was a luxury they could not afford. Their existence depended on the uncertain salmon run, and a handful of tobacco to trade with other tribes may have meant the difference between survival and starvation.

A man of definite and often unshakable opinions, Tod sometimes did not search far for the truth. Compared with his more intransigent fellow officers, however, Tod was enlightened indeed. During his time at McLeod Lake, he gradually fell under the influence of Chief Factor William Connolly who had no illusions regarding the lack of power of the Hudson's Bay vis-à-vis the Indians. If it had been their intention to do so, the natives of New Caledonia could easily have forced the Europeans back across the Rockies. For that reason, many of Tod's anecdotes concern not his physical strength or endurance when pitted against the Indian, but his cunning and resourcefulness.

* * * * *

Because Tod and his contemporaries were convinced of the superiority of European culture, Company officers failed to look seriously at aboriginal society. With little European contact save the one or two servants occasionally assigned to the fort, Tod suffered under the burden of cultural isolation. He would later claim that his separation from his native language was so complete that he eventually lost the ability to use spoken English, conversing instead in a mixture of Gaelic, French and Indian dialects interspersed with a few words of English. Whether this was true or not is uncertain, but it seems clear that Tod's loneliness was causing him to sink deeper and deeper into depression.

Although his trip to Fort Vancouver may have briefly rallied his flagging spirits, it was not long before Tod's mood again became darker. The time he spent in the company of friends like John Work and Frank Ermatinger only underlined the social pleasures long denied him at McLeod Lake, and it was with a mixture of anger, frustration, and self-pity that he wrote Edward after his return:

> It is evident that neither a successful return of Beaver skins, merit, nor length of service, will give one a chance for promotion in this hateful employ. That feathering thing called favour will always make those, who have nothing but honest worth to

John Work. (COURTESY BCARS, 4324)

recommend them, Kick the beam. Do you know that I consider myself very ill used and I think I have just cause to complain. ... It is from not Knowing how to better my condition that, in a manner, compels me to remain in their service. I was once a great builder of castles in the air but, for the most part, I have now given it up as unprofitable speculation.[15]

As the bleak months passed, the simple pleasures that had been so important to Tod gradually lost their appeal. The flute he had once been so keen to play was now all but silent — the sheet music Edward had sent him remained unopened. Adding to Tod's general misery was his deteriorating physical health. "I have otherwise, this winter been frequently unwell — long and frequent fasts, I suspect, have nearly distroyed [*sic*] the powers of digistion [*sic*] in me," he wrote Edward.[16]

Edward's letter from London did little to cheer Tod, for his friend was also despondent. Despite his own low spirits, Tod felt obliged to pass along to the younger man a full measure of advice. "What is most to be dreaded is that feverish state of mind in which You seem too often to indulge [and] beware, my friend, & let me beg of You to remember that all earthly things are mere dust & ashes when bro[ugh]t in competition with good health."[17]

Although Edward had half expected to remain in England, the visit was not a success, probably because of his father's displeasure with the decision to leave the security of the Hudson's Bay Company. Four months after arriving, Edward was again on board a ship, this time bound for Quebec City. Disembarking on 22 May 1829, Edward went to Montreal where he remained a few days before travelling on through Kingston, York, Penetanguishene and Niagara. The purpose of these wanderings was to find a place to settle, but none of the communities seemed suited to him. He returned to Montreal at the end of October for the winter.

In the spring, Edward returned to his search; on 1 July 1830 he arrived in the little village of St. Thomas. "The principal building in it," he wrote in his journal, "is a neat little Episcopal Church & it contains two Stores, two Taverns, Blacksmith's Shop, Tailor & I suppose from 20 to 30 dwelling Houses."[18] The village had been founded 13 years earlier as part of a land grant given to Colonel Thomas Talbot in exchange for promoting settlement along the north shore of Lake Erie. St. Thomas was situated on the road connecting the market town of London with Port Stanley. The surrounding land, beyond the boundaries of the village, seemed well suited to agriculture. Under the moderating influence of Lake Erie, the climate was mild, and the fine clay loam soil was almost completely free from stones. With his own savings and those of his brother, Edward opened a general store on Talbot Street, the community's main thoroughfare.

Tod, despite his lack of economic prospects outside the Company, intended to follow Edward. He wrote in early April 1831, "I have determined on quitting it this spring but I fear I cannot without disobliging them [the Company]. I will therefore be compelled in a manner, I fear, to remain one Year more, thou[gh] by doing so I am fully aware of the ill consequences to myself."[19] As he had predicted, his departure from New Caledonia was not easily achieved. Frank wrote Edward the following year that "Tod and [clerk Charles] Ross are very ill and are allowed to leave New Caledonia via Peace River."[20] Later in the letter, after furnishing Edward with the names of the clerks transferred out of the Columbia Department, Frank added, "They appear careless about bringing him [Tod] on; in fact, I fear they are disposed to keep him back altogether."[21] Tod's departure was delayed by Chief Factor Peter Warren Dease, who had succeeded Connolly as superintendent of New Caledonia. Despite Tod's failing health, Dease did not wish to give up a clerk with his experience and abilities. Upon the expiration of his contract, the Company was obliged to furnish him with transportation to York Factory, and this Dease did, albeit in the meanest spirit. Tod was given only one large freight canoe, an elderly interpreter and two paddlers — a number entirely insufficient to carry the heavy canoe, as well as provisions and Tod's personal possessions, over the many difficult portages that lay ahead of them. Regardless of the difficulties, Tod was determined to turn his back forever on that worst of all territories, New Caledonia, a land which for nine years had laid waste to his body and broken his spirit.

One day near the middle of May 1832, Tod climbed on board the canoe which waited for him at the landing directly below Fort McLeod. He never wrote of his feelings at the time, yet he was leaving New Caledonia without his country wife — a woman whom he once claimed had meant much to him. Although "divorces" of this sort were common within Company service, it should be noted that Hudson's Bay men often did take their Indian and mixed-blood wives with them when they were retired or transferred. Indeed, Tod had only to look as far as his longtime friend, John Work, to find a man made of different stuff. After his early sexual adventures Work was to form a stable and long-lasting relationship in 1826 with Susette Legace, a Spokane woman who bore him ten children. "I am aware that my family, being natives of this country, would not be fit for society, but that gives me little concern," Work wrote, "[for] they are mine and I am bound to provide for them."[22]

Tod had crossed the Peace Portage once before — in 1823 with Stuart. The trek had been gruelling, even with the assistance of the Rocky Mountain Indians who fortunately had been camped on the portage. This time there seemed to be little chance that Tod and his small crew would be able to transport the huge canoe and its contents over the mountainous path. However, luck was with him again, and he came upon an Indian encampment on the trail. During negotiations with the Indians, Tod made sure not to alert them to the desperation of his plight — in a seller's market, the charges for their services would surely have risen.

Tod and his party continued along the Peace as far as Lake Athabasca where they met the fur brigade bound for York Factory. The remainder of the journey was uneventful. After almost a decade in New Caledonia, Tod found York Factory a potent tonic. He wrote Edward a month after his arrival: "I came down here [and] fell in with old friends by whom I was Kindly received; with them I eat, drank & laughed until I found my health & spirits almost completely restored."[23]

At York Factory, Tod was surprised to find the governor had changed his attitude toward him. Simpson, who had previously been hardly able to conceal his dislike for Tod, had become friendly. During his interview, Simpson tried to dissuade Tod from resigning. Simpson's about-face, however, had probably more to do with his fear of losing a good clerk than a change of attitude. The expansion of the fur trade west of the Rockies had left the Company without enough experienced officers. Whatever the governor's personal feelings, there was no doubt that Tod was a good clerk who had done his job well under the most difficult conditions. Concerning Tod, Simpson wrote in his employee evaluation book that year:

> Has experienced much privation in New Caledonia which has injured his constitution & destroyed his health. ... considers himself neglected and overlooked in the Service and is dissatisfied. ... Is not generally liked* but I think has claims to promotion and may in due time succeed in attaining a Chief tradership.[24]

Meanwhile, Tod's friends, too, tried to dissuade him from severing his connection with the Hudson's Bay. In the end Tod agreed to stay on, but he reached the decision with little enthusiasm. Now almost 40, he saw the opportunities for success rapidly retreating. To remain a clerk at a hardship posting like Fort McLeod was beyond his endurance. His only chance was to be given a chief tradership. With the additional money a commissioned officer received, Tod could plan an early retirement and live in comfort. Yet he had no assurance he would be promoted — there were clerks who spent their entire careers without obtaining a commission. To leave or to stay on: either decision was a gamble. "I am like a losing gamester — I gain scarcely anything," he wrote Edward. "Yet the hopes of better fortune at some distant period induces me to continue the game."[25]

* This is not entirely true. Although Tod had little difficulty making enemies, he also made many friends. Simpson used this phrase as a kind of a code to identify employees he personally disliked.

Chapter Six

SHE IS SUBJECT TO A MENTAL AFFLICTION

In the late autumn of 1832, Tod was put in charge of the Split Lake post in the Nelson River district, about 125 miles southwest of York Factory. He was not there long, however, before he was involved in an incident with his second-in-command, a longtime employee named Andrew Wilson. The details of Wilson's firing are not clear, but some time in 1833 Tod charged him with drunkenness and dismissed him on the spot. The governor was not at York Factory at the time, but Tod had little difficulty receiving Chief Factor John Charles's approval of his actions. While Tod and Charles had overstepped their authority, the matter seemed trivial and was soon forgotten. Tod appeared to have recovered his health, and made a good adjustment to his new posting. In 1833, Thomas Simpson, the governor's cousin, gave Tod his qualified endorsement, describing him as "a man of excellent principle," albeit of "vulgar manners."[1]

Tod's singing companion from Fort McLeod was apparently soon forgotten, for not long after his arrival at Split Lake he was sharing his bed with a local woman. For entertainment, he organized dances attended by his men and some of the local Indians. Such events undoubtedly gave him an opportunity to display his talents on the violin, for Tod was a man who craved attention. Yet, still without his commission, he remained deeply dissatisfied, and east of the Rockies, it was not difficult to find a liberal measure of Hudson's Bay rum to drown one's sorrows.

During the trading season of 1833-34, Tod established Fort Seaborn, a minor post in the Nelson River district. In the spring of 1834, he was sent with the fur brigade down the Nelson River to York Factory. His boat had hardly been secured at the landing when he was met by his friend, Chief Trader Nicol Finlayson, who took Tod's hand and shook it warmly, and told him he had at last received his commission. While he had long hungered for promotion to chief trader, Tod's next letter to Edward hardly mentioned his good news. Although prepared to share his years of misery with his friend, Tod was less willing to lay open the odd moments of joy.

Unlike Tod, Edward's brother Frank did not receive his hoped-for promotion. Frank too believed that he was entitled to a chief tradership, and as the years passed he increasingly felt ill-used by the Company. Part of Frank's difficulty was due to his penchant for trouble. While he was at Fort Thompson in the spring of 1830, Frank had entered into a relationship with Cleo, an Okanagan woman. Their affair was stormy, and when Cleo finally left him for an Indian lover, Frank was enraged. Fearing reprisal the couple fled, but Frank sent the fort's interpreter, a man by the name of Lolo, after them. "My resolution was formed and he [Cleo's lover] was punished with the loss of his ears," Frank wrote Edward.[2]

Frank's action created a furore among the Indians and in a short time word reached Fort Vancouver. In his report to Simpson, Chief Factor John McLoughlin stated that while he did not favour Frank's action, "still if the Indian had not been punished it would have lowered the Whites in their [the natives'] estimation."[3] The fact remained, however, that Frank had increased tensions between the Europeans and the Indians and he was removed from Fort Thompson. In his place the Company sent Chief Trader Samuel Black. A worse choice could not be imagined, for Black was hardly the person to mend strained relations between the Indians and Europeans — his record proved that.

* * * * *

With Tod's promotion came a year's leave, which he took almost immediately. At York Factory on 28 August 1834, he boarded the Company's ship *Prince Rupert* shortly before it began its return voyage to England. Among his fellow passengers were his friend Robert Seaborn Miles, the chief accountant at York Factory, and a young Welsh woman, Eliza Waugh. Little is known about Eliza's reasons for coming to the Company's territories. Tod later implied that she had worked in some higher capacity for the Hudson's Bay, but it seems that Eliza had gone as a personal servant, in the employ of a Protestant missionary, Reverend David Jones, and his wife "at the particular solicitations of Mrs. Jones and her friends" to Red River in 1829.[4]

For the 39-year-old Tod, the six-week journey was eventful — he developed a romantic relationship with Eliza. When the vessel anchored off Portsmouth early in the morning of 10 October, the two parted; Eliza stayed with friends while Tod and Miles arranged transportation to London. Tod had never been to England, and the contrast between the bustling city of Portsmouth and the wilderness communities to which he was now accustomed surprised him. Here, the familiar polyglot language of the fur trade — the mixture of Gaelic, French and Indian dialects as well as English — was neither spoken nor understood. The rude but practical clothes of the frontier were also nowhere to be seen. Instead, men were dressed like dandies in knee breeches and leather boots ornamented with dangling tassels.

The coach to London on which he and Miles were booked was of a design that he had never seen and he marvelled at its smartness.

Eliza Waugh Tod. (COURTESY BCARS, PDP3242)

Yet he also found the differences between "civilized" England and the frontier somewhat daunting. While Miles, who had made the journey to London many times before, preferred the comfort of a seat inside, Tod climbed up and took a place behind the coachman. After many years on the open frontier, the sudden crush of people inside the carriage would have been too much to tolerate.

From his vantage point on the roof he had a good view of the green, rolling, southern English countryside, different not only from the Hudson's Bay territories of North America, but even from his own Scotland. In his native land there was a hard edge to the hills that was entirely missing here. Of particular interest were the towering windmills that occasionally broke the horizon — structures Tod had previously seen only in books. On the road, the coach passed one of the marvels of the age — a lumbering steam carriage that transported freight between Portsmouth and London. This was the last of its kind, so the coachman said. These heavy vehicles were very slow, frightened the horses and made deep ruts in the roads; it had become apparent to the English that steam transportation on land required iron rails.

The pair reached London that same evening, and while Miles continued on to deliver his dispatches to the Company offices, Tod booked a room at the Green Dragon Inn in Bishopgate, a favourite stopover for Hudson's Bay officers. Alone for the first time since leaving York Factory, Tod faced the challenge of ordering supper for himself. So out of touch had he become with European fare that the menu placed before him was a document in a foreign language. Tod had no idea what many of the dishes were, and the approach of the waiter caused him considerable trepidation. Gradually though, he acquired the skills necessary for survival in his new environment.

During this time Tod had the chance to explore many of the attractions of the city, and aided by a map he walked the streets past shops whose windows held all manner of merchandise he scarcely knew existed. Occasionally he climbed aboard one of the new omnibuses which plied routes around the town. Even for Londoners, the horse-drawn vehicles were still a novelty — they had been introduced only five years earlier. He was also pleased to note that regardless of the distance travelled, the fare remained only sixpence.

On 22 October 1834 Tod was honoured with an introduction to Governor Sir John Henry Pelly and the Committee of the Hudson's Bay Company: an indication of his new status within the organization. Some time after his arrival Tod met Eliza again, and they were married in London. That the marriage took place there rather than near Eliza's home in Wales may suggest that the union was arranged without the approval of Eliza's mother, Letitia Waugh. Although she had lately fallen on hard times, the Waughs once had been well-connected — Eliza's father had been governor of Caermarthen County Gaol, and her uncle an officer in the East India Company. After the ceremony, the bride and groom travelled north to Scotland where Tod saw his parents for the first time in 23 years.

John and Eliza received a warm reception at his home, and he and his new wife visited many old friends and neighbours. Tod undoubtedly had long relished this moment, for he was returning home in triumph. His acid-tongued mother had been proven wrong: far from being a ne'er-do-well as she had once charged, he was now a commissioned officer in the Hudson's Bay Company. There must have been a bitter sweetness in this visit, too, for the Scotland of his childhood could no longer be thought of as home. As a youth Tod had rebelled against his parent's drab, narrow existence and as he noted, their world had changed but little since he left. Now, after he had experienced the openness of North America, life in this little Lowland village seemed all the more confining. Even before his return to Scotland, Tod had recognized that the path he had chosen took him in one direction only. "I have long since given up the thoughts of going to lay my bones in the land of my Fathers," he had written Edward in 1831. "I must seek some retired spot, where my savage habits & mode of life will be less under the eye of ceremonial observance, and where my liberty is not likely to be hemmed by Game laws."[5]

Tod noted that his bookish father had added a few expensively bound volumes to his library. The years had only increased the older man's delight in Burns, a poet also dear to the heart of his eldest son. At his parents' home, Tod experienced a pleasure long absent from his life — for the first time since leaving Scotland he savoured the smooth flavour of scotch whisky that was a far cry from the long familiar Hudson's Bay brandy.

After receiving permission from the Company to return with his wife, Tod arranged passage for two on a packet bound for the United States. On 24 February 1835, the couple boarded the ship at Liverpool, and, after a satisfactory voyage, given the time of year, they reached New York. John and Eliza, though, spent little time in the American city, preferring instead to leave almost immediately for Lower Canada.

The few weeks Tod spent with Eliza in Montreal were perhaps the happiest time in his life. Without the burdens of work or family the newlyweds were free to enjoy the pleasures of the city. In Montreal, too, were many of Tod's old friends from the fur trade whom the couple visited. On one occasion, he and Eliza took an excursion to the picturesque fortress city of Quebec. Tod had acquired a good knowledge of French in the fur trade, and as a result felt very comfortable wandering the narrow streets of the old town. With spring break-up, however, he and Eliza had to return to Hudson's Bay territory.

In the months following his return, Tod filled in as temporary replacement at various posts, and consequently he and Eliza were often on the move. They were at the old Nor'Wester headquarters, Fort William, on 22 May where Tod wrote the governor concerning his posting for the upcoming season. Simpson replied on 4 June, "You are already down in our Minutes of the Council for the Columbia, but on account of your being accompanied by Mrs. Tod, there is a difficulty about a passage up the Athabasca Rive[sic]."[6]

Tod discovered that an almost forgotten incident had come back to haunt him — more than a year after he had been fired by Tod, Andrew Wilson, the post master at Split Lake, had decided to go directly to see Governor Simpson, who was then at Red River, and formally appeal his dismissal. The governor arranged for depositions to be taken from Wilson and another employee who had been at Split Lake at the time. Tod, who had left for Britain, had no idea that Simpson was building a case against him, and by the time he found out it was too late.

On 17 June, Tod arrived at Norway House where the Northern Council had convened an inquiry into the Wilson firing. Regarded as an outstanding servant, the former post master had obviously found favour with the governor. Tod, as usual, had not. The hearing had all the appearances of a trial in which Tod, not Wilson, was the defendant. A deposition was introduced in which another servant at the post, David Garson, swore that he had often seen Tod intoxicated. During one expedition, he claimed that Tod took an eight-gallon keg of rum, all of which save five quarts was finished in 22 days. Garson, however, said he had seen Wilson drunk on only one occasion — on the day the post master discovered that his wife was having an affair with Tod.

Yet the evidence was ambiguous. Garson admitted that he had never seen his master so intoxicated that he could not attend to his duties. Further, he never saw Tod drunk after the winter. Tod, of course, had a weakness for alcohol, and given his state of mind after arriving in the east, it could hardly be surprising that he imbibed. In his deposition Wilson claimed he got along well with Tod, until the incident with his wife. He stated he believed that the tryst had been arranged by Tod's companion who evidently wished to change places with the other woman. Wilson himself was not at the proceedings; he had died in a boating accident earlier that year.

On 18 June the council, "after careful examination of the evidence adduced by the said Andrew Wilson to prove his innocence, [came] to the unanimous conclusion that the charge against him is unproven & unfounded." While the outcome was not a surprise, the council went a step further by ordering that Wilson's wages for the last year of his employ, a total of £40, "be charged forthwith to the account of John Tod."[7]

While Wilson's exoneration may have been proper, Tod had every reason to conclude that he had been badly treated.* The evidence against him was hardly conclusive, nor did he have an opportunity to produce his own depositions. Later, in a letter to Simpson, Tod belatedly cobbled together his case. As well as other pieces of evidence, Tod forwarded a letter from another Company servant, John Isbister, regarding Wilson's improper conduct, but for Simpson, the new evidence was not sufficient to "disturb the decision of the Council."[8] The stain on Tod's record almost certainly ensured that he would receive no further promotion.

* * * * *

Tod and his wife left Norway House on 20 June 1835 and reached York Factory on 3 July. They remained at the northern depot for three weeks before again setting off for Norway House, which they reached on 16 August. After spending another three weeks at this post, they were off again, this time to Berens River, 300 miles to the southeast. Simpson had considered sending Tod and his wife to the Saskatchewan district, but this did not come about, possibly because by then Eliza was pregnant.

On 3 December 1835, they were at Fort Alexander, Bas de la Rivière Winipic, where Eliza gave birth to a daughter whom the

* In his memoirs, Tod implies that his problems arose from his failure to institute proper discipline, and blames Chief Factor John Charles for Wilson's firing.

couple named Emmeline Jane, "a fine healthy child."[9] All was far from well, however. As Tod wrote Edward:

> You will no doubt be grieved to hear that my matrimonial affair has already involved me in consequences very distressing indeed. ... The fact is Mrs. Tod's state of health, or rather I should Say Mind, is Such that I must return with her again to England by the fall Ship as already settled with the Gov[erno]r. She is subject to a mental affliction, and tho' she appeared entirely recovered during the greatest part of this preceding Winter, and until very lately when Symptoms again [recurred, I] decided my taking this step would be most judicious for us all three.[10]

Eliza's problems may have begun before she became acquainted with Tod. Tod's friend, clerk William Sinclair, seemed sufficiently familiar with her behaviour to remark in a letter to Edward, "Our friend Tod, has Married a *half Cracked Brainid* [sic] *Chamber Maid*, since he was about it I think he Might have Choosed a better Companion for life [as] they already show symptoms of discord between them."[11]

Tod had good reason to delay his departure as long as possible. The cost of such a journey, he lamented, "will no doubt go far in exhausting the already delapsed State of my finances," but there seemed little alternative.[12] Moreover, although he reluctantly agreed to Tod's leave, the governor was decidedly unsympathetic. "John Tod," Simpson wrote James Hargrave in 1836, "has been a most useless and troublesome man of late. ... He requires more luxery [*sic*] and attention, I understand, than any governor of Rupert's Land would be indulged with; let him have all that is fit and proper, but not one iota more."[13] Simpson, it should be noted, had much on his mind that year, for York Factory was experiencing the outbreak of a mysterious disease that had sent more than a few officers to their beds.* Tod's absence could not have come at a worse time.

As result of the staff shortages, Tod was sent to Oxford House, in the Island Lake district. The establishment was familiar to him — he had been posted there 16 years earlier during the warfare between the Hudson's Bay and North West companies. Tod had planned to

* The outbreak may have been scurvy which results from an inadequate intake of vitamin C contained in fresh fruits and vegetables. During the winter of 1835, the Company reduced its ration of fresh provisions to its employees.

remain at the post with Eliza and the baby only a short time, but once there he decided to stay on. In the end, the Company's difficulties as a result of the illness at York Factory, together with his own desperately strained finances, prompted Tod to put off his journey to England. That Eliza had shown some improvement also gave reason for delay.

Unfortunately, once he had agreed to stay, there was no turning back and Tod was committed to remain with Eliza until at least the following spring — a very long and trying time as it turned out. As winter approached her condition worsened to the point where she became violent and uncontrollable. So difficult had she become that he could find no one at the post willing to help him manage her. He remained in constant fear that she in her unbalanced state would do harm to either his daughter or himself. "In circumstances so particularly [depressing] and without human aid and consolation," he wrote Edward, "You can form no idea of the anguish of my mind."[14]

As the brief northern spring began, Tod again made plans to take Eliza and Emma to Britain. In late July, accompanied by his wife and baby, he left Oxford House for York Factory where they took passage on the *Eagle*. The voyage could hardly have been pleasant, for burdened not only with the care of his unstable wife and infant daughter, Tod had reluctantly accepted another responsibility. On 18 August 1837, before leaving York Factory, he had been sworn in as a constable for the purpose of escorting a prisoner to London. Tod's prisoner was a Company servant, a Cree named Creole Lagrasse. Lagrasse had been implicated in the murder of 11 Indians, members of the Hare tribe, at Puant Lake in the McKenzie River district on 26 December 1835. For some reason it was decided not to transport all the accused together. Two others charged with the crime had left earlier for London.

It was unusual that the Company should take on the expense of a British trial, but in 1837 the Hudson's Bay believed that the cost was justified. With the laissez-faire economic doctrine currently in favour, the British government's resolve to support unpopular mercantile concerns such as the Hudson's Bay was fast fading. The case was undoubtedly intended as a publicity exercise — to show the Company as an effective administrator of British laws.

On reaching the English Channel, the *Eagle* faced severe October headwinds that drastically slowed its progress. As the vessel approached the English coast, Tod made arrangements with the crew of the pilot vessel to disembark with his prisoner at Brighton.

After handing Lagrasse over to Company authorities, he planned to return to the *Eagle* as quickly as possible so that he could assist his wife and daughter ashore.

Despite the ghastly nature of Lagrasse's crimes, Tod seems to have regarded his companion as a harmless fellow and allowed him considerable freedom on board the ship. In order not to alarm the crew or his fellow passengers, he had claimed that his companion was his servant. As the pilot boat wound through the many ships anchored in the English Channel, Lagrasse was clearly impressed by what he saw, and asked whether all these vessels in the harbour belonged to the Hudson's Bay Company. It was not until about midnight that the two men landed at Brighton. Lagrasse continued to wear his native dress, which included a buckskin shirt, leggings made from antelope hide, and ornate moccasins, and those passing by on foot or in carriages stared in astonishment. The pair made their way along the dimly lit streets to the Sea House Inn where Tod booked rooms for the night. After a long day, both men went to bed immediately, each to his own room. The night passed quietly until Lagrasse got up to use the outdoor latrine. When he returned, he realized that all the doors to the rooms leading off the corridor looked the same. He solved his dilemma by opening each unlocked door to determine if it was his room. "It may be imagined what thoughts possessed those who saw the poor fellow's head and coutenance [*sic*]," Tod noted later.[15]

In the morning, Tod made preparations for leaving, but not before he had prevailed upon his host for a favour. The cost of their pilotage had been almost ten pounds, and Tod found himself without funds to pay their bill or secure a coach to London. Fortunately, the Hudson's Bay Company name still carried considerable weight even in Brighton, and few inn keepers would have wished to offend the representative of such an august firm. The man obligingly not only lent Tod enough to cover his bill and coach fare but advanced him five pounds for expenses.

After breakfast, the prisoner and his escort waited in the entrance hall for the arrival of the coach, and Lagrasse again became the centre of attention among his fellow passengers. He submitted good-naturedly to attentions of the onlookers, many of whom could not resist touching his clothing, ornamented with animal claws, porcupine quills, and beads. Once the coach arrived, Lagrasse swung up to occupy the seat next to the driver while Tod took a seat at the rear.

The distance between Brighton and London is short, and Tod tipped the plodding driver a small amount to speed the journey. By late afternoon the coach had reached the outskirts of London. Tod had chosen to lodge at the Green Dragon Inn, the hostelry where he had stayed during his visit to London in 1834. After placing Lagrasse in the care of a waiter at the inn, Tod took a carriage to the home of William Smith, the Hudson's Bay Company secretary, and gave him the dispatches that he had carried from York Factory. That his wife and daughter were left unescorted on board the *Eagle* continued to weigh heavily on his mind, and at his urging the secretary agreed to have Lagrasse arraigned the following day.

Early the next morning, Smith arrived with a man whom he introduced as Mr. Crosse, the Company's solicitor. Tod observed that both visitors were attired in the latest London finery — high top hats with curled brims, long frock coats with thick fur collars and shirts with sharply pointed collars that poked out from under ample scarves. When they met the prisoner, Smith and Crosse were taken aback by Lagrasse's appearance. Tod could not help but see the irony in this meeting. Had the circumstances been reversed and the oddly dressed pair had found themselves at York Factory, they undoubtedly would have received the same fearful response from the fort's inhabitants.

When Tod and his companions reached magistrate's court, Lagrasse was formally arraigned on the charge of murder. As elsewhere, the prisoner's appearance caused a sensation — the officers of the court crowded around him for a closer look. Tod noted that the courtroom was a shabby affair, and the lawyers, despite their pedestalled pretensions, were unimpressive. The horsehair wigs they wore made their heads look misshapen. Even the lawyers seemed to have little respect for tradition, for they had allowed their once-pristine wigs to become soiled and bedraggled. The events in the courtroom would have mattered little to Tod, for with his duties as constable at an end he had expected to return immediately to the *Eagle*. Instead, he was ordered by the magistrate to remain in court, for without Tod as translator, the case could not proceed. Rather than informing him that he would be needed for the proceedings, Smith and Crosse had gone to the magistrate. Frustrated and angry, Tod had no choice but to remain at court.

The outcome of the case against Lagrasse is not certain. At the meeting of the London Committee in October, Smith stated that the accused had confessed and been bound over until 10 November. In the meantime he was to be held at Clerkenwell Prison. Despite the Company's desire for publicity, the trial was all but ignored by the leading London newspapers.

The following day, Tod was again aboard the *Eagle*, which by now had made its way to London Docks, where he escorted his wife and child ashore. Tod's movements after leaving the ship are not entirely clear. He had intended to place Eliza and Emma in the care of her relatives, and once they arrived Eliza may have stayed briefly with her brother in London before going on to her mother's home in Caermarthen, Wales. Although Tod had hoped to leave both his wife and child there, the further burden of her grandchild was unacceptable to Letitia Waugh. In her disturbed state of mind Eliza required considerable care and Mrs. Waugh was a woman of advancing years and limited financial resources. When he left for North America again the following year, Tod had little choice but to take his daughter with him. In the meantime Emma remained with the Waughs while her father returned to London.

Thus relieved of the direct responsibility for his wife and child, Tod spent much time in the public rooms of the Green Dragon, the George and Vulture, and other drinking spots favoured by Hudson's Bay employees. Away from the scrutiny of the governor and with ready access to alcohol, Tod was free to drink as much as he wished, and there is no doubt that the amount was considerable. He gradually enlarged his social circle to include drinking companions who were not Company men. One such new acquaintance was a Highlander who had served in the British army before retiring to London and Tod took pleasure in trading tales of adventure in the far-flung outposts of the British Empire.

On one occasion, Tod and his friends went farther afield, to Upper Thames Street near London Bridge, where they enjoyed the night spot called the Shades. The establishment was known for the quality of its wines, served in silver tankards, and — a new idea in 1830s London — for a price, guests could have the band play whatever tune they wished. Overall, however, Tod was not impressed by the establishment. During the evening, he got into an argument with another patron, a German, whom he claimed had expressed his dislike for the Highland tunes ordered by Tod and others. In the heat of the moment Tod was surprised to find himself insulting his antagonist in Cree.

Tod's Hudson's Bay commission increased his position within class-conscious British society, but his lack of formal education, together with his years in the North American backwoods, meant that he was likely to commit the occasional social error. It seemed to him that these blunders never escaped the notice of Secretary William Smith, who made the most of Tod's failings. Smith was a practical joker whose humour was often at the expense of rough-edged field officers like Tod. Yet, it was also true that Smith handled the personal accounts of Company officers, and it was to him that officers had to turn for expense money. For this reason the often quarrelsome Tod carefully avoided a confrontation with the secretary.

Another source of conflict was Smith's attempt to control Tod's life. Although Tod was on furlough, the secretary preferred to keep him close at hand, using the excuse that members of the London Committee might want to see him on short notice. After enduring Smith's stalling tactics for some time, Tod found a room in suburban Islington, and set about seeing all the attractions of early Victorian London. One of his favourite places was Hyde Park where he would walk to Rotten Row near Kensington Gate and watch the London gentry gallop their horses over the loose gravel track. Tod came to admire the deftness of the English equestrians whose skills he thought compared favourably to the Nez Percés Indians of Oregon, the greatest riders he had ever seen.

Tod's visit to London had come at a time when social tension throughout Britain was increasing. With the breakdown of the rural subsistence economy, thousands of people poured into the cities and towns and, lacking adequate sanitation, the urban areas were incapable of supporting the expanding population. The depression which had begun in 1836 made the situation even worse as factories laid off men, women, and children. The extent to which Tod was aware of the suffering around him is not clear, but the unrest certainly occupied the minds of middle-class Londoners. The death of the profligate William IV in June 1837 had placed his niece Victoria on the throne, and it was the general opinion in the public houses, Tod wrote, that the change was welcomed.

While he was in London Tod also prepared a will in which he named his infant daughter Emma as sole beneficiary. His mixed-blood son James who, although almost fully grown, was still at Reverend David T. Jones's boarding school at Red River, was cut out — in the event of his father's death, the boy was to be withdrawn from class immediately and sent to live with his mother. The final cost of his education was "to be paid from any funds which may be in the hands of the Company."[16] The executors of his estate were William Smith of the Hudson's Bay and John Greenshields of Liverpool, a relative of Tod's. A well-connected mercantile family, the Greenshields had prospered with the expansion of the British Empire over the globe. To deal with their personal accounts in the hands of the Company, Hudson's Bay officers commonly named the Company secretary as executor of their estates.

After completing his will, Tod travelled north to his parents' home. This time, however, his visit was short and it was not long before he had made plans to return to North America. In early January 1838, he went to Liverpool to board the packet for New York. In Liverpool to meet him was Eliza's sister Jane, who had brought Emma. The separation from the Waugh family was not easy for the child, and Emma, who had known only an unstable mother and difficult father, clung tenaciously to her aunt.

The sailing of the ship closed a chapter in Tod's life. He would never see Eliza again.

Chapter Seven

ONE OF THE MOST APPALLING CALAMITIES

Soon after landing at New York in early 1838, Tod went on to Lower Canada where he had made arrangements to place Emma with another relative, Samuel Greenshields, who was a successful Montreal dry-goods wholesaler. While Tod never defined the nature of his kinship with the merchant, it seems likely that Greenshields was related to his mother: the Todds maintained close ties with both the Liverpool and Montreal branches of the Greenshields family. Samuel Greenshields appears to have immigrated to Lower Canada from Liverpool about 1820, and was one of the men responsible for rescuing the flamboyant Colin Robertson from his Montreal creditors in 1821.

After he left Emma at Greenshields's home on St. Paul's Street, Tod took advantage of the few months' leave remaining to visit his old friend Edward Ermatinger. Following the difficulties of the past months, he found the hospitality of his longtime correspondent most welcome. Edward had recently married, and Tod met for the first time his friend's young wife Achsah, or "Axie" as she was usually called. The sister of Anglican minister Mark Burnham, Axie was 12 years her husband's junior. Tod was much impressed with Axie, for her cheerfulness was a pleasant counterpoint to Edward, whose mood was sometimes dark. After a difficult start, Edward's general store had prospered and by the time of Tod's visit he had also taken over as the St. Thomas agent for the Bank of Montreal.

Tod turned to Edward as a financial manager to invest his Hudson's Bay earnings. He was not alone in looking toward Edward to manage investments; the former clerk had built up a large clientele of Hudson's Bay officers. In their isolation, clerks, chief traders and chief factors had little choice but to rely on agents to manage their affairs, and as a former officer himself, Edward was well-situated to offer such services.

Tod had made his journey to Canada at a difficult time. During the previous year, revolts had broken out in the colonies of Upper and Lower Canada. In each colony, the reason for unrest was the same: a privileged oligarchy that exercised considerable economic and political control. West of the Ottawa River, the focus of much of the anger was Lieutenant-Governor Sir Francis Bond Head, whose government had openly served the interests of a small group of clergy, businessmen and colonial officials known as the Family Compact. Opposed to Head was a radical newspaper editor, William Lyon Mackenzie, whose paper called for the formation of an American-style democracy. Faced with the governor's intransigence, Mackenzie and his followers turned to open revolt, and on 7 December 1837 the rebels met government supporters at Montgomery's Tavern, a few miles from Toronto. Unfortunately for the rebels, Mackenzie was better at talk than tactics — his forces were quickly scattered. Although Mackenzie escaped, many of his supporters did not, and, during the following year, 19 of his lieutenants were hanged.

At the time of Tod's visit the political situation in the Canadas remained volatile. Edward did nothing to calm matters — during the rebellion he had served as a loyalist paymaster and justice of the peace. After the government's victory, Edward was not prepared to forgive the rebels. He openly condemned not only Mackenzie and his lieutenants, but anyone who had been in sympathy with their cause. Edward's friends, many of whom had served in the militia, were also staunch loyalists, and in such a highly charged atmosphere, Tod considered it wise to keep his opinions to himself.

While politics occupied much of Edward's time, he retained his passion for music, and the Ermatingers' small frame house on the corner of Walnut and Port Stanley streets was very much the centre of St. Thomas's musical circle. In the evenings Tod's flute and Edward's violin were often part of an impromptu orchestra that included many local musicians. As they played, Axie and other guests would gather on the floor to watch them. The short time Tod spent with the Ermatingers was undoubtedly pleasant, but the purpose of his visit went beyond his desire to see his old friend. The increase in his income as a result of his promotion meant that it would be possible to take a comfortable retirement in a few years. Tod had planned, after he retired, to settle near his friend, and this visit gave him a chance to look over the area around St. Thomas. The location was well-suited to Tod's retirement plans. Edward, who also dabbled in real estate, agreed to act as his agent in the land purchase. It was not possible for Tod to act immediately, though, for at the moment he was short on funds. Tod's last trip to Britain had taken most of his savings, but the income from his one-half share in the fur trade would be enough to buy farm land in a few years time. "I am in hopes," Tod wrote Edward shortly after leaving St. Thomas, "... that the returns of '35 and '36 which were sold last Winter, and the splendid Trade of this Year ... will leave you something to work on."[1]

Tod did not intend to leave any land he purchased unimproved and unproductive during his absence, and during his last trip to Scotland, he had already discussed his plans with two of his brothers, Simeon (Sym) and James. The details of Tod's scheme were never completely settled, but there was probably a general understanding between them that for their work on his land Tod would later provide some favour. As part of the agreement Tod would pay their passage to Canada and, given the hard economic times in Scotland, the idea was well received. Sym, who wished to have land of his own, was particularly eager to emigrate to Canada.

Tod was not the first among Edward's friends in the fur trade to consider retirement in St. Thomas — longtime clerk Thomas Dears had arrived there from the Columbia in 1838, the same year as Tod's visit. A pathetic figure, the clerk was frequently in difficulty with his superiors as a result of his mismanagement of the trade. At retirement, Columbia fur traders who had Indian spouses usually took up land in the vicinity of Fort Vancouver where there was tolerance of mixed-blood families, but Dears made it clear that he intended to take his Indian wife and family to St. Thomas. On discovering Dears's plans, Frank Ermatinger, who also planned to retire near his brother at St. Thomas, was scandalized. "I am for having him near us, but it is his wife," he wrote Edward. "I should like to form a little neighbourhood in your quarter by and bye, and would not like to see anyone in it with whom we could not freely associate."[2]

Dears also faced opposition closer at home, for his wife had no desire to leave the Columbia to live among the Europeans. The slow-witted clerk solved his dilemma by direct action — he struck the woman over the head, and while she was unconscious put her in the canoe to begin the trip east. Even Frank, who had his own well-deserved reputation for brutality, found Dears's behaviour shocking.

At the opening of the navigation season, Tod left once more to return to the Hudson's Bay territories. The Company had decided to send him west beyond the Rockies again, this time to the Columbia territory. Tod proceeded from St. Thomas to Port Stanley on Lake Erie, where he took passage on a ship bound for Amherstburg, near the mouth of the Detroit River. At Amherstburg he renewed his acquaintance with Captain Campbell, a young military officer whom he had first met at Edward's home. The two travelled by wagon to Detroit, arriving there at noon on 14 April 1838. During the recent uprising in the Canadas, American sympathies had been with the rebels, and tensions between the United States and Britain continued to run high. As a member of the British army, Campbell could not enter the United States except by travelling incognito, and thus he was dressed as a civilian when he crossed the American border.

In Detroit, Tod found that he and his companion were looked upon with distrust. Since the whereabouts of Mackenzie and the other rebels who had escaped to the United States were of obvious concern to Lieutenant-Governor Bond Head, he sent agents into the United States in an effort to locate them. The consequence was that the Americans were on the lookout for British or Canadian visitors whose behaviour seemed suspicious. Whether Campbell went as a spy or simply as a tourist is not certain, but it seems likely that if he was on an intelligence mission, Tod would not have been informed. At the hotel, Tod was pleased to find that he was treated with politeness, although Campbell had the misfortune to lose seven pounds in American dollars to a street pickpocket.

The day after their arrival, Tod took passage on an American Fur Company steamer bound for Mackinac Island at the western end of Lake Huron. Prior to boarding he had spent many hours in a futile search for a book on agriculture for his friend Dears, a newcomer to farming. Campbell, however, promised to take up the quest later when he returned to Canada. As the ship set out on Lake Huron the weather became increasingly unpleasant and strong head winds eventually forced it to put back to the St. Clair

River. Since he was unable to discover "a decent Yanky on board" with whom he could strike up a conversation, Tod found his passage all the more tedious.[3]

On 22 April, the ship reached Mackinac Island, where Tod was obliged to wait several days for another vessel to take him on to Sault Ste. Marie. While he was able to find accommodation at the home of an old Nor'Wester who had retired to the island, the meals were not entirely to his taste. "I am getting fast into training for the Campaign which may yet be before me — fish a[nd] potatoes, morning, noon, & night, constitutes our daily [sub]sistance," he complained to Edward.[4]

Tod remained at Sault Ste. Marie through much of May, waiting for a boat to take him on to Hudson's Bay territory. When at last the canoe arrived, Tod crossed Lake Superior and took the route north along Lake Winnipeg where, on the way, he met Dr. John McLoughlin who had travelled east from Fort Vancouver. The doctor was at the beginning of a furlough that would take him to Britain, and the two officers breakfasted together. The Montreal-born McLoughlin was a strong supporter of Louis-Joseph Papineau and the rebels of Lower Canada, and during the meal, made no secret of his sympathies. "I took the liberty to say in a jocund way that it was fortunate for him he had not been with me last winter," Tod wrote Edward, "otherwise I should have most probably been now carrying an account of his trial for the gratification of his friends."[5]

Travelling northeast, Tod went on to Oxford House where he awaited the boats returning from York Factory. From there he and his party headed southwest to Norway House, about ten miles from Lake Winnipeg where the brigade took on additional people and supplies. More than 60 men, women, and children made up the party that year — a large number, for the usual complement was less than a dozen.

In charge of the brigade was Chief Factor John Rowland who was returning to his post at Fort Edmonton. Many in the party were new recruits who, with their wives and children, were heading for the Company's Columbia operations. A few travellers, though, had no direct connection with the Hudson's Bay. Two Catholic priests, François Blanchet and Modeste Demers, had received the Company's permission to begin missionary work west of the Rockies. This was against Hudson's Bay policy, but on McLoughlin's urging the London Committee finally relented and agreed to allow the Oblates passage to the Columbia in 1838. The purpose was to counter the influence of the American Protestant missionaries who had been streaming into the Columbia. While the Hudson's Bay could keep out British subjects, it could do little to stop the American influx, for the land west of the Rockies remained under joint occupancy.

Also accompanying the brigade were two botanists, Robert Wallace and Peter Banks. They had been sent from Britain by the famous plant specialist William Paxton to gather tree specimens suitable for the English climate. During his stay at Norway House Wallace fell in love with Maria, one of Governor Simpson's mixed-blood daughters, and after a brief courtship, they left together for the Columbia.

On 26 July 1838, the travellers pushed off from the shore of Lake Winnipeg to begin the journey west. Ten days later they reached Fort Constant on the Saskatchewan River, and stopped briefly before following the river's north branch as far as Fort Edmonton. Already they had travelled over a month, but much more was to come — the most difficult part of the journey remained. Tod's years with the Hudson's Bay had accustomed him to the hardships of the trail, but many of those with him were not used to such difficulties. In their report to the Archbishop of Quebec, the two priests provided a sketch of what they faced:

> We know how toilsome [this] manner of travel is. To spend days and occasionally entire nights sitting in a cramped position; to endure the inclemency of the seasons, the wind, the pouring rains; to shoot rapids without number, often at the risk of one's life; or perhaps to make long portages through woods, rocky terrain and marshes; to camp without shelter in cold and damp places; to gulp down in haste a wretched and unsuitable fare ... that is a summary of the life of the missionaries on their way to the Northwest.[6]

Before reaching Fort Edmonton the brigade suffered its first loss — one of five children belonging to post master Pierre LeBlanc and his wife Nancy died. Little about the incident was recorded but, as tragic as the loss was, it was only a harbinger of what was to come.

Wallace, the young botanist, intended to marry Maria Simpson when they reached Fort Edmonton, but John Rowland was reluctant to allow the wedding to go on. The couple had not received the blessing of Maria's father, Governor Simpson. (Rowland need not have worried, for since Simpson's own marriage to his cousin Frances the governor had taken no interest in his country children.) Before the brigade left, however, Rowland relented and the couple were wed.

With Rowland remaining at his Fort Edmonton post, Tod was in charge of the brigade. He and his party continued on by horse across the long Assiniboine Portage that connected the Saskatchewan with the Athabasca River system. Even with the aid of animals their passage was difficult — thick forests, muddy bogs, and steep ravines made up the terrain — and the 85-mile portage took five days. From Fort Assiniboine the brigade again took to boats as they made their way along the Athabasca River. Unlike the Peace River which Tod had followed during his journey to New Caledonia in 1823, the more southerly Athabasca route was strewn with rapids and reefs that impeded the journey. On 2 October they reached Jasper House, the Company post that stood in the shadow of the Rocky Mountains. Here the brigade usually transferred to horses for the journey over the mountain barrier, but there were only a few animals available at the post.

Fortunately, many wild horses ranged around the post. Tod ordered that a large corral be built in which he planned to trap the animals. The task was not as easy as he had hoped, for every time the horses were driven near the corral they would veer away. Several days went by before they were at last able to close the gates on the herd. Since there was not enough time to break the horses properly, they were simply lassoed and pulled to the ground, and the packs tied to their backs. Crude halters were then fitted over the animals' heads and the leads tied together. To prevent a general stampede, two or three of Jasper House's tame pack animals were placed in front and the recently captured broncos followed after. Yet even by horse, the journey over the mountains was gruelling. Simpson, who with a small party had taken the Athabasca Pass on his visit to the Columbia in 1824, described it "as bad and dangerous as it can well be."[7] Tod had even greater difficulties, for his party was larger and less experienced than the governor's.

Unused to their role as carriers, the horses shied and threw off their burdens. Time had to be spent rounding up the animals again and re-tying their packs. When they reached a stream that was too deep to be walked through, the horses had to be unloaded and allowed to swim, but the transport of people and cargo was more difficult — rafts had to be built to float them across the water. On days when it was necessary to make several river crossings, the brigade travelled only a few miles.

On 10 October they reached a pair of deep mountain pools known as the "Committee's Punch Bowl." Tod watched two streams flow out of the miniature lakes — one ran east toward the open prairie and the other west toward the Pacific: they had reached the continental divide. As they travelled on, the trail which wound between the great glaciated mountains seemed to get narrower, as if the granite cliffs were about to close in on their columns. Finally, after a steep descent, the brigade reached the place where the cold waters of the Canoe River emptied into the Columbia.

Boat Encampment, as the spot was called, was where the brigade usually exchanged its horses for canoes to take it down the Columbia River and, as expected, Chief Trader Archie McDonald had sent two vessels up from Fort Colvile to assist in transport. However, with such a large party, the craft were entirely inadequate. Tod decided to split the brigade into three sections. The first part, made up mostly of the freight, was loaded into the larger boat and sent on with its crew directly to Colvile, almost 200 miles down river. The smaller craft, carrying freight as well as a complement of voyagers, the two missionaries and a clerk, young John McLoughlin, Chief Factor McLoughlin's son, was sent as far as Maison des Lacs, a new outpost the Company was establishing on the Upper Arrow Lake, about 125 miles down stream. There the voyagers were to discharge their passengers and freight and return to Boat Encampment where they would pick up the third section of the brigade and continue on to Fort Colvile. The plan had not been well thought out, for to remove everyone from Boat Encampment, the smaller craft had to be grossly overloaded. Moreover, for whatever reason, Tod chose not to remain at Boat Encampment with most of his brigade, but to leave with the first boat for Fort Colvile. Since the other officer, McLoughlin, went with the second section to Maison des Lacs, the travellers who remained at Boat Encampment — mostly servants and their families — were left leaderless.

On 16 October, two days after leaving Boat Encampment, the second craft, containing McLoughlin and the two priests, reached Maison des Lacs. The voyagers quickly unloaded the cargo and set off again upriver. The outpost was hardly a suitable stopover. The fort was still in the early stages of construction, and offered no satisfactory accommodation — the two missionaries and McLoughlin had to spend the nights in tents. They would, however, be better off than the remainder of the brigade still at Boat Encampment.

On 20 October the boat with guide André Chilifour in charge completed its return upstream to the mouth of the Canoe River. To accommodate everyone remaining at Boat Encampment, 26 people had to be crammed on board. The journey went without incident until the boat reached the first major rapids along this section of the Columbia, known as the infamous "Dalles des Morts," a stretch of white water that narrowed to no more than 60 feet across. The "rapids of death," as Dalles des Morts has been translated, were well named, for 21 years earlier, in 1817, they had been the scene of a tragic incident involving seven Nor'Westers returning from Boat Encampment.*

The Dalles des Morts on the Columbia River, near Revelstoke, BC. (COURTESY NAC, PA31772)

* Due to the danger of the passage, the travellers had come ashore and allowed their cargo-laden canoe to be taken through the rapids with a rope to manoeuvre it. Some distance into the white water, however, the guide line snapped and the craft was dashed on the rocks where it broke to pieces. With their supplies lost, the men's only hope was to search for local Indians who could help them. Unfortunately, they found no people, and one by one the men perished.

110

For safety, Chilifour sent the passengers and some of the cargo ashore to be portaged around the rapids. The unaccompanied craft was sent through the rapids. Even in this lightened condition, the boat was damaged in the current and almost swamped. It was retrieved and the water emptied out, but the cargo that had been left on board was soaked and now weighed much more. With everyone again on board, the gunwales were hardly above the surface of the water.

After what they had witnessed at the Dalles des Morts the passengers remained apprehensive; however, there was little choice but to go on. They had travelled less than 50 miles when another stretch of churning water came into view. Compared to the last obstacle, Little Dalles should have been only a minor difficulty, but the sight of their boat being almost destroyed at Dalles des Morts had unnerved many of the passengers. As the vessel neared the rocks that broke the surface of the water, waves began splashing over the sides of the boat. There was still time to consider making for shore, but Chilifour, faced with unloading the boat again, chose instead to head into the current. This was a costly mistake for some of the passengers were so frightened that they began standing up, which threatened to capsize the boat. Chilifour restored order just as the craft shot through the most dangerous stretch of white water. Before the vessel had reached safety, however, the botanist Wallace stood up and stripped off his coat. Panicked, he intended to swim for shore, which now seemed deceptively close. Taking up his young wife in his arms he jumped overboard. The sudden shift of weight caused the boat to overturn, throwing everyone into the cold Columbia waters.

The death toll was high. Twelve people — almost half of the passengers and crew on board — drowned. The victims included Wallace and his wife Maria, the second botanist, Banks, and nine other men, women and children. For the shocked survivors, there was little that could be done but to haul the boat on shore and begin a search for their missing companions. The Columbia, though, was reluctant to give up its dead. Only the bodies of three children were ever recovered — nine others were never found. After repairing their battered vessel, the wretched party continued on to Maison des Lacs where the children were buried.

When Tod reached Fort Colvile on 20 October, he was unaware of what had taken place upriver. Archie McDonald dispatched another boat to retrieve McLoughlin and his two companions at Maison des Lacs. The second craft carrying the Boat Encampment passengers should have arrived a few days later, but of course it did not. The survivors reached Colvile on 6 November, by which time Tod had left for Fort Vancouver.

The Company did not hold Tod officially responsible for the deaths, but many of the survivors did. At Boat Encampment he had abandoned his responsibility to the men, women and children he had led since Fort Edmonton, and the result was what Archie McDonald called "one of the most appalling calamities we have experienced in the Columbia."[8] The Columbia had cost André Chilifour and his wife two of their three children. (Only their third son, Joseph, survived.) Nancy LeBlanc's loss was even greater. To the passing of her baby earlier on the journey, she had to add the deaths of her husband Pierre and three of her four remaining children.

On 28 February 1839, Tod wrote to Edward from the Columbia for the first time. Other mutual friends, including Archie McDonald, had written Edward about what had happened on the Columbia, so the contents of Tod's letter must have struck him as surprising. Of the incident at Little Dalles, Tod said nothing.

* * * * *

Tod's return west meant that he had the chance again to see old friends. It had been almost a decade since he had shared the company of Edward's brother Frank, and the younger Ermatinger had put on considerable weight. "When he made his appearance here," Tod wrote Edward, "it was in the dusk of the evening & from his dress — a foraging cap, blue [cloak] in the Island Lake style, a broad leather belt shining with grease & fastened in front by a large brass buckle — it was not easy I assure you, to recognize him."[9] After leaving Fort Thompson, Frank had spent time among the Flathead Indians in the Oregon interior. Although he was a successful trader, the Company failed to promote him.

Another mutual friend, John Work, had been far more fortunate — he received his chief tradership in 1830, and in 1834 succeeded Peter Skene Ogden in charge of trade along the Pacific Coast. Work, like Frank, was showing his years. He had lost most of his hair and become very thin, although Tod was pleased to observe that his spirit remained as lively as ever.

During the absence of Dr. John McLoughlin, James Douglas had been placed in charge of the Columbia Department. Tod remained

112

at Fort Vancouver as assistant to Douglas until the autumn of 1839, when McLoughlin returned. Although in his memoirs Tod spoke warmly of McLoughlin, during his time in the Columbia he and the doctor were frequently at odds. Unlike many other officers, Tod was not impressed by McLoughlin's paternalistic manner. Writing Edward in 1841, Tod claimed that the reason Frank was overlooked once again for promotion was "I am convinced owing entirely to your friend the Doctor — that man appears to me to have as great a share of duplicity as he has egotism."[10] That the two were of opposite temperament may have contributed to their mutual dislike. McLoughlin, as Columbia veteran George Barnston recalled, "could fall out and be again friends with anyone in the course of 48 hours, but the West Country Scot 'John' liked to stick to his point till all was blue."[11] Of course, Tod rarely found authority palatable, even when wrapped in the mantle of fatherly concern.

After McLoughlin's return, Tod was sent to manage the Puget's Sound Agricultural Company's farm at Cowlitz. Begun in 1834 as a subsidiary of the Hudson's Bay, the agricultural operation was intended not only to encourage immigration from the British Empire to the territory, but to develop its own large-scale farming operations in the Columbia. In 1839, an agreement between the Hudson's Bay and the Russian-American Company, the enterprise that controlled the Alaskan fur trade, had secured a ready market for farm produce, and the purpose of the Cowlitz Farm was largely to meet the Russian contract.*

Tod's selection as head of the farm seems strange, for he had little knowledge of agricultural practices. While he dreamed of retiring to his own property at St. Thomas, he was interested in assuming the role of gentleman farmer. "Keep in mind ... my views are merely to live, not to make money," he had once cautioned Edward.[12] The Company's choice as manager should logically have been John Work, who had been born on Geroddy farm in County Donegal, Ireland, and who never quite managed to free himself from the lure of the soil. Work, though, was very important to the success of the fur trade and Tod was not. After the Little Dalles disaster, his personal stock had fallen to a new low. Though most of the chief factors and chief traders were shareholders in the farming enter-

---

* Hudson's Bay posts inland received little benefit from the Company's farms, for the produce was mainly for export. At places like Fort Colvile, Fort McLeod and Fort St. James, employees continued to supplement their ration of dried fish with whatever could be coaxed from their own garden plots.

prise, the commissioned officers regarded the agricultural company's chances of success as small.* In 1838 Douglas warned the London Committee that "a farm in this part of the world cannot be managed with the same apparent economy of means, as in civilized countries, where the agriculturist may, at will, call in the assistance of various trades that minister to his wants."[13] In addition, a large number of menial workers were necessary for the planting and harvesting of the crops, but labour in the Columbia was scarce.

During the spring and summer of 1839, Tod supervised the ploughing of over 200 acres. Nearly 300 bushels of wheat were sown in the first season, while another 135 acres of land were cleared of bush. Cattle had been imported from California. The breed, called simply "Spanish cattle," was difficult to manage, provided little beef and gave almost no milk. They made up for their deficiencies, however, through their resistance to disease and by their prolificacy.

Pigs, sheep and horses were other animals on the farm, with the latter kept mainly for breeding purposes, although the British naval officers visiting Fort Vancouver occasionally rode them for sport.

As Douglas noted, all was not well at the farm. "This has been a year of trial at the Cowlitz, abounding in difficulties, amidst which the gentleman in charge [Tod] has done all that could be expected," he wrote London in the autumn of 1839.[14] One problem was that the sod did not give easily under the plough. A drought which lasted the entire summer contributed to the difficulties, and in the end yields were small.

The following spring, McLoughlin's report sounded a little more optimistic: "I am happy to say that [Tod] had sown this fall 275 bushels which, looks uncommonly well."[15] Yet though the land was fertile, the operation was never an economic success and some years Cowlitz failed even to supply enough grain to meet its contract with the Russians. Although it controlled half a continent, the Hudson's Bay Company seemed incapable of making money at anything other than furs.

By 1840, the Cowlitz operation was not Tod's only agricultural interest. Edward had purchased 200 acres in his name on Port Stanley Road, the planked highway connecting St. Thomas to Lake Erie. "I have been taxing my memory to the utmost ever since I received this piece of news to endeavour to bring to my recollection the appearance & situation of this spot, and for the life of me, tho' I

* When Puget's Sound's shares failed to sell well in Britain, the London Committee put pressure on its senior employees to purchase the stock.

have a tolerable recollection of that of Widdifields [farm] I have none of my own [land]," Tod wrote Edward. The property came with a rude house, where Tod intended his brother Sym to live after he arrived from Scotland. Tod also made it clear to Edward that he expected his friend to oversee the operation of the farm. "I have written him to apply to you for his wants — plough, harrow, oxen etc. and to be guided by your direction in all matters of importance relative to the farm."[16]

Fearing the labour would be too difficult for Sym alone, Tod planned to recruit James, his 22-year-old son, to assist with the farm. Now employed by the Company, James had been sent out to Fort Vancouver where he worked as a carpenter and millwright. With paternal pride Tod noted that in the views of both McLoughlin and Douglas, James "bears an excellent character."[17] Tod hesitated about making final plans for James, however. It was not until 1841 that he wrote Edward: "James is to be put to work immediately on the farm at whatever you may consider most necessary to be done there. I believe you will find him an able & willing lad and tolerably efficient either as plough-man or ploughmaker."[18]

His youngest child, Emma, remained in the care of his relatives in Lower Canada, and if not entirely a doting father, Tod did continue to provide for her and to take an interest in her wellbeing. "Should you visit Montreal in the course of the summ[e]r I shall take it kindly could you find the time to call at Mr. Sam[ue]l Greenshields and see my little Emma," he wrote Edward in 1838.[19]

It was Emma's mother, however, who remained Tod's greatest concern, for the cost of maintaining her was an unwelcome drain on his accounts. Seven months after Eliza's return to her mother, Letitia Waugh wrote the governor and Committee in London to explain that the family was now in a difficult financial position. The local doctors had recommended that Eliza be placed in an asylum but this was impossible because "the sum allowed by Mr. Todd [sic] for her support is very inadequate, more especially as she requires the constant attendance of a proper person to take care of her." If Tod himself was not able to contribute more to Eliza's care, she asked that the Company would "grant such assistance as may alleviate her greatly to be deplored situation."[20] After all, the letter implied, the Company had some responsibility in this matter, for before going to Hudson's Bay territory, Eliza's health was perfectly sound.

While the Company was not eager to undertake the cost of Eliza's care itself, the Committee was prepared to discuss the matter with

Tod. In his reply dated 28 February 1838, Committee Secretary William Smith advised Mrs. Waugh that Tod would be made aware of her situation, and a few months later Tod agreed to increase his contributions for Eliza's care to £15 twice yearly. As Eliza's husband, Tod was kept apprised of her condition. "My unfortunate wife," he wrote his friend, James Hargrave, in 1843, "is still in the same unhappy state of mind in Tharbortons assylum [sic]." He was able to add, though, that Emma was "very well with my relations in Montreal, and by all accounts I have received, making good progress with her education."[21]

Not surprisingly, given the state of his finances, Tod did not look upon a request for another expense with much favour but in 1839, like other commissioned officers, he had received a circular from Chief Factor Donald Ross requesting donations for the purchase of a silver service for George Simpson in honour of his contribution to the fur trade. The gift was an opportunity for some of the officers to ingratiate themselves with Simpson, for the contributors and the amount of their pledges would be known to the governor. Tod proposed instead that the gift be made not from individual officers, but as "a general thing and that a service of plate be voted to him from the fur Trade; for which, all acknowledge, he has done so much."[22] Since the gift would be made on behalf of everyone, Simpson would not be aware of individual donations. His idea received, however, little support from Ross and his associates. As might be expected, those who had prospered under Simpson's stewardship were the most liberal in their offerings. Doctor John McLoughlin, whose power within Hudson's Bay territory was second only to Simpson's, contributed the then-enormous sum of £50. Tod, in the end, gave nothing.

* * * * *

In the summer of 1840, when Tod arrived at Fort Vancouver for the meeting of the Columbia Council, he discovered an epidemic had broken out. The cause of the illness was unknown at the time, but the symptoms included pain in the bones and joints, and high fevers that alternated with severe chills. While the Europeans sometimes died, the mortality rate among the Indians was considerably higher. For the natives, Tod noted in his memoirs, "The universal panacea ... was to have the infected parties placed in a sweating house for 15 or 20 minutes, & then plunged into cold water, — the worst possible treatment for the disease. Many were taken out dead."[23]

By 1840, the illness had already devastated so many Indians that the two priests, Blanchet and Demers, noted in their report "in one of their villages that the survivors, not being able to bury the bodies that had piled up there, were obliged to destroy them by giving them over to the flames to preserve the surrounding country from infection."[24] The illness, which was later discovered to be malaria, had been introduced to the Columbia by an American ship, the *Owhyhee*, which visited in 1830. Located as it was on the north bank of the Columbia, Fort Vancouver adjoined low, marshy land that was an excellent breeding ground for the mosquitoes that carried the disease. Tod was drafted to minister to the sick — Europeans and Indians alike — and he did not contract the disease, but many of the senior officers were stricken, including Work, Douglas, and even McLoughlin himself.

Work, particularly, was experiencing a run of misfortune. In the spring of 1840, an accident almost cost him his life. While putting in his garden plot at Fort Simpson, on the north coast, Work fell across a tree stump, thereby weakening the muscles of his abdomen. The injury was not serious, but a tumble from a tree a few months later made the condition worse and his intestines herniated through the rupture. As he wrote Edward, while stuffing the colon back into the cavity, "I injured the intestines or some of their coverings which brought on an inflammation and I was for five days at the point of death."[25] Eventually he recovered, but it was two months before he was out of his sick bed.

While he was at the council meeting, Tod received news that he would be transferred again to New Caledonia in the fall. His time on the Cowlitz farm had not been wasted. "My short stay here," he wrote Edward, "has afforded me an opportunity of gaining considerable practical knowledge in farming which I trust to make good use of hereafter."[26] He did not look forward, though, to his return to New Caledonia. "What I would not give to be along side you & Mrs. Ermatinger this very night, with a long pipe & flaggon [sic] of brandy," he wrote Edward in his last letter from the Columbia.[27]

Chapter Eight

HE MERITED DEATH AT OUR HANDS

In the autumn of 1840, Tod accompanied the York Express as far as Fort Okanagan on the Columbia. From there he headed north on the brigade route to Fort Thompson in the Kamloops Valley. On his way, Tod passed many Indian camps. Despite its aridity, the Kamloops Valley supported a large Indian population, for the greater rainfall in the surrounding mountains encouraged game and the many lakes of the region were well stocked with fish. In the late summer and early fall, salmon usually were a sure and plentiful source of food to be dried for the coming cold winter months. The natives, members of the Shuswap tribe, occupied much of the Kamloops Valley and surrounding lands in what is now southern British Columbia. In turn, the Shuswap were made up of about 20 bands, most of whom maintained a nomadic existence during the summer months. In winter, the bark or reed-covered teepees were replaced by semi-permanent sod-covered lodges.

During the period of North West Company control, the Kamloops Valley had been a rich source of furs, but gradually the beaver were depleted. Dried salmon, however, remained an important commodity of trade between the Indians and Europeans. By 1840, some of the natives had begun to plant potatoes, both to supplement their own diet of roots and berries, and to trade with the Hudson's Bay men at the fort. Still, many of the fiercely independent Shuswap remained deeply suspicious of the Hudson's Bay traders — not surprisingly, since the Europeans in charge usually favoured intimidation over diplomacy in their dealings with the Indians.

When Tod visited, the post was under the command of Samuel Black who had taken over after the departure of Frank Ermatinger ten years earlier. Black had done well in Company service; in 1837, the former Nor'Wester had been promoted to chief factor and placed in charge of all the posts along the upper Columbia.

When Black's friend, Chief Factor Peter Skene Ogden, now at Fort Stuart, accompanied the New Caledonia brigade through the Kamloops Valley, the two men who had once terrorized the Hudson's Bay had an opportunity to recall their former glories. Ogden, though, had changed — he had become a hard-working and dedicated officer who was well respected by those who served under him. His friend had not. Black could be pleasant when it suited him, but underneath the superficial *bonhomie* was the bully of former days. Black appeared to enjoy making an enemy of his nearest neighbour, Alexander Fisher, the chief trader at Fort Alexandria. His letters to Fisher were clearly intended to enflame the passions of his humourless subordinate. When Tod arrived in 1840, however, Black held his dark side in check and Tod was much impressed by the hospitality he showed.

It was only when Tod reached Fort Thompson that he learned of his final destination. A letter waiting for him from Ogden placed him in charge of Fort Alexandria following Fisher's transfer east. During Tod's visit, a disturbing incident occurred — early on the morning of their departure, as he and his companions said farewell to the trader and his family, Tod suddenly had a premonition something terrible was about to happen to Black. He never recorded what had happened, but the experience deeply affected him. Not wishing to alarm them, Tod said nothing to Black or his wife Angelique.

The trail to his new post was difficult — he continued along the South Thompson by horse until the river joined the Fraser. There he followed the Fraser north almost to its junction with the Quesnel River, a distance of nearly 200 miles. Although trade with the surrounding Indians was small, Fort Alexandria was important for supplying the more remote forts farther north.

The winter of 1840 had begun early and with little else to occupy his evenings, Tod read copies of the Canadian newspapers forwarded by Edward. As an owner of Canadian property, Tod had begun to take greater interest in events in the province to the east. After the 1837 Rebellion, the British government had moved quickly to appoint John Lambton, first Earl of Durham, to prepare a report on the affair. The result of Durham's inquiry was presented to the British House of Commons on 11 February 1839. Although the commissioner demonstrated little understanding of the plight of the French-speaking population of Lower Canada — he had received only the views of the privileged English-speaking minority — he was better able to grasp the grievances of the predominantly English-speaking settlers of Upper Canada. One of Durham's principal recommendations was the implementation of responsible government as a means of ending the power of the Family Compact, the small and influential elite that had long dominated Upper Canadian politics. As Tod recognized, Durham's report would weaken colonial ties to Great Britain. "I think it probable that the British possessions in N. America will not remain long in the position of dependencies on the Mother Country," he wrote Edward.[1] Unlike the United States, which had gone its own way, he argued that an independent Canada must become a part of the British Empire.

For Edward, though, the notion of limited Canadian sovereignty was unthinkable, and the report's call for a few modest steps toward self-rule was to him an expression of the greatest radicalism. The last straw for Edward was Durham's decision to have the charges against most of the remaining rebels dropped. The uncompromising tone of Edward's letter of the previous year was deeply disturbing, and Tod felt obliged to reply on 1 March 1841: "It has always appeared to me ... that few things in this world tend more to generate feelings of uncharitableness toward our fellow creatures than patriotic zeal."[2] But even years later, Edward remained unwilling to forgive those who had supported the rebel cause.

After a setback resulting from the 1837 Rebellion, the St. Thomas area had again become a destination for British immigrants, and Edward, who sold almost everything the new arrivals needed, continued to prosper. Some time after Tod's visit, Edward demolished his old frame house and erected an imposing brick structure. Far away in New Caledonia, Tod's thoughts were on St. Thomas. During the long winter evenings at Alexandria, Tod developed his plans for the farm at St. Thomas, Canada West (as Upper Canada was now called). "I should like to get more acres cleared," he wrote Edward, "and such other improvements as may occur to you." Perhaps because of his experience on the Cowlitz farm, Tod was a strong believer in maintaining a system of crop rotation. It was also his intention to establish a small dairy farm with perhaps a few horses, but there was much to do in the meantime. The property still lacked an adequate farmhouse and Tod hoped to have a new building completed before his retirement. To this end, Edward was asked to send building plans. The house, Tod envisioned, would be "of moderate size, to contain a dining room, parlour, library, kitchen & four small bed rooms."[3]

Tod still faced a major problem: by 1840, he had no word from Sym. Since it was long past the time Tod had expected him to arrive, it seemed increasingly likely his brother had changed his mind about the venture and had stayed in Scotland. Until Tod's son James arrived from the Columbia, there would be no work done on the property unless he hired a local hand — a possibility he considered reluctantly because of the cost. The role of absentee property owner was becoming increasingly frustrating, but he could not afford to retire immediately.

* * * * *

On 2 March 1841, Alexis Laprade, a servant from Fort Thompson, arrived at Fort Alexandria. The shaken man reported that Chief Factor Black had been murdered by an Indian, but he had no idea whether the death was a single incident or the beginning of a general Indian uprising. With good reason the Company had feared trouble, for some Indians remained hostile to the incursions of the fur traders into their land. On an earlier occasion, Black had had his horse shot out from under him. The details of what had taken place at Fort Thompson were thin — Laprade did not know what had happened to Black's family or the other employees at the fort. Following the death of his superior, he immediately headed north for Fort Alexandria.

With only a few men, Tod felt there was little he could do. If the Indians were prepared for serious trouble, he and his companions had small chance of survival. Yet, regardless of the danger, he considered he had no choice but to return immediately to Fort Thompson. Before leaving, he quickly scrawled what he believed might be his last words to Edward:

> I am going to start immediately to take possession. I consider
> it not merely as a point of duty to do so without waiting to

consult any of my colleagues, but from a desire to save the lives of the men of the place. Should all go well with me I shall drop you a few lines from thence.[4]

With Laprade and two of his own servants, Tod headed south on horseback along the banks of the Fraser. The journey was not easy — by now two or three feet of snow covered the ground — but the four men made good time, reaching the post in a little over three days.

As they approached, Tod cautioned his companions to wait outside while he entered alone. It did not take him long to find the victim. Black remained where he had been shot, with, as Tod claimed, his wife Angelique and children still weeping over the frozen body.

Other than the trader's family, the fort had one remaining occupant, Jean Baptiste Lolo, a former Hudson's Bay interpreter who had stood guard over the Company's property. Lolo's origins are not entirely clear — although he may have been from the Kamloops Valley, it seems more likely he was an eastern Indian who had moved west with the fur trade. A valuable employee, the interpreter had been able to move easily through the camps of the Shuswap and gather intelligence for the Company. Lolo, though, had recently not renewed his contract with the Hudson's Bay.

Tod made a brief inspection to determine the angle of the shot, after which Black's body was wrapped in a horsehide blanket and placed in a rough-hewn coffin for burial. He and his men then made an inventory of the post stores. Nothing had been taken from the supplies, which meant that robbery was an unlikely motive, and according to Lolo, the reason for Black's death was not a mystery.

The murder was the indirect result of an argument that Black had had with Tranquille, one of the Shuswap chiefs. During the previous summer, Tranquille had asked Black for a gun that was kept at the fort, a gun supposedly belonging to another hunter. The trader refused and the matter appeared to end, but in early January 1841, Tranquille came again to the fort and asked for the weapon. When Black would not give it to him, an argument broke out. There seems little doubt that the tactless trader deeply insulted the proud chief, for the old man stormed angrily from the post and returned to his camp at Pavilion on the Fraser River. A short time later, Tranquille suddenly became ill and died. Recalling the incident with Black, the chief's relatives attributed his passing to the trader's bad medicine.

Aware of the hostile feeling toward him, Black tried to appease Tranquille's family by sending several servants to attend the chief's burial, but it was too late. Tranquille's wife demanded vengeance and began goading the old man's 18-year-old nephew, Kiskowskin, to restore the family honour. Undoubtedly aware that killing Black would bring the wrath of the Hudson's Bay upon him, the young man hesitated, but after several days of the woman's harangues, he gave in. Taking his gun, he and two companions rode to the fort.

The three visitors arrived about noon and went directly to the reception hall where they sat quietly. As Tod later discovered, many of Black's servants were away from the fort at the time and there were few people to notice the three men sitting there. Edward Montigny, one of those remaining behind, did notice that one of the men seemed ready for trouble, and he reported his suspicions to Black. Despite the warning, the trader took little notice and continued about his duties.

Servant Alexis Laprade, who had spent most of the day sorting potatoes in the cellar under the reception hall, was also aware of the visitors. To get to the compound's various rooms, Black frequently crossed through the hall, and from time to time, he would talk to his servant through the open trap door. Eventually Laprade saw two of the visitors depart, leaving Kiskowskin seated alone in the gathering gloom of the winter afternoon.

A little while later Black entered the hall where the visitor remained. Before the trader had passed out of sight, the young man took the gun he had concealed under his coat, braced himself against the fireplace chimney and pulled the trigger. Black, who had just stooped to go through the doorway to his living quarters, was struck in the back — the ball passed through his chest and embedded itself in the wall opposite him. He crumpled at his wife's feet. The shooting panicked the remaining servants who scattered in the directions of the nearest forts.

With such a limited force, Tod could do little to apprehend the fugitive himself, but within a few days, reinforcements arrived from other forts in the district. Since his own post was unprotected, Tod made plans to return to Fort Alexandria once it was clear that tension in the Kamloops Valley had eased somewhat. The task of catching Black's murderer was given to Donald McLean, a clerk with a reputation for violence. McLean, Tod recalled later, "in his youth having served on board a man of war, was not scrupulous in his idea of justice & was therefore a likely man for the work. He was used to making raids on Indians." When the suspect was not captured, McLean's practice was to "take their horses, break their canoes, & commit such like depredations."[5]

McLean failed to turn up new leads, so the Company removed its men and most of the stores and left Fort Thompson in the hands of Lolo. McLoughlin was aware that the most effective means of retaliation was simply to pull out of the fort, thereby denying trade goods to the Indians of the area. In this case, however, Fort Thompson was on the trail through which the New Caledonia brigade had to pass, so a failure to quickly pacify the local Indians threatened the Company's route to the Columbia. The Hudson's Bay thus faced the difficult task of punishing Black's murderer without further angering the local Indians. To end the crisis McLoughlin looked toward Tod rather than other officers such as Chief Trader Donald Manson who was more inclined to act rashly.

On 3 August 1841, Tod arrived with Chief Factor Peter Skene Ogden and a small party at Fort Thompson where they were greeted by Lolo and his family. While the occupants of the post had suffered much hunger and hardship during this time, Tod noted that the buildings locked by the Europeans when they departed remained secure. Although he never entirely trusted Lolo, Tod was nonetheless impressed by his strength and courage.

The summer was extremely hot and very dry, the unpleasant conditions made worse by smoke from brush fires some miles down the valley. Depending on the direction of the wind, the haze was sometimes so thick the sun could not be seen. About noon on 5 August, Ogden and Tod mounted up and rode off to meet the Columbia brigade. They camped along the trail overnight, and early the next day came upon the party of men and horses travelling north. While Tod continued with the brigade, Ogden, with men and supplies destined for Fort Thompson, rode on ahead. As they crossed the river some miles from the fort, Ogden and his companions suddenly found themselves in the middle of a large party of Indians. There is no record of what took place, but the meeting was far from cordial; unbidden, Ogden and his men were given an escort to the gates of the fort. Near the safety of the stockade, the officer turned and began haranguing the Indians about their protection of Black's murderer. When Ogden had finished, the Indians did not seem impressed — the chief factor was met by a wall of stony silence.

After Ogden left for Fort Alexandria with the brigade on 9 August, Tod once again assumed command of Fort Thompson.

During the spring and summer, the Indians of the Kamloops Valley had been deprived of ammunition, making it difficult for them to kill enough game to meet their needs. (After embracing European weapons, the Indians seemed to have difficulty making the transition back to the old ways of hunting.) Tod believed their concerns for the coming winter would make the capture of Tranquille's nephew easier, for the Indians would now be less willing to hide the fugitive.

During the summer, Tod also intended to begin building a new post, which would be called Fort Kamloops, on the river bank opposite the existing post. While Fort Thompson was large and well-fortified, there was much wrong with it. "Never in the whole course of my travels in this country have I beheld a place that exhibited a more complete picture of desolation than the present establishment," he wrote shortly after his return to Fort Thompson. "The buildings have apparently been long in a state of decay and notwithstanding the props by which they are supported are fast tottering to the ground."[6]

Remaining behind with Tod was a clerk, D. E. Cameron, and nine servants. The capture of Tranquille's nephew was Tod's priority, but he was also eager to begin the construction of the replacement post. During Black's stay there, he had allowed the fort to fall into disrepair, with scrub bush and grass springing up just beyond the palisade. The vegetation was not only tinder for the approaching fires, but also provided excellent concealment for anyone wishing to attack. The first task was thus to clear the poplar and willow thickets from around the fort. The work was made difficult not only by the thick smoke continuing to hang over the valley, but by a strange sickness affecting Tod's men. Those who came down with the disease suffered a high fever that, at least on one occasion, brought on convulsions. To increase the discomfort caused by the heat, smoke and sickness, officers and servants alike were plagued by swarms of mosquitoes invading the fort every morning and evening.

By 19 August, the blazing forests were becoming a concern to everyone at the fort. "Wood, which had been squared for a store[house] some time last winter," Tod noted in the Fort Thompson journal, "and which I was to raft down the river, is now found to have been all consumed by fire."[7] The flames were so close that the forests nearest the old fort were on fire. Fortunately, by early September, the fires had begun to die down. The servants continued to work on the new fort, but the charred

125

forests meant it was now much more difficult to secure good logs for the stockade and buildings.

The annual salmon run had reached inland as far as the Kamloops Valley by the middle of August and the local Indians were participating in their usual feast. To supplement their own food stocks, the traders traditionally purchased a few fish from the Indians who brought them to the fort, but Tod did not wish to give the impression that it was business as usual. "They will, I apprehend," he wrote on 27 August, "be sadly disappointed by and by when they find we do not intend sending out parties of our people to collect them as formerly. On those occasions they were in the habit, on the slightest provocation, of shooting our men's horses."[8]

Yet Tod was also intent on improving relations with the Indians of the Kamloops Valley. With Lolo's help, he obtained an inventory of the property that had been taken or destroyed earlier by McLean and his men during their raids on Indian camps and he began making restitution. But the great stumbling block to normalized relations was still Tranquille's nephew. Tod decided to offer a substantial reward in trade goods to the Indian who provided information leading to the suspect's capture.

As Tod had hoped, reports on the whereabouts of Kiskowskin began to reach the fort. He sent Cameron to follow up leads and on 1 September, the clerk and a party of armed servants rode 80 miles to Cache Creek where they raided a small Indian camp. While they found one of Kiskowskin's wives and several of his children, the wanted man was not there.

In an effort to force Kiskowskin's hand, Cameron took one of his children hostage — an act that not surprisingly threw the entire Indian camp into an uproar. The clerk and his men picked up the child and rode off to make camp 15 miles away where they waited for the man's return. When they raided the Indian encampment two days later, Kiskowskin still had not come back. Faced with little choice, Cameron returned the child to its mother. Cameron's seizure of the child was an isolated action, done without Tod's approval, but it further impaired relations between the Indians and Europeans.

On 6 September Lolo, who had recently put his mark upon a new three-year contract with the Company, was sent to persuade an Indian named Grand Gule to seek out and capture his fellow tribesman. Since Grand Gule seems to have had the complete trust of Tranquille's nephew, it is likely that they were related in some way. If this were the case, Grand Gule did not appear to value his blood ties highly. Tod hoped that for a price he would sell out the wanted man.

Lolo returned later with news that Grand Gule had agreed to capture Kiskowskin the next day. For Tranquille's nephew to be taken by one of his fellow tribesmen was, of course, desirable — the Company would not be held directly responsible for the capture. When the time came, however, Grand Gule chose to remain in his lodge rather than confront the fugitive. "We are now resolved therefore on making no further application to him on the subject but entirely on taking the villain on our own resources," wrote a frustrated Tod.[9]

Once captured, Kiskowskin's fate would be all too apparent. As Tod wrote in the Thompson River journal, "it [is] our intention ... to have him brought to the fort and hung by the neck."[10] The Company's summary execution of Indians accused of murdering Europeans had long bothered Tod, but he was nevertheless prepared to carry out the act. As an officer, he would have had to follow Company policy.

Meanwhile, tensions between the Europeans and Indians continued high. On 9 September, one of the servants cutting hay on the bank of the North Thompson opposite the post came rushing back to the fort considerably excited. He claimed he had seen two Indians watching him from a hiding place in the grass. Lolo and Cameron returned to the spot, but could find nothing to support the man's claims. "It is evident that the fellow, who is an arrant coward, must have taken flight at two strange horses who were quietly grazing at a short distance from him," Tod concluded.[11]

On 11 September, Tod received word that the fugitive and his two wives had left to hide in the mountains. Cameron and his men, including Lolo, rode off in pursuit while Tod remained at the fort with only two servants. The hunt was a job for younger men. The next morning, Tod found a number of Indians had set up camp at the fort gate. When he spoke to them, they reported they had seen the suspect riding back toward the fort. "I don't believe it," Tod noted in the fort's journal, "however I intend to keep watch in the night and have given the Indians encamped around us [instructions] to keep close to their lodges during the night as I had determined to fire on the first person I should happen to see sculking [*sic*] about the bushes."[12] As he had suspected, Tod saw no sign of Kiskowskin during his all-night vigil.

By now it was mid-September and autumn was coming to the Kamloops Valley. While the days remained hot, by evening a chill was in the air, and on some mornings, frost covered the ground. The annual migration of thousands of water birds south for the winter was well under way. During the day, many Indians came to the fort to ask for ammunition, which Tod refused to supply.

Cameron and his men returned to Fort Thompson about noon on 17 September after trailing the suspect to the mountains beyond Cache Creek. Although they tracked Kiskowskin as far as the snow line, they eventually lost his trail. Disappointed, Cameron could do little but return to the post. That Tod was unable to capture Tranquille's nephew was only one of many concerns, for about this time, news reached him that a Hudson's Bay messenger had been attacked as he rode between Forts Colvile and Okanagan. The servant was fortunate to escape with his life. With the unrest to the south, it would be difficult to maintain the communication and brigade route between New Caledonia and the Columbia district. Tod could only hope that Indian tempers would cool.

Since there were no new reports concerning Tranquille's nephew, the servants returned to the task of constructing a new post. On 21 September, they were preparing to retrieve logs rafted on the river as far as the construction site when they saw two men appear on the opposite bank of the North Thompson. After they crossed the river, the pair confessed to deserting from Fort Alexandria. While desertion was a serious offence, the incident had been made worse by the theft of Company property — they had taken two Company horses which they had apparently lost during their flight south. The servants, Grand Louis and a man identified only as Lolo's nephew, had allowed themselves to be robbed by the Indians at Green Lake, about 80 miles north of Fort Thompson. With much else on his mind, Tod also had to decide what punishments to impose on the hapless pair.

Also on 21 September, he received a servant carrying a message from Chief Factor Ogden at Stuart Lake for Fort Vancouver. It was usually Tod's responsibility to supply a runner to relay the dispatch as far as Fort Colvile, but in the current situation the man's life would be in grave danger. Tod spent several days considering the problem.

The next day, Lolo's nephew was brought into the compound; his clothes were stripped off and his wrists tied to the gates of the fort. Then as Tod noted in the Fort Thompson Journal, he was "well flogged."[13] Although not beaten, Grand Louis would go with the messenger to Fort Vancouver where he was to be sent out of Hudson's Bay territory. Since he would accompany the messenger south through hostile territory, this might have been regarded as punishment worse than a lashing.

On 23 September, the blue skies disappeared behind a heavy, grey-black curtain, and the air carried the hint of the first storm of autumn. By nightfall, rain had started heavily, and in the morning, the North Thompson was muddied and swollen. The following day the storm continued, with the wind blowing sheets of rain against the decrepit buildings of the old fort. Tod could not delay sending out the Vancouver packet long, but it was clear he did not want the two men's deaths on his conscience.

Before dispatching them, Tod sent Cameron to Chief Nicola's camp to ask him to come to the fort. Nicola, a Thompson River Indian, was the most powerful chief in the area, and Tod hoped he would agree to accompany the Hudson's Bay men as far as Fort Colvile. Nicola's presence, Tod believed, would offer some protection, for the Indians to the south might have been reluctant to do harm to the chief and his companions. But when Nicola failed to arrive at the fort, Tod was forced to send his servant, Edward Montigny, and the deserter, Louis, to Fort Vancouver without escort. He advised Montigny to beware of the Indians at the Forks, but the two men completed the journey without incident.

There was little further news about Kiskowskin until the morning of 27 September, when Tod received word that the fugitive had taken refuge in the hills beyond the fort. He immediately cancelled plans to send a trading party to Fraser Lake, but rather than dispatching Cameron and his men on what might have been a wild goose chase, he decided to wait.

The following day, Tod learned that the fugitive Kiskowskin was with Grand Gule, the Hudson's Bay's erstwhile agent. It was still hoped Grand Gule would capture the young man himself, but it was easy to understand why he had chosen not to act alone. Black had not been popular with the local people, and there were many Indians who had helped the young man escape. Grand Gule did not wish to incur the anger of his people. With winter coming on rapidly, though, and without powder and shot, the natives were paying a high price for their loyalty.

On 30 September, Grand Gule and a number of Kiskowskin's relatives arrived at the fort. Through an interpreter, Tod lectured them for sheltering the fugitive. Before riding off, Grand Gule had a few words with Lolo. What they discussed was not reported, but the next day Grand Gule returned to the fort alone. During a meeting with Tod, he agreed that for a reward in trade goods he would help capture his fellow tribesman. Grand Gule knew Kiskowskin's hiding place and a plan was worked out. During the night, when everyone was asleep, Grand Gule would sneak into the camp and disarm the fugitive. Cameron and his men, who would be waiting near by, would then have no difficulty taking the man prisoner.

On 2 October, the weather was overcast but still mild. In the afternoon, Tod watched as Cameron, Lolo and three other men cut out five horses from the corral, mounted up and rode off. One other rider had now joined the party: a young man who was the son of Nicola. That such a prominent chief as Nicola was tacitly supporting the action did not bode well for Tranquille's nephew. The fugitive was becoming increasingly isolated.

The next day, more than 20 Indians arrived at the fort and took up positions in the reception hall. The visitors said little, but remained seated, fixing their pipes and slowly drawing in the tobacco smoke. As Tod learned after speaking with them, they had been told by Grand Gule to stay at the fort until they received word on the fate of Kiskowskin.

On 4 October, Tod awoke to the usual grey dawn. The sky was heavily overcast, and a steady downpour, turning earth to mud, made travel difficult. By afternoon the rain had stopped and blue sky appeared through breaks in the clouds. Cameron and the others had been gone two days, and Tod by now had anticipated some word from them. By nightfall, however, there was still no message.

Life at the fort went on as usual. On some nights, Indians carrying torches stood on the banks of the Thompson spearing the last few spawning salmon — a scene Tod could watch from the walls of the stockade. Such fishing, though, was best carried out on calm, dark nights, and this evening the weather had changed — the clouds had blown away to reveal a starry sky. The next morning passed uneventfully. The servants who remained with Tod went about their chores, while in the reception hall, his Indian guests smoked their pipes and maintained their silent wait. Finally, in the late afternoon, Cameron and his men appeared — without a prisoner.

After they left the post, all had gone according to plan. Cameron and his men had ridden west and, at nightfall, set up camp. The following day on the trail to Cache Creek, the posse met Grand

Gule who was to guide them the remainder of the way. The journey was arduous, for by afternoon, the rain had drenched the riders. Not long before evening, they reached the brow of a hill that looked down upon a small creek in a valley. This was supposed to be the location of the fugitive's camp. Cameron and his companions dismounted and waited for darkness. As the light faded, they could see the blaze of a campfire in the distance, and in the stillness of early evening, the sound of voices.

Quietly Cameron and his men moved forward, but their way was blocked by the creek they had seen earlier. Tying up their horses on the near bank, they moved along until they found a spot where it was possible to ford the stream. With the others waiting in the darkness, Grand Gule crept forward into the Indian camp to steal the weapons. In the light of the fire, everyone seemed asleep. When Grand Gule returned with the weapons, he claimed Kiskowskin had called out to his wife that he dreamt the white men were coming. Cameron and his companions then rushed the camp. In the melee that followed, the unarmed man was taken easily.

On the return journey, Cameron decided to save time, against Lolo's advice, by crossing the headwaters of the South Thompson River in a canoe. Several of the men were ferried across the river before Kiskowskin and his two guards were put in the boat. For some reason, they failed to tie their captive's hands, and when the canoe was half way across, he suddenly moved about wildly, upsetting the vessel. The two guards almost drowned, but their captive managed to reach shore without difficulty. As he stood on the bank, however, one of the posse saw him and fired. Severely wounded, Kiskowskin jumped into the river, but was caught in an eddy and drawn under. Cameron and the others watched from the shore, and when it was obvious the fugitive would not rise to the surface again, they left. The body was never recovered.

For the Europeans, Kiskowskin's death was just retribution for Black's murder and Tod was able to write in the Fort Thompson journal, "This event appears to have caused little excitement in the minds of those in our immediate vicinity. They all acknowledge he merited death at our hands."[14] After receiving the news, Tod went to the hall where he delivered a short speech explaining to the Indians how the man whom the Hudson's Bay accused of Black's murder had died. For his betrayal Grand Gule was paid off in trade goods, some of which he distributed among his relatives. Grand Gule's prestige would rise even further — a few months later he was made a chief of the Shuswap tribe.

In his almost 30 years in Indian territory Tod had changed from the impetuousness of youth to the caution of maturity. Gone was the individual who was prepared to act on the most insubstantial evidence: Tod, in middle age, considered the circumstances carefully and acted wisely. His capture of Kiskowskin was accomplished as a result of careful planning. Unlike so many of his colleagues who held positions of authority with the Hudson's Bay, Tod believed in the judicious use of persuasion over the application of brute force.

In November 1841, with the operations at the post returning to normal, Tod was replaced at Fort Thompson by Chief Trader Donald Manson. Although later he was often at odds with Tod over the way Indians should be treated, Manson was nonetheless impressed by his colleague's handling of the Black affair. After his return to the fort, Manson noted his approval in a letter to the governor:

> ... from what I can see and learn, the Sushwaps [sic] and other tribes in the vicinity of this establishment are now in pretty good order, and apparently well disposed to us, and certainly (when we look back to the very different state of things in this quarter, during the past few years, when it was no uncommon thing for the Indians to draw knives on the late Mr. Black inside the Fort, and, invariably grossly insult and rob his men when ever they met them on the route) I think Mr. T. is justly intitled [sic] to every praise for his supperior [sic] management and arrangements in having effected such a desirable change in so short a time. ...[15]

The following spring, Tod returned to take command of Fort Alexandria. After his experience at Fort Thompson, he could look forward to the relative quiet of the Fraser River post, yet his respite there was short. The murder of another Hudson's Bay officer at a distant outpost would again result in Tod's return to Fort Thompson.

Chapter Nine

I Do Not Wish to Incur Their Contempt

Fort Alexandria, by Hudson's Bay standards, was a comfortable posting. As well as its own gardens, the establishment had a small herd of cattle which supplied meat and milk to the table, and a water-powered mill in full operation which ground grain into flour. Yet his isolation from his old comrades continued to weigh heavily on Tod. Such luxuries as the fort supplied he would willingly give up, he wrote his friend James Hargrave, for a "sociable night's crack wi' ye man."[1] At Alexandria, Tod turned again to music for comfort. The flute which he had purchased many years earlier now made hardly any sound at all. Undaunted, he still continued to practise with the instrument. To impress the Ermatingers when he saw them again, Tod attempted to learn one of the more demanding pieces in his collection of sheet music — the overture to Rodolphe Kreutzer's *Lodoïska*, arranged for two flutes. He hoped to play it as a duet with Edward.

By the spring of 1842 Tod was 47 years old. His long brown hair had thinned and was turning grey. The years of privation had so conditioned him that even when provisions were plentiful, he ate little. He could also see the effects of this difficult life in the face of his longtime friend John Work who, he noted, was now "a queer looking *chap* — of his hair, there remains but three small elflocks which protrude, far between, over his coat and neck, and the point of his nose is actually coming in contact with that of his chin."[2]

Many of the men he had long known were already dead. Thomas Simpson, the governor's cousin who had distinguished himself as an arctic explorer, had died two years earlier, apparently by his own hand. Chief Trader Pierre Pambrun, who had served the Company almost as many years as Tod himself, had recently died as a result of a fall from a horse at Fort Nez Percés. For Tod, however, the hardest blow was the loss of his old friend Thomas Dears. In 1839 Dears had come down with a condition that was probably incorrectly diagnosed as gout. In a year he was dead. "An event so unexpected, so unlooked for by me was a shock to my heart from which it did not soon recover," Tod wrote Edward.[3]

Others less close to Tod, however, seemed to be prospering. In 1839 the London Committee had moved to make George Simpson governor-in-chief of all Hudson's Bay territories. While the title conferred no increase in power — he had in fact long controlled the Company's entire North American empire — Simpson's prestige increased. Two years later he was given an even greater honour: a knighthood from Queen Victoria.

John McLoughlin's star, too, continued to rise. When he visited England in 1839, the chief factor met the London Committee who came away much impressed with him. As a result he was appointed chief superintendent of the Hudson's Bay's empire west of the Rockies. The doctor's increasing power and prestige, though, had done nothing to change Tod's opinion of him. As he wrote Edward in 1842:

> [McLoughlin] is a character for whom I entertain the most deadly hatred — God forgive me — not from any unkindness I have received from his hands — far from it, but from a knowledge of his treatment of others. He of all men I know in this Country is the very last I should put any dependence in.[4]

The agreement signed the previous year between the Hudson's Bay and the Russian-American Company had given the English enterprise a ten-year lease on the narrow finger of land stretching from Mount Fairweather in the north 350 miles down the Pacific coast, and in his new position McLoughlin had been charged with bringing this territory into production. In 1840, he sent James Douglas on board the Company steamer *Beaver* to take over the Russian company's operation at Fort Stikine. There Douglas left two clerks and ten servants to build a new fort on the site. One of the officers posted to Stikine was John McLoughlin, Jr., the doctor's son who had accompanied Tod on the ill-fated journey to the Columbia in 1838.

Although the Hudson's Bay's control of the panhandle was an opportunity for greater profits from the coastal trade, the Company faced new threats to its western empire. In 1840 the ship *Lausanne* had brought 51 American settlers to bolster the small settlement in the Willamette Valley, Oregon, while six or seven more families had occupied land near Fort Walla Walla. Equally unwelcome was the talk of war between Britain and the United States. In February 1839, lumbermen from Maine and New Brunswick clashed over timber rights to the land on the disputed boundary along the Aroostook River. Such a conflict, Tod argued, was "an event most devoutly to be deprecated by all us Fur Traders, as the result could hardly be other than fatal to our interests in the Columbia." Once American trappers were no longer constrained by the treaty between the United States and Britain, Tod believed, scores of them would pour in and attack Fort Vancouver, which would be "easy prey to their Rifles."[5] While the matter was eventually sent to arbitration, tensions between the two countries remained high.

The fur trade was also experiencing harder economic times. In Europe after 1839, silk gradually replaced beaver as the major constituent of men's hats, with the result that the value of the fur fell on the London market. Between 1836 and 1839, Company profits from New Caledonia fell almost one-third. Tod was hardly blind to the changes in the trade. As he noted in a letter to Edward in 1845:

> The old Factors, are clearing out with the utmost haste. Some years ago one would have imagined that they were immoveable [*sic*] fixtures — necessary appendeges [*sic*] to the Indian trade — with such tenacity did they cling to their respective charges, [but] now however the case is reversed, and their greatest anxiety seems now to get away — guided, no doubt, by the same instinct that teaches rats to leave a falling house.[6]

The Company had built a successful empire upon fur, but in the west it seemed unable to exploit the territory's many other resources successfuly. Tod had been a reluctant investor in the Hudson's Bay's Columbia agricultural subsidiary, and it now seemed apparent that his money was lost. "You are no doubt a share holder in the Puget Sound Co[mpany]," he wrote his friend James Hargrave in 1842. "I too, have that misfortune, and next to my unhappy marriage there is nothing in this world I regret more than having joined it."[7] The reason for its failure, Tod believed, fell squarely upon the shoulders of McLoughlin who had been paid a substantial bonus to oversee its operation.

Tod's brother Sym had arrived at Montreal in 1840, but Tod was surprised to learn that he was not alone — he had brought along one of their sisters. While he had not objected to Sym's fare, Tod begrudged the expense of the second passenger. The money had been advanced by the Greenshields family, Tod's relatives in Montreal, whom he would be expected to reimburse. The Greenshields, he grumbled, "like most others in the Civilized world, think Nor Westors [sic] possessed of a mine of inexhaustable [sic] riches."[8]

Sym, Tod learned, had failed to make a favourable impression on Edward. Although disappointed, Tod did nothing to counter his agent's assessment. "My expectations of him [Sym] were never Sanguine," Tod wrote Edward, "and from Your account of him, tho' it is short, I have little hope for him as a farmer, and after the assistance he has had, should he not be able to support himself and his Sister, the Farm I think had better be sold."[9] In March 1842 Tod was not sure whether his son James had arrived in Canada West. After Edward's assessment of Sym, Tod wondered how James would be judged. If he failed to display much talent for agriculture, Tod asked Edward to find him a job as a carpenter — the trade for which he had been trained. "In James, in as far as regards the powers of intellect heredity transmission appears to have had its full force," Tod wrote, referring to James's mother, Catherine Birston. "You will not find him a bright character, he has however been represented to me as having little of the general character of his country man, but a well disposed and hard working lad."[10]

* * * * *

On 31 July 1842, Tod returned to Fort Thompson. The reason for his transfer was the killing of a Company clerk at Fort Stikine in the territory the Hudson's Bay had leased from Russia: in April, Dr. McLoughlin's son, John, had been murdered at the post. Young McLoughlin, of course, was no ordinary clerk, and shock waves ran throughout the far west. The circumstances surrounding his death were not clear. According to the Company servants at Stikine, McLoughlin was a drunken despot whose behaviour was so brutal that it had driven some of his own men to kill him. However, while there may have been questions regarding the young man's character — a few years earlier in Montreal he had run up a number of bad debts — there was little indication that McLoughlin was the monster his men had claimed.

Following the murder, Governor Simpson, who was visiting the North Pacific coast as part of his journey around the world, was among the first on the scene. The results of his investigation placed the blame on the victim, for McLoughlin, Simpson concluded, was a morally bankrupt individual given over to drunkenness and cruelty. Further, the governor wrote the London Committee, "I am constrained to say that from what [Chief Factor] McLoughlin knew of his son's previous conduct, he ought never in my opinion to have been placed in charge of Stikine."[11]

Simpson's concerns may have had more to do with politics than a desire to see justice done. The case fell into murky legal ground — although the Hudson's Bay had leased the land, the murder had happened in Russian territory. The governor clearly did not wish to cause difficulties for the Company's foreign landlords. The investigation was superficial at best — Simpson concluded only that one man, a servant named Urbain Heroux, was responsible for the crime.

Not surprisingly, the doctor, who was deeply affected by the loss of his son, did not agree with the governor. In McLoughlin's opinion, Simpson himself was partly responsible for what had happened, for he had sent away the only other officer at Fort Stikine, clerk Roderick Finlayson, to Fort Simpson. In the face of unruly subordinates the young clerk was left without support. Chief Trader Manson, who was hurriedly sent to Stikine, was charged with interviewing the men remaining at the post and taking the suspects to the Russian authorities at Sitka where they would stand trial. As a result of Manson's transfer, Tod received a letter from Chief Factor Peter Skene Ogden ordering him to take charge of Fort Thompson.

Tod reached the post on 5 August and found a vast number of Indians gathered there. With Manson transferred and D.E. Cameron, the clerk, at Fort Vancouver, Lolo was in charge. Although the returns had been poor, Tod was pleased to learn that the Shuswap had been peaceful. During the summer the Indians had helped the Hudson's Bay men raft the logs for the new fort down the river. After Tod had left for Alexandria in the winter, the work on the new fort had been continued by Manson, but the pace was slow. The structure was to be surrounded by a 15-foot-high palisade, while two bastions would guard the perimeter. Inside, the plans called for a trading hall, fur-storage shed, barracks for the servants, kitchen and mess facilities, as well as a separate house for the officer in charge. Outside the walls there would be a fenced garden plot as well as a large corral for the horses. As yet, however, nothing had been built, for the job of obtaining the timber necessary for the outside walls and buildings had not been completed.

A week after Tod's arrival, Cameron returned to Fort Thompson with Chief Factor Ogden and the brigade. With them was a familiar face: Reverend Modeste Demers, the Oblate missionary who had accompanied Tod during his disastrous journey across the continent in 1838. The Roman Catholic priest had received permission from the Company to spread his faith among the Indians of the Kamloops Valley and New Caledonia. The following day Tod was pleased to note that Father Demers intended to continue on to New Caledonia with Ogden, rather than remain at Fort Thompson. "The object of the missionary is no doubt praiseworthy," he wrote in the Thompson River Journal, "but their endeavours to convert the natives has [sic] hitherto produced no good effect, nor while they pursue their present system will they either succeed in making them Christians or useful members of society."[12] Tod's remarks reflected the attitude of most fur traders toward Christian missionaries, for with the coming of the evangelists the Hudson's Bay lost influence over the Indians.

Under Cameron's direction the men continued felling trees for the new fort and floating them down river. Manson had intended to build the post some distance from the confluence of the North and South Thompson rivers, but Tod felt that it would be too far from the salmon fishery. As a result he and Cameron chose a location on the west side of the North Thompson River near the junction. This turned out to be a poor decision, for the land was subject to flooding.

For a second year Tod endured the summer at Fort Thompson. Again the semi-arid Kamloops Valley baked under the intensity of the August sun. The leaves of the trees that lined the river bank did not stir, for even the cooling afternoon breeze was absent. On 19 August, a slight breeze from the southwest arose, but now the air was heavy with smoke. "The neighbouring hills," Tod wrote, "all on fire which have a splendid appearance enduring the darkness of night."[13] Since the bush had been cut back around the post Fort Thompson was in less danger, but Tod must have watched the progress of the flames with some apprehension.

The summer was at first easier to bear, for retirement was one year closer. Unfortunately though, the arrival of the brigade with the mail from the east changed everything. "In a letter from Miss Jean Greenshields dated Aug. '41," Tod wrote Edward, "I am informed of the arrival of my father, Mother & Sisters *Tee tote* in Montreal with their subsequent departure thence for St. Thomas for the express purpose of joining Sym on the farm."[14] Also accompanying his parents and three sisters was his brother James.

Although he later claimed in his memoirs that he had urged his family to emigrate, this was not correct — their arrival took him by complete surprise. "As they have undertaken this step on their own accord and in direct opposition to my wishes, so repeatedly expressed to themselves" he wrote Edward, "I must beg to caution You against making them advances beyond which my means can nor will admit of."[15] Tod felt ill-used, for now even if he wished, he was unable to dispose of his St. Thomas property without making provision for his family. Reluctantly, he told Edward to purchase several milk cows and a sheep for his family's use. "This last movement of theirs," he wrote sadly, "will detain me I apprehend not less than five Years longer in the Country, and in a Service of which I am most heartily tired."[16] In fact, Tod was never to return to St. Thomas to see his farm, his family, or his friend, Edward.

* * * * *

The farm continued to be a drain on his income, and to make his situation worse Tod was being pressured from another quarter — Eliza's mother had fallen behind in the payments to Warburton's, the private asylum where her daughter was kept. Demanding payment, the manager of the institution had written to Hudson's Bay Company secretary William Smith who in turn contacted Tod. In addition to the £30 per year he contributed to Eliza's care, Tod paid for shares in the Hudson's Bay's Puget Sound subsidiary. Since his financial records are not complete it is impossible to determine the amount paid to Edward for the farm operation or the credit provided his parents through the Ermatinger general store, but it is

clear that by 1840 he was hard-pressed for money. The payout for
the 1838-39 season was only £249, little more than half what it had
been the previous year.

Tod had earlier corresponded with Simpson on the subject of his
wife's transfer to St. Luke's asylum where she would be maintained
at public expense. The governor had applied to Benjamin Harrison,
treasurer at Guy's Hospital (with which the asylum was affiliated),
but at the time Eliza's relatives in Wales did not want her transferred to London. Tod may have used their reluctance as an excuse
to suspend payment to the private institution where she was kept,
but Eliza's mother was not able to meet these obligations on her
own. Moreover, as the manager of Warburton's was well aware,
Tod, as Eliza's legal husband, was ultimately responsible for the
cost of her care. In 1842, Tod once more appealed to Governor
Simpson for assistance:

> ... By a letter which I lately received from Mr. Smith, it
> appears that she is now in Warburtons assylum, [sic] and that
> gentleman I am further informed, now threatens me with prose-
> cution for refusing to contribute more towards her support
> which situated as I am at present with two aged parents and
> four sisters on my hands, I really cannot afford. I humbly
> intreat [sic] you to oblige me so far if possible to carry into
> effect the result of your former arrangement. ...[17]

Simpson, on Tod's behalf, wrote to Harrison again on 28 June
1843, noting not entirely honestly that "the poor man is quite
broken hearted, & notwithstanding all his labors & toils in this
country for between 25 and 30 years, he is still absolutely worse
than penniless."[18] The application was successful (not surprisingly,
since the treasurer had been for many years the deputy governor of
the Hudson's Bay) and on 6 November 1844, Eliza was admitted to
St. Luke's asylum.

Some months later Tod wrote acknowledging two letters he had
received from the governor, "in both of which you have had the
kindness to announce the consumption of an affair of indeed paramount interest to me, in as much as it has removed from my mind a
weight of anxiety, with which it had long been oppressed, and also
relieve the pecuniary obligation, which my small means could not
afford."[19] Tod seemed little concerned with the morality of his
actions. The public asylum had been opened for the poor who were

unable to pay for the care of their relatives, and although short of cash, Tod was hardly a pauper.

At St. Thomas, Edward was facing his own difficulties: a series of business setbacks combined with a rancorous split with his partner and store manager, Samuel Price, contributed to the onset of one of his periods of despondency. "How distressing and disheartening was it for me to find a friend whom I have so long regarded with esteem & affection, Speaking the language of dispair [*sic*]," Tod wrote in 1843.[20]

In his darkened mood, Edward turned for solace to religion. Not one to advance by half measures, he maintained his mainstream Anglican faith with the zeal of a missionary. Tod, who during his years of isolation had long studied the Bible, had his own strong opinions about religion. "I have this winter read & reread with deep & intense interest, the New Testament, the result of which is that I have calmly, but resolutely discarded from my mind all Creeds, and doctrines founded by heads of Sects some of which I consider little less than impious," he wrote in reply to Edward.[21] Not surprisingly, the worst of all creeds in Tod's mind was Calvinism, the religion of

Edward Ermatinger. (COURTESY NAC, C51628)

141

his childhood. The belief "seems calculated to give a dark, stern & gloomy character to devotion as if it was intended to subdue men's minds and consciences by terror alone, which [I] am convinced has done much harm, and is probably ... the cause of that scepticism that has prevailed so much amongst the Scotch."[22]

While some of his colleagues may have relished the isolation of New Caledonia, Tod did not, for he needed companionship. He rarely saw his friends, but their letters helped to fill a void in his life. Since his return west of the Rockies he had avoided permanent sexual relationships — the reason was probably due to his plans to settle in St. Thomas. Unlike his late friend Dears, Tod was unwilling to fly in the face of racial bigotry. Yet, with the arrival of his own family at St. Thomas, Tod's hoped-for escape from New Caledonia was eliminated. "How ardently do I wish I was once more along side You and Mrs. Ermatinger," he had written Edward in 1842, "but must not think of it while there is such a concourse of my needy relations near You — they would devour me up in less than a twelve month."[23]

About the time his new quarters were completed Tod began a relationship with Sophia Lolo, a young woman who was probably the daughter of Lolo. Despite the great difference in their ages — in 1843, when Tod was almost 50, Sophia, or Martha as he often called her, was only 16 or 17 years old — the relationship appeared remarkably stable. Sophia gave birth to Mary, the couple's first child, in 1843.

While in his letters to Edward Tod failed to mention his country marriage to Sophia, there were hints that he had a renewed interest in family matters. The birth of a daughter to the Ermatingers in 1842, prompted Tod to write the following year, "My humble request is . . . that You procure a little work entitled 'A Treatise on the Psychology and moral management of Infancy' by Dr. A. Comb. Knowing You as of old, it is too much to expect that You Yourself will read it, but am sure Mrs. Ermatinger will, & I venture to say it will repay her well of the trouble."[24]

* * * * *

In the spring of 1842, Donald Manson sailed north to Fort Stikine on board the Company schooner *Cadboro* to investigate young McLoughlin's murder. Also on board was Chief Factor James Douglas who was returning one of the men, a servant named Pierre

Kanaquassé whom Simpson had let go without charges, to Fort Stikine. Since Kanaquassé had been implicated in an earlier attempt on his son's life, Dr. McLoughlin had decided not to allow him to leave the territory but to return him to the site of the murder for questioning with the other suspects. Under questioning on board the *Cadboro*, the servant volunteered a statement that exonerated young McLoughlin — the clerk had been killed, Kanaquassé claimed, because of his refusal to allow his men out of barracks to mix with native women.

At Fort Stikine, Manson's murder investigation led nowhere. Only two of the accused were ever taken to Sitka for arraignment because, according to Manson, the only vessel available to him could not accommodate all the prisoners. This was only an excuse — the real reason was more likely that he did not wish to appear to be working too actively on the doctor's behalf. For Manson, who was well versed in the politics of the Hudson's Bay, Simpson was a more fearful enemy than McLoughlin — the governor still held tightly to the reins of power in North America.

Dissatisfied with the second investigation, McLoughlin continued to hold Simpson responsible for the loss of his son. As the months passed, he began writing long, rambling letters to friends and acquaintances complaining about the wrongs that had been done to his son's reputation. Simpson, for his part, adopted an attitude of quiet forbearance in the face of what he seemed to regard as the doctor's bizarre behaviour.

Tod took no satisfaction from the split between the two giants of the Hudson's Bay. While he disliked both men, the conflict served only to undermine the western fur trade. As he wrote Edward:

> ... how the matter will end, is at present uncertain, but assuredly our interests can never be looked after, when two of the first two Characters in the Country are so much at variance — every allowance ought to be made for the feelings of a father, in such a case as this, but I fear the Dr. has not only compremised [*sic*] his dignity in this affair but has also failed to excite the Sympathy of the greater part of his friends, from his very excess.[25]

In New Caledonia, Tod was a distant witness to another clash of wills — this time between his brother and his best friend. Since Sym's arrival, the relationship between him and Edward had deteriorated and each man now attempted to enlist Tod's help against the other. Sym, it seemed, had a full measure of his older brother's irascibility. Even Tod's mild-mannered son James, who had finally arrived at St. Thomas, could not agree with his uncle and eventually quit the farm. The letters to Tod from the family were no doubt intended to turn father against son. James, Tod wrote Edward in 1843, "thinks [I] am told, he has been treated with cruelty, because he has not been made a gentleman! I am sorry that he should entertain such an erroneous impression, for God knows, all my plans hitherto with him, have been with a view to his ultimate good."[26]

The arrival of Tod's brother James with the family caused more difficulty, for the young man had ambitions to go into business for himself — a goal which his brother John had at one time encouraged. Of James, also, Edward formed an unfavourable impression. Tod noted that Edward had already been convinced by a "nearer acquaintance" of James's "total incapacity to succeed in the line of a merchant even of the lowest class."[27] Thus denied a role in business, Tod's brother was consigned to hard labour on the farm. Given their recent arrival in Canada it seems likely that the report originated with another family member.

Unsatisfied with the vagueness of his understanding with his brother, Sym had written Tod in 1842 requesting that the agreement by which he managed the farm be formalized. Instead of dealing with the matter himself, however, Tod chose to place negotiations in Edward's hands. The negotiations were made more difficult by the terms Tod had proposed. "I think ... if he has the farm rent free during the lifetime of his father & Mother, he ought to be satisfied," he wrote Edward.[28] Because Tod could not judge Sym's true worth for himself, he did give Edward the power to offer his farm manager a better deal. Knowing the attitude of the two men toward each other, though, it is difficult to imagine how the matter could have been resolved to everyone's satisfaction.

Whether consciously or not, Tod had begun to distance himself from his St. Thomas relatives. In his letters to Edward they had become not his own, but "my father's family." He was not entirely ungenerous toward his parents, for he continued to allow them to draw on his credit at Edward's store. There is little doubt, however, that he was ashamed of his origins. Although he had spent most of his life in the wilderness, he had risen to the rank of a commissioned gentleman. Tod's position within the Company, together with his friendship with Edward, would have guaranteed him admittance into the best St. Thomas drawing rooms, and the presence of his rustic family would have been a singular embarrassment to him. "For goodness sake," Tod warned Edward in 1843, "don't lead them [his family] into Company, and above all the old woman."[29]

Edward for his part had been more than willing to point out the shortcomings of Tod's brothers Sym and James. While Tod seemed to readily agree with Edward's assessment of them, it was true that his friend's indictment implicitly carried a personal slight to Tod himself. He was, after all, from the same mold. He received letters from his family putting forward their side and damning Edward's handling of matters, which also undermined Tod's faith in his agent. Sym, Tod wrote Edward, "says You compelled him to give up his wheat for half a dollar when he was offered Seven Shillings York for it at his Barn door."[30]

The first signs of tension came as early as 1842, when Tod received a letter in which Edward admitted facing business problems. News of Edward's distress was upsetting for Tod since he had authorized his friend to withdraw a large sum from his account with the Hudson's Bay for investment. Tod broached the subject during Frank's visit to Fort Thompson in 1843 and the following year Frank wrote to his brother in St. Thomas:

> I believe Tod sent you an order to draw a thousand pounds. If you draw it I hope you will keep it so that it will be available to him when he wants it. I saw Tod last spring and he mentioned this sum to me. Not ... however with distrust, but I would perceive that your letters of the spring before had made an impression on him.[31]

The seeds of doubt had also been sown in the letter Tod had received from Edward's former partner, Samuel Price. With his note to Tod, Price included a copy of an assessment of Edward's business dealings written by a man named Killisan. It was these comments that most damaged Edward's reputation, for Tod believed that unlike Price, Killisan had no personal axe to grind with his friend. "I certainly never intended, nor could I have believed, You would have brought me in at the Tail end of Your bad debts, in the manner You appear to have done," Tod wrote Edward in 1843.[32]

Yet, in isolated New Caledonia, Tod had little chance to grasp the reality of the situation. As a businessman of extreme political beliefs, Edward had made many enemies. His intention to start a newspaper the following year as a voice for his reactionary views probably was the nucleus that united many of his foes. He had run for the legislature in 1841, but had been defeated by lawyer Thomas Parke. With his own paper to galvanize public opinion, Edward was a greater threat. As his disaffected former business partner, Price had knowledge of Tod's dealings with Edward. The identity of Killisan, a man whom Tod apparently respected and regarded as unbiased, remains unknown. He was not a local landowner, nor was he a St. Thomas merchant. Tod, though, was deeply affected by the allegations contained in the letter, and in 1845 revoked Edward's power of attorney. The farm was placed directly under Sym's control. In his letter to Edward, Tod made his feelings apparent:

> On receipt of this [letter] also, I have to request that my name be entirely erased from Your Books as I solemnly protest against all further transactions between Yourself & our family, or others, on my account. Should they think proper to deal in Your Store, to which I have not the slightest objections, it must be on their own account — not mine.[33]

There is no evidence that Sym was behind Price's attempt to smear Edward, but Tod's break with his friend seemed to work to his brother's advantage. The sum of £20 that was credited to Tod in the store books was to be given to "my brother Sym *in cash*."[34] The interest on the capital Edward had been asked to invest, Tod wanted forwarded to John Greenshields of Montreal for Emma's education. "As the duties of a father are deeply impressed upon my mind, any event causing disappointment in the foregoing arrangement, could hardly fail to give me uneasiness," Tod wrote.[35]

At the end of one of two letters he sent to Edward in March 1844 — letters full of anger and suspicion — Tod included a final curious plea: "In writing to Your friends in this Country, I have to beg that You will say as little as possible about any of them [his family at St. Thomas]. Altho' I have no desire whatever to Court the Sympathy of Mankind, Yet as poverty seems to be a reproach with some people, I do not wish to incur their contempt."[36] This line seems strange: since Tod had provided, albeit grudgingly, for his family's comfort, giving them a start at least equal to many other immigrants to Canada, his concern about poverty is exaggerated. Yet it is easy to understand his shame. Despite his recent business setback, Edward was one of the most prosperous men in St. Thomas. Having outgrown the small store and post office on Talbot Street, he had constructed an impressive, three-storey brick building across the street. From there he carried out his other business activities, including banking, real estate, and insurance. He was also a man of education whose house was the centre of St. Thomas's cultural life. By comparison, the Todds had few advantages. Neither brother was in Edward's league — although a good worker, Sym wanted little more than to own the land he farmed; the slow-thinking James had ambition but lacked ability.

As exposed as he was, Tod did not wish his kin to be used as pawns in a public dispute with Edward. Tod habitually kept his private life to himself — "I was not aware that Tod had a batch of connections on his farm, as from his last Letters I had learned nothing of the sort," wrote a surprised Robert Miles to Edward in 1844.[37] Edward had been given entry into his life, but now that their friendship was on the verge of collapse, Tod was aware of his vulnerability.

Due to the slow exchange of the mail, Tod would not have received Edward's reply to the allegations contained in his letter until late in 1845. From Tod's response, it seems that Edward had

Edward Ermatinger's house in St. Thomas, built around 1840. (COURTESY NAC, PA26920)

147

successfully refuted Killisan's charges. Tod's letter to Edward dated 20 March 1846, was uncharacteristically short:

> I have received Your note ... and whatever injustice I may have done You by Yielding too implicitly to the impression disigned [sic] by that letter, I now hasten to make to You all the reparation, a person in my remote situation Can, by Candidly acknowledging my error, and fully acquitting You of the foul calumnies it contained. However deeply I may lament the loss of our past friendship & Correspondence, still I beg You to understand that the foregoing statement is not made with a view to induce You to resume them, (that must depend entirely on Yourself) but simply to assure You that you are fully exonerated in my own mind of Mr. Killisan's false accusations.[38]

Edward, however, did not forgive his friend. The letters that had gone on between them, the plans made, the confidences shared, stopped abruptly. The gulf that now separated them remained unbridged for more than a decade.

Chapter Ten

A PERFECT EDEN

The conflict between Simpson and McLoughlin came to a head in 1844 when the London Committee removed the doctor from his position as sole head of the Columbia Department. Faced with a humiliating demotion, McLoughlin did what the Company no doubt had intended: he submitted his resignation. In his place, London appointed chief factors Peter Skene Ogden, John Work and James Douglas to the three-person Board of Management.

In the same year Donald Manson returned from Fort Stikine to take charge of the territory of New Caledonia from Peter Skene Ogden. It is somewhat surprising that for a quasi-military organization, the lines of authority within the Hudson's Bay were not always well defined. After Samuel Black's promotion to chief factor in 1837, he had been put in charge of a number of "Indian posts of the Columbia" that included Forts Thompson and Colvile. After Black's death, his inland empire was broken up and Fort Thompson was again placed under Chief Factor Ogden's jurisdiction. Yet, the Kamloops Valley post seems to have retained a degree of its former autonomy. Although they travelled together to Fort Vancouver, the Fort Thompson brigade was regarded as separate from New Caledonia's. Tod seemed to have little trouble accepting Ogden's authority, for the latter was highly regarded by his men. Manson, however, was another matter, for he was never given the rank of chief factor that had always gone with the job of superintendent of

New Caledonia. Moreover, although both men were chief traders, Tod had held the rank longer, and was therefore senior to Manson. Given the volatile personalities of both officers, there was little chance of compromise.

On the surface, the source of friction was the difference in their attitudes toward the Indians. Like Samuel Black and Donald McLean, Manson was an advocate of brute force in dealing with the natives, an approach Simpson had once dubbed "club law," and Tod, as has been seen, was not. In fact, the men harboured petty jealousies toward each other, and the Indian question served only as a flash point to ignite long-standing animosities. Thus it was that a relatively minor occurrence touched off a running feud that continued for years.

In 1844, both men travelled with the brigades from New Caledonia and Fort Thompson to Fort Vancouver. Earlier that year, Tod had injured the Achilles tendon of his right heel, and was going to Fort Vancouver to receive medical treatment. As senior officer, he was nominally in charge of the brigade, but as superintendent of New Caledonia, Manson's position carried the most weight. In the beginning there was little difficulty; each man tended to his own responsibilities.

The brigades had ridden south about 80 miles from the Kamloops Valley when they came upon a large party of Indians camped at a fork of the Okanagan River. As was common practice, the Hudson's Bay men passed out small pieces of tobacco to the natives in a gesture of good will. Tod took advantage of the halt to speak with some of the chiefs, for he had decided that he and his men would spend the night in the Indian camp. The elders warned Tod that some among them would wish to steal his horses, but he was not to be dissuaded. He believed he had come to know the natives well, and that to take advantage of their hospitality was his best course.

When Tod told his colleague what the Indians had said Manson was very upset, and made it clear that before nightfall he intended to put as much distance between himself and the natives as possible. Manson and his men rode off, leaving Tod and his group behind.

As evening approached the Indians cleared a campsite for Tod's party while the brigade horses were taken to graze with the Indian ponies. Tod passed out more tobacco among his hosts and after supper everyone bedded down for the night. The Indians were pleased that some of the Hudson's Bay men had camped among them, for it displayed an element of trust often missing from race relations in the west. Tod was not concerned about his horses — the theft of property from those who had sought the Indians' hospitality would have been a breach of etiquette — and indeed in the morning all the pack animals were returned to him.

When Manson finally stopped to camp at nightfall, however, he had three horses stolen before they had their packs removed from their backs. He managed to get two of the animals back, but the furs they were carrying were never recovered. Manson had been in Company service 30 years, but, as Tod claimed in his memoirs, "he never learned anything of H. B. Co. (Indian) character."[1]

Although the dissension between Tod and Manson put the entire brigade in turmoil, they reached Fort Vancouver without incident. On the return journey, however, the entire crew of one boat deserted before reaching Fort Walla Walla. What exactly took place is unknown but apparently only the mediation of a Jesuit priest who was travelling with the brigade prevented matters from becoming worse. "This circumstance shows the impolicy of this Department having no head," McLoughlin wrote the London Committee a few months before his retirement.[2] The governors, though, took no notice of his concerns.

* * * * *

As the years passed, the Hudson's Bay found it increasingly difficult to carry out its operations in the Columbia Department. American immigration, which had begun as a trickle in the 1830s, was a flood by 1845. The number of new arrivals in that year alone was nearly 3,000. These settlers were reluctant to recognize the rights of a company they regarded as a foreign occupier of American territory. Tensions increased when two Hudson's Bay employees were murdered by an American in a dispute over the ownership of property. The killer's escape probably avoided an open clash between the camps, but on the diplomatic front the United States was becoming more assertive in its demands for exclusive control of Oregon Territory.

The Company's own half-hearted attempts to attract immigration from Britain and the Empire had met with failure, and it was clear that it would not be long before part of the Hudson's Bay's western territories would be under the American flag. Already, in the spring of 1843, James Douglas, on board the *Beaver*, had crossed from Fort Nisqually on Puget Sound to the southern tip of Vancouver Island.

On land overlooking a well-protected natural harbour, he chose to construct a new Company post. Fort Victoria, as it was eventually called, was intended to be a replacement for Fort Vancouver and for that reason it was constructed on a large scale. The pickets surrounding the fort were 20 feet long and three feet thick, while some of the buildings were two and three storeys high.

In anticipation of conflict between Britain and the United States over the Columbia, the Hudson's Bay began moving its cattle and horses north to Kamloops. Many of the horses had been on the farm Tod had managed at Cowlitz, and as the animals arrived he amused himself by pretending that after a long separation, he was once again greeting old friends. Among the herd of horses were 200 brood mares, and Tod, who had a particular fondness for horses, was pleased to see the birth of many fine foals the following spring.

The increase in grazing animals in the valley, though, led to a greater number of predators. The wolf packs were quick to add to their numbers, and it was not long before the men tending the stock reported losses to Tod. The potent poison strychnine had been used elsewhere by the Company to control wolves, and Tod sent to Fort Walla Walla for a supply. The advantage of the substance was that although somewhat bitter, its taste was not so disagreeable as to warn animals away; the difficulty was that hungry humans were also likely to find the poisoned bait appealing. As a precaution, Tod decided to add the bait to wolf traps since it was against Indian law to rob these devices. He further demonstrated the poison's effectiveness upon a hapless dog that had acted as taster — after consuming the morsel the animal suffered an agonizing death. The Indians who had witnessed the event were much affected by what they had seen. As he was to discover later, however, he had failed to realize the full extent of their concern.

As a final precaution Tod ordered his men to set out the strychnine-laced bait at sundown and to retrieve it early the next morning. The poisoned traps created no difficulties until one morning one of the servants, a man named Camille who had been working at one of the camps squaring logs, was sent back to the fort to obtain more provisions. Instead of gathering up the poisoned pieces from the trap and replacing them with untainted meat as he was supposed to do, he only freshened it by adding a piece of salted salmon on top of the horse flesh bait. Later that day one of the local natives came along the trail, and noting the bait in the trap, prepared a meal for himself. Had he only eaten the fish he would have been unharmed, but the hungry traveller went on to consume the large chunk of horse flesh that contained the strychnine.

When Camille returned with his supplies he noted the man writhing in the grass beside the spot where he had placed the salmon. Realizing what had happened, he ran back to the fort to tell the officer in charge. Tod, who had spent many hours poring over Buchan's *Domestic Medicine* and similar books, got a bottle of blue vitriol from the post's medicine chest and followed his servant back to the spot where the man lay convulsing. Because strychnine acts on the nervous system, the victim's teeth were tightly clenched, and it was only with a great deal of effort that Tod was able to force his mouth open and pour in the medicine. As intended, the vitriol caused him to retch violently and bring up the poisoned meat. Though the man survived, it was some time before he had recovered completely.

The incident increased the tensions between Indians and Europeans in the Kamloops Valley. The natives felt they had been right to fear the Hudson's Bay's poison. Like the diseases that had come with the white men, strychnine crept up and killed almost silently, and an enemy could be laid low without the murderer being present. The incident only confirmed what the chiefs already suspected — the substance was another weapon in the European arsenal.

As word spread to the surrounding villages, hundreds of natives came to see the victim who was still recovering at the fort. When Tod appeared they began to harangue him, demanding that he explain why he was now poisoning them. Tod carefully explained that the reason he lived among the Indians was to trade furs: he could not carry out his business if he poisoned his Indian suppliers. Beside, he added, if he had planned to murder them he would not have waited all this time — he would have done it years ago. The strychnine was to kill the wolves that took not only the foals belonging to the Company, but the animals belonging to the Indians as well. If his native neighbours wanted the guilty person, Tod claimed, pointing to the victim, it was this man. He had committed the offence of stealing food from traps.

The chiefs, who until then had not been entirely receptive to Tod's arguments, suddenly seemed to see the victim in a new light. By robbing a trap, the man had committed a serious breach of custom. Although he had defused a volatile situation, Tod was not entirely pleased with his argument. The fault also rested with his servant who had failed to pick up the bait in the first place, and, of course, with himself for not ensuring that proper precautions were taken by his men. So that a similar incident would not happen again, Tod made sure that warning marks the Indians would recognize were placed beside the wolf bait.

* * * * *

In 1846 the long-simmering dispute between Britain and the United States over the Columbia boundary almost resulted in war. The election of the jingoistic Democrat James Polk as president a year earlier seemed to set free the forces of expansionism. Although the Americans had demanded the land as far north as 54° 40', which would have fixed the boundary only a few miles south of Fort McLeod, their claim to the territory beyond the north bank of the Columbia River was weak. The British government, though, had little stomach for conflict with the United States, and an 11th-hour agreement established the boundary at the 49th parallel. While the settlement favoured the United States, the British succeeded in retaining the southern tip of Vancouver Island, which extended below the 49th parallel.

The Hudson's Bay was not forgotten in the settlement. For the loss of some of its western territory, the Company received $450,000 in gold from the United States government, but the money was a long time in coming: it took more than 25 years for the United States government to settle the Hudson's Bay's outstanding land claims for the loss of its property in Oregon Territory.

At first, the loss of the Oregon Territory made little difference to Tod at Fort Kamloops. The fur brigade continued to make the long journey south to Fort Vancouver. Although as part of the settlement, Britain retained its right of navigation on the Columbia River, the Company found itself required to pay American duties on goods shipped by way of its fort. The obvious alternative was the Fraser River, which empties into the Pacific Ocean a few miles north of the 49th parallel. The main obstacle was the Fraser Canyon, a long and difficult stretch of high cliffs and white water that made the river all but impassable.

In May 1846, the officer in charge of Fort Alexandria, Chief Trader Alexander Caulfield Anderson, set off to find an all-British route to Fort Langley near the mouth of the Fraser. His first attempt was to follow the Lillooet River overland as far as Harrison Lake

Alexander Caulfield Anderson. (COURTESY BCARS, 2228)
which in turn drained into the Fraser. While Anderson completed
the journey, the route was not practical for pack animals, which
meant the Company still lacked a usable route from New Caledonia
to the Pacific.

* * * * *

The new post, Fort Kamloops, which Tod had begun not long
after the death of Samuel Black, was completed about 1846. It was
comfortable enough, with its own gardens irrigated by a series of
ditches. A system for transporting water was necessary for crop
survival in the semi-arid climate of the Kamloops Valley but, despite
its gardens, the fort remained heavily dependent on dried salmon,
which was traded with the Indians.

While Tod kept on generally good terms with the Indians of the
Kamloops Valley, his relations with other tribes were sometimes
difficult. This was particularly true of the Cayuse Indians whose
territory was farther south. In the late summer of 1847 Tod sent
most of his men to obtain dried salmon from the Indians at Pavilion
on the Fraser River, about 80 miles from the fort. The party
included almost everyone from the post; only Tod, his family, and
one mixed-blood boy, evidently the son of one of the servants,
remained behind. Also riding out to join the party was Lolo, who

had remained at old Fort Thompson on the opposite side of the river where he traded with the Indians living near the post.

Not long after the expedition had departed, Tod was surprised to see Lolo riding in the gate. When Tod asked why he was not with the others, the interpreter explained that on his way he had met an Indian acquaintance who had warned him against accompanying the Europeans to the Fraser. The man said that the Indians at Pavilion were prepared for trouble, and when the Hudson's Bay men arrived at the fishery, they were to be given no salmon. Thus warned, he returned to the fort without seeking out his European companions, who were riding into trouble.

Tod claimed later that he did not know the reason for the Indian anger. The interior Indians correctly blamed the white interlopers for the devastating measles epidemic that was then sweeping the west. Unlike the Europeans, the Indians had no immunity to the disease. First to fall victim to native anger in 1847 was Methodist minister Marcus Whitman, his wife and 12 others who were murdered at their mission near Fort Walla Walla by the Cayuse Indians. The epidemic enflamed resentment among many interior peoples, and for a time it appeared that war with the Indians was inevitable.

After hearing Lolo's story Tod had to consider his next move carefully. To cancel the Pavilion expedition was impossible since Fort Kamloops depended on its yearly supply of dried salmon. Yet, although he did not entirely trust the interpreter, he could also not afford to disbelieve Lolo's story. Early the following morning he and the servant's son saddled up and rode off toward Pavilion. Before leaving, Tod placed the materials necessary for smallpox inoculations in his pocket. He had heard of an outbreak of measles among the Indians to the south, and while he could not inoculate against measles, the epidemic could still be used to his advantage.

Since the first party had to manage 60 horses, some of which were burdened with trade goods, Tod was able to catch up with his men at Hat Creek, about ten miles from Pavilion. There they remained overnight and the next day he rode ahead to Pavilion. Before he reached the camp, however, he hid in the woods at a spot where he could observe what was happening. What he saw was not heartening. No women or children were to be seen at the camp, only men with painted faces, brandishing guns and knives.

When his men caught up with him, Tod told them to remain where they were. He did not intend to hide their presence, however, for he ordered them to build a fire that produced plenty of smoke. In

Jean Baptiste St. Paul Lolo and his family at Kamloops, 1869. (Courtesy
BCARS, 2007)

the meantime he mounted his horse and rode alone into the Indian
camp. Surprised to see a lone European, the Indians demanded to
know where he was from and whether he had come for salmon. Tod
denied the real purpose of his visit, but said instead that there had
been an outbreak of measles to the south and that he would vaccinate
the camp against the disease. Tod then prepared his needle and began
to scratch the Indians on their right arms. He had chosen the place
for the inoculation carefully, for he realized that once their arms
were scratched, the Indians' discomfort would leave them uninter-
ested in swinging their arms in an assault upon the Europeans.

In fact, the fear of measles was enough to quell their anger, and
before long a number of Indian women appeared with offerings of
salmon. Tod refused the gifts, but suggested that they might wish to
trade with his men while he continued the inoculations. Perhaps, he
offered, their camp could be found by the smoke of their fire. By the
time he had scratched about 70 arms, Tod was sure that all danger
had passed, and after instructing them on how to continue the task,
he returned to his camp. There he was pleased to discover that his
men had obtained the year's supply of fish in trade.

This often-repeated tale presented Tod in a way he wished to be
seen — as the cunning fox who could outwit a more powerful but
less crafty opponent. As the story was repeated, Tod substituted

smallpox for measles, for Europeans could not appreciate how gravely the Indians regarded the latter disease. Smallpox, though, was certainly feared among the white population, and it was thus possible to see why Tod's inoculation ruse was so successful. In his 1878 memoirs Tod added a footnote to the affair:

> About 2 years ago, I paid a visit to New Westminster on business, & whilst there an Indian came up and held out his hand to me. I refused, [and then] he asked didn't I know him ... he was one of the Indians whom [I] had vaccinated a long time ago. Of course recognizing the poor fellow now, I gladly shook hands with him.[3]

Tod's telling of the vaccination incident does not depict the interpreter Lolo in a favourable light. Given his loyalty and bravery in the past, the interpreter seems to have behaved entirely out of character. There is little doubt that with the exception of Tod himself, Lolo was much respected by the Europeans at Kamloops.

* * * * *

His duties at the fort fell heavily upon Tod's shoulders and he continued to dream about quitting the territory forever. While he retained ownership of the property at St. Thomas, he had given up his plan to retire there, for, with his marriage to Sophia, he had undertaken new responsibilities. Refusing to consider additional farm expenses, he had written Edward in one of his last letters that "other objects more near & dear to me, and whose claims on me are therefore paramount to all others, will not admit of my making any further outlay."[4] With the birth of Mary, Tod had the opportunity to enjoy fully his role as father. Although he was not new to fatherhood, his other children were almost strangers to him. James had apparently remained in Canada West while Emma continued to live with the Greenshields family in Montreal.

He had much else on his mind. The quarrel between Tod and Manson that had begun in 1845 grew more intense, and as their mutual antagonism increased, each officer complained directly to the governor. In 1847, Simpson replied to one of Manson's letters:

> ... the misunderstanding between you & Mr. Tod, which called forth some remarks from me last year & has led to long

explanations from you and that gent[lema]n this season, is very
much to be regretted & must have placed you both in a very
awkward point of view with strangers. I have no doubt you
were both to blame, but the subject is now of such an old date
that no benifit [*sic*] can arise from discussing the matter; it is,
however, to be hoped that similar difficulties may not recur. ...[5]

The two men eventually reached an accommodation, but their
mutual dislike remained apparent. In his memoirs Tod failed to
acknowledge his colleague's important role in the New Caledonian
fur trade. "Another man Manson used to be with me at New
Caledonia," he wrote dismissively.[6] While Tod himself was often an
irascible individual, it was also true that Manson had no difficulty
making enemies — his quick temper contributed to his unpopularity
among fellow officers in New Caledonia.

In May 1847, Tod was host at Fort Kamloops to Alexander
Caulfield Anderson and his party who were once again setting off in
search of a brigade route to the Pacific. This time, after a series of
wrong turns, they followed an old Indian trail that bypassed the
worst part of the treacherous Fraser Canyon. As Anderson himself
recognized, the new way was usable only with the greatest difficulty,
but the Company had to persevere with it. Over the next few years
several changes made the New Caledonia trail more serviceable.

With the loss of the Oregon Territory in 1846, the Company
planned to shift its headquarters north to Fort Victoria, but it did
not officially control the land on which the fort was situated — the
British government had never ceded Vancouver Island to the
Hudson's Bay. When news of the Company's petition for the island
reached the London newspapers, it raised a furore, for in an era of
free trade, the old monopoly had fallen out of favour with the
British public. Nevertheless, in 1849 the Company was granted
proprietary rights to Vancouver Island. The terms of the deal were
not entirely in the Hudson's Bay's interest because in exchange for a
ten-year lease, the Company was required to open the island to
British immigrants.

Given the Company's dismal history as a settlement agent, the
government attempted to ensure that it would fulfil its contractual
obligations. The agreement was limited to ten years, but if the
Company had failed to establish a colony in half that time it would lose
its control of Vancouver Island. In addition, the Company was
expected to pay the costs of the colony's civil and military administra-

tion. However, even when it was in its own interests to encourage settlement, the London Committee found it impossible to change old habits. Rather than favouring immigration, the Company was prepared to allow Vancouver Island to revert to the Crown in five years.

While the Company remained opposed to settlement, it continued to try to diversify its operations beyond fur and agricultural produce. Salmon was a readily available staple, but efforts to find a satisfactory method of preservation had been largely unsuccessful; a few barrels of the salted fish were exported to Hawaii. The resources of Vancouver Island's forests, though, were far more valuable. The British navy was already a major purchaser of the giant coastal firs, which were used for ship's masts and spars, and after 1849, California became a ready market for the lumber and shingles the Company produced. But it was the mineral resources of the west coast that captured the imagination of the Hudson's Bay. Reports of coal deposits on Vancouver Island had been made as early as 1835, but it was not until 1849 that the resource was exploited. The impetus was the rush of settlers to the Oregon Territory. Ships returning around Cape Horn needed coal for their boilers, which the Hudson's Bay agreed to supply.

When it began development of the resource, however, the Company made a serious mistake, for the site it chose was on northern Vancouver Island. The error was not surprising since no one in the Hudson's Bay's employ knew much about coal. To work the deposit, the Company brought in seven Scots miners to the site near newly constructed Fort Rupert. As it turned out, though, the coal was soft, the seam difficult to exploit, and the living conditions primitive. Only after the Company's mining activities were shifted to Nanaimo, in 1852, was the black mineral produced in quantity.

* * * * *

In late spring 1849, Tod and his family travelled with the Fort Kamloops brigade to Fort Langley. The route via the Squa-zowm River, which had been pioneered by Alexander Caulfield Anderson in 1847, must have been difficult for Sophia and the children. The previous year, the hardships of the journey had led one member of the brigade to take his own life. Tod, too, probably found the journey difficult for he was ill. While the nature of his complaint is not clear, it may have been the beginning of chronic kidney disease. During his last years at Fort Kamloops Tod had been under considerable strain, for the arrival of American settlers in Oregon Territory continued to anger the interior tribes. If the conflict spread north, Fort Kamloops, due to its proximity to the American border, was a likely battle site.

Leaving his wife and children with James Murray Yale at Fort Langley, Tod continued on to Fort Victoria where he met Chief Factor James Douglas, newly arrived from Fort Vancouver. What the two men discussed is unknown, but Tod soon left by ship for Fort Nisqually on Puget Sound where he arrived on 17 July. In charge of the post was William Fraser Tolmie. Although not a qualified doctor, Tolmie had had some medical training and acted as both trader and physician. The following day Tod travelled to Fort Vancouver where he remained until 3 August; then he returned to Fort Nisqually in the company of Captain Walter Colquhoun Grant, who was on his way to take up land near Fort Victoria. Captain Grant would be the colony's first independent settler. A few days later Tod returned to Fort Langley and brought Sophia and his family back to Nisqually. Under Tolmie's care, Tod remained on medical furlough. He was not confined to bed, and to relieve his boredom he occasionally accompanied Tolmie during the latter's visits to the outlying settlements. On one occasion, Tod and two servants from the fort rode to the Sequallitch River to look for a suitable location for a proposed sawmill. On returning to the post, Tod passed his recommendations on to Tolmie.

In the early morning of 16 October, Tod sailed on the Hudson's Bay schooner *Cadboro* for Fort Victoria. The occasion was the wedding of his old friend, Chief Factor John Work, to his longtime country wife, Susette Legace. Performing the rites was Reverend Robert Staines who had recently arrived and had accepted the dual responsibilities of chaplain and schoolteacher. Tod and Douglas witnessed the marriage certificate. The couple had been together more than 20 years, but for the sake of the status of their daughters, who were now at a marriageable age, they had agreed to the ceremony. Soon after, Work took his place on board the canoe for the return journey to Fort Simpson, a distance of more than a thousand miles. Susette remained at Fort Victoria where their children attended Reverend Staines's school. Tod returned to Nisqually where he briefly took command of the post during Tolmie's absence at Fort Victoria.

While his condition showed improvement, by the spring of 1850 he was still too ill to return to the rigours of Fort Kamloops. Rather than remain longer at Nisqually, however, Tod applied for a three-year leave of absence that would be followed by retirement. "I have lost all inclination of returning again to the Service," he wrote Simpson in March 1850.[7] During his time on Vancouver Island Tod had been impressed by the gentle, rolling countryside around the fort and hoped to settle there. The difficulty was the Company's asking price for land "which ... appeared to me, and most others here ... so exorbitant as to amount almost to a prohibition, and to a man of my slender means, would be little short of ruin."[8] Tod's obvious course was to move south to Oregon Territory where land could be obtained from the American government at little cost. However, his longstanding distrust of Americans made him reluctant to follow "the example of others here who have also been long in the employ of the Company, and have already become American citizens and taken up extensive claims on Yankee land."[9] Tod hoped that the London Committee would consider offering land to its retiring employees at reduced prices.

In June 1850 Simpson replied that "although 3 years leave previous to retirement is a greater indulgence than is usually accorded to retiring officers, yet, in consideration of your declining health and from a desire to terminate your long connexion with the concern in a liberal and agreeable manner they [the Northern Council] have consented to your request."[10] Although the governor praised Tod's desire to settle on British rather than American territory, the price was firm. In fairness, Simpson had no control over Vancouver Island land costs, for the Hudson's Bay only acted as an agent of the British government, and colonial land prices were an element of a broader Imperial policy devised by the political economist Edward Gibbon Wakefield.

Wakefield believed that Britain's colonies could best be managed through the creation of a small, powerful, property-owning elite which maintained tight control of the political and social institutions. Land ownership would thus be restricted to already affluent immigrants who would pay the high price of one pound per acre. However, even the well-off had no intention of throwing their money away purchasing land on Vancouver Island when land in Oregon could be had at a fraction of the cost. For retiring Hudson's Bay officers, like Tod, with large families, the price was steep. In the end he chose to homestead at Point Roberts, a tip of land jutting south of the 49th parallel. Tod may have picked this spot because the location of the final border had not been determined; this gave him some freedom since neither the United States nor Britain could claim undisputed ownership.

In July Tod received a visit from James Douglas who wanted retired senior officers to take up land on Vancouver Island rather than in the United States. Taking advantage of the deep suspicion with which many Hudson's Bay officers regarded Americans, Douglas presented his case for settlement on British territory. Tod did not record what the chief factor had said, but his opinions were well known. His point was that while no immediate payment was required for American homestead land, settlers did not receive title to their property for ten years, and it was impossible, he claimed, to say whether the United States government would fulfil its part of the agreement a decade hence. "I would rather Pay a pound per acre for land with a secure title and numerous other advantages," Douglas wrote, "than have a farm for nothing with ten years torturing suspense."[11]

Tod did not trust Douglas's motives, believing that his old comrade's desire for him to settle near the fort had more to do with post security than friendship: in the event of an Indian rising the chief factor would be able to count on aid from the surrounding farms. This view, though in keeping with Tod's suspicious disposition, was probably unfair, for unlike his superiors in London, Douglas hoped to fulfil the terms of the agreement with the govern-

Fort Victoria. (COURTESY BCARS, 10603)

ment and establish a viable colony for new settlers. In his opinion, the southern tip of the island was most desirable. "The place itself appears a perfect Eden," Douglas had written in 1843 "and so different in general aspect, from the wooded, rugged regions around, that one might be pardoned for supposing that it had dropped from the clouds into its present position."[12] His early letters to London were optimistic, but the price of Vancouver Island land remained the major stumbling block to settlement. In 1850, however, Tod decided to take Douglas's advice and move to Vancouver Island.

Tod and several other potential Hudson's Bay settlers had originally marked out land on the Metchosin Plain, about six miles from Victoria, but fear of the natives, and the distance from the fort, made them change their minds. Tod decided instead on land between the Company's Uplands Farm and Fort Victoria. Despite its cost, Tod was pleased with his purchase. He wrote Simpson the following year that "the land is tolerably good, and situation pleasant and healthy and as I now begin to feel a growing fondness for the island with all its primitive wilderness it is likely that I shall remain and take root therein."[13] There is no doubt that Douglas gave Tod a preferred site, less than half an hour's ride from the fort.

The new head of the Vancouver Island government was Richard Blanshard, a man chosen not by the Colonial Office, but by the Company. The London Committee had intended to appoint James Douglas to the position, but in the face of objections to this apparent conflict of interest, an outsider was given the role. It was not until Blanshard arrived at Fort Victoria in March 1850 that he discovered the impossibility of his situation. With none of the institutions of colonial government in place, including the courts, police and public works, the governor was expected to administer this remote backwater of the British Empire. In the entire Fort Victoria area, Blanshard discovered, there was only one independent colonist: Captain Grant who had settled at Sooke, 25 miles from the fort.

Douglas and other officers who had long been a law unto themselves saw Blanshard as an obstacle to their traditional exercise of power. The Company continued to operate as before without reference to British colonial policies — the new governor was intended to be little more than a figurehead. It is hardly surprising that in less than a year the frustrated Blanshard submitted his resignation to London.

By the summer of 1851 the colony had lost its only other permanent settler: Captain Grant had given up the idea of farming his property. Since the Hudson's Bay had no retail competition on

Richard Blanshard, first governor of Vancouver Island. (COURTESY BCARS, A01112)

Vancouver Island, Grant had to pay what the Company called "stranger prices" for goods he purchased at the fort, a situation that probably contributed to his increasing financial difficulties, and to meet his expenses, Grant was forced to sell many of his personal possessions. As a former Company employee Tod had the advantage of discounts on his own purchases. (It is not surprising that later settlers resented the privileges Tod and his fellow retired officers seemed to take for granted.)

In the spring of 1851 Tod had occupied his property, but had not yet paid the purchase price. He had put up security in lieu of payment, pending approval from the Company's London headquarters. However, word was slow to come — a situation Tod found increasingly frustrating. Blanshard, in his letter to his own superiors in London, noted in 1851 that Tod had begun to cultivate his acreage under a verbal agreement with Douglas, but "finding that he cannot obtain the said title, nor even a written promise to furnish it, he is becoming alarmed, has discontinued the house he was beginning to build, and talks of leaving the colony."[14] Despite his threats, however, Tod did not give up his land.

On 20 January 1852, Tod finally received title to his 109-acre farm. The cost to him was £109: the maximum price the Company was permitted to charge. Tod had chosen to build his house a few hundred yards back from the shores of Oak Bay, at a spot known as "The Willows." On clear days, he had an excellent view of the magnificent, snow-covered volcano of Mount Baker across the water on the American mainland.

Tod's small house was constructed from lumber produced by the Company's primitive, water-driven sawmill, which now operated not far from the fort. Nails, which would have been hand-forged by the Company's blacksmith, were used sparingly, the frame being put together with carefully cut mortices. Among the few items imported from England were the panels of glass which made up the latticed windows. In most rooms, walls were plastered over hand-split laths — a job probably done by local Indians. At the front of the house, which overlooked the ocean, the windows were quite large, but elsewhere Tod was more economical: in other rooms, the small mullioned frames let in little light.

At first, meals were prepared on a plain fieldstone fireplace that was later covered over with a more impressive rock facing. It is not difficult to imagine Sophia preparing the Sunday roast on a great iron spit set into the mortar. After the hardships of his 40-year career with the Hudson's Bay, Tod planned a less arduous retirement. He had the opportunity to indulge his passion for music. He had given up the flute — possibly because of the loss of his teeth due to age — but he continued to play the violin. As the population of southern Vancouver Island increased he could look forward to more amateur musicians to accompany him. While Tod's location offered considerable privacy, Fort Victoria was only about three miles away and he frequently made the journey to the post to visit with his longtime Hudson's Bay colleagues. Also,Tod had not forgotten another lifelong pleasure — reading. When Governor Blanshard departed for England on 1 September 1851, he did not take his entire collection of books, and Tod was pleased to add the remaining volumes to his own growing library.

Although no longer young, Tod embarked on raising a large family. By 1851, eight-year-old Mary, his eldest daughter by Sophia, had three younger brothers, John Jr., Alex and Isaac. Since James, his oldest son, also lived with him at this time, the new house must have seemed crowded, but after Fort Kamloops, they at least felt safe. While the local natives were occasionally restless, Tod and his family were not threatened.

The fort was only a few minutes' ride from his house, and since many of his old friends remained in the service, the journey to buy supplies was a chance to engage in fur-trade gossip. It is impossible to know how much he missed the letters from Edward Ermatinger, but Tod did receive word on his activities by way of his son James, who continued on good terms with Edward. Contrary to Tod's fears, Edward continued to prosper as a St. Thomas merchant, postmaster, and banker. In 1851 he quit the Bank of Montreal to organize a new financial institution, the Bank of the County of Elgin. In 1844 Edward had been finally elected a Conservative member of the Legislative Assembly of Canada West, but in politics, he was not a success. Unable to forgive or forget what had happened in 1837, he objected to the fact that many of the rebels now sat in the House. In 1847 he was defeated and never ran again.

Following his split with Edward, Tod seems also to have ended his friendship with Frank Ermatinger. After 1844, Frank's letters to Edward make no mention of Tod. Since the two brothers were close, it would not be surprising if Frank had taken Edward's side in the quarrel. In 1846 Frank was transferred from the Columbia Department to York Factory. During his years in the west, Tod had gradually lost contact with many of his friends who had remained at eastern posts. His contact with his family in St. Thomas also lessened, and happenings half a continent away had become remote.

In October 1851 Tod celebrated his 57th birthday and he continued to be active. Regardless of the weather he walked down the slope from his house to the shores of Oak Bay where he would strip off his clothes and take a regular early morning swim. At first, the noise of the water crashing against the rocks on his beach was unfamiliar. He knew the sounds a river made as it spilled and tumbled through its course, for he had long paddled the rugged highways of New Caledonia. But the ocean was different: the waves on his beach did not sing the same complex harmonies. As time passed, though, Tod came to prefer the Pacific's bass rhythm to the intricate trebles of the inland waterways. Oak Bay had become home.

Chapter Eleven

MY FACE IS PAINTED

On accepting Richard Blanshard's resignation, the Colonial Office appointed Hudson's Bay Chief Factor James Douglas in 1851 to take his place as governor of Vancouver Island. There was really little choice, for even from as far away as London it was clear that Blanshard had been governor in name only — the real power rested with Douglas and the Hudson's Bay Company. Supplies were purchased at the Company post, children attended Hudson's Bay subsidized schools, medical services were supplied by the Company physician, and even transportation to and from the colony was usually by way of Company ships.

For the dozen or so settlers who had taken up Crown land on Vancouver Island, however, Blanshard was a symbol of an authority independent of the Hudson's Bay. Few of the new arrivals believed that the chief factor would be any more than an agent for his employer, the Hudson's Bay. When news of Douglas's appointment arrived, some settlers petitioned Blanshard not to carry out the Colonial Office directive, but there was nothing he could do.

Earlier that year, Blanshard had appointed Tod to the new, three-member Legislative Council which would act in an advisory capacity to the governor. The two other members were an independent settler, Captain James Cooper, and James Douglas, who represented the Company. When Douglas was appointed governor a few months later, his place on the council was filled by Chief Factor Roderick Finlayson, who was in charge of Fort Victoria.

A major task facing Tod and the new council was the establishment of a colonial judicial system. With no qualified lawyer practising on Vancouver Island, the council had to appoint lay citizens to act as justices of the peace. To complicate matters, few residents of Vancouver Island held the land qualifications British law required for appointment to these posts. For this reason, the council was forced to waive the property requirements and ask only that the appointees be "faithful and true men loyal to Her Majesty the Queen, of experience in business, and of good repute in the Counties where they reside."[1] The four new justices were permitted to levy a fee of one pound per day as court costs in all civil cases.

After Tod's arrival in 1850, the colony grew steadily, if not spectacularly, and by 1854 the European population of the town of Victoria was over 300. Few of the new arrivals were independent settlers, for the cheap land of Oregon Territory continued to be attractive to most British immigrants. During this period, both the Hudson's Bay and its subsidiary, the Puget's Sound Agricultural Company, expanded their operations on Vancouver Island. The Hudson's Bay had brought several hundred indentured labourers to work its land. While many men deserted for California's 1849 gold rush, the workers who stayed earned a bonus of 20 acres at the end of their five-year contract. These labourers, together with retiring clerks and the few servants who could afford the price of colonial land, were some of the earliest settlers. Agricultural land purchases had to be a minimum of 20 acres, which at one pound per acre was more than a year's wages for the lower ranks of servants. For this reason few Canadiens, or Kanaka workers the Company was bringing in from Hawaii, settled on Vancouver Island.

By 1852 the colony was showing its first sign of independence from the Hudson's Bay Company. The arrival of a surveyor, Joseph Despard Pemberton, permitted the laying out of a town site beyond the walls of the fort. The town lots, though, were regarded as too expensive by most potential purchasers. Only the Company had the resources to buy up large tracts of Victoria land.

Beyond the town boundaries, senior Company officers were major purchasers of land. About 1852, John Work purchased 583 acres north of the fort and during the next few years gradually acquired more property until by 1858 he was the largest individual landowner on Vancouver Island. Other major buyers were Chief Factors Roderick Finlayson and William F. Tolmie, as well as Douglas himself, who purchased 300 acres not far from Beacon Hill.

One notable arrival in 1852 was Dr. J. S. Helmcken, a young physician who had briefly served at the Company's coal-mining operation at Fort Rupert. On 27 December, Helmcken married Cecilia Douglas, the governor's eldest daughter. As a council member, leading settler and Douglas's friend, Tod probably attended the reception, which was the social event of the year. Relations between Douglas and Tod had become somewhat strained, however. The price of land had remained a sore point not only for Tod, but for the other large landowners as well. Although there was nothing Douglas could do, since the price had been set by the Colonial Office, many of his fellow officers took their resentment out on him.

Major property owners were not alone in their complaints against Douglas and the Hudson's Bay — other colonists also had grievances. The Hudson's Bay's retail monopoly was an on-going source of anger. Because many of the immigrants had no idea what faced them at Fort Victoria, few had brought along stocks of necessities, including seeds, flint, needles and thread, with the result that they had to pay high Hudson's Bay prices for these goods.

In 1853 the number of executive members of the Legislative Council was increased to four when Chief Factor John Work was appointed. With Work's presence, the voice of the independent settler was proportionally smaller. Although Douglas could not control Captain Cooper, he expected little opposition from the other members of council.

Douglas's most outspoken critic was the Reverend Robert Staines who, in 1853, was the moving force behind a petition calling for an end to Hudson's Bay rule and the formation of an elected assembly. While the governor was aware of Staines's opposition, he was disappointed to discover that Chief Factors William Tolmie and Roderick Finlayson, as well as retired Chief Trader John Tod, were among the signatories. "They did so before I was informed of their intention and would then have recalled the act, of which they are heartily ashamed, had they not been restrained by the fear of ridicule," Douglas wrote his superiors in London.[2]

Given the length of their acquaintance, Douglas must have found Tod's betrayal particularly galling, but the latter had always been distrustful of power, even when wielded by friends. Moreover, the role of the governor's "rubber stamp" would not have come easily to the outspoken Scot. In truth, except for their long years of Hudson's Bay service, the two men had little in common. Douglas had a serious turn of mind and obviously enjoyed the pomp and ceremony of his colonial position. Meals taken at the officers' mess at Fort Victoria were formal affairs where levity was discouraged. When Tod attended these dinners, however, his wry sense of humour sometimes undermined Douglas's strict decorum. At one such mess, Tod told the governor and assembled guests that when he was a young man at Island Lake he had celebrated Wellington's victory over Napoleon at Waterloo in 1815 by firing a round from his fort's cannon. However, news of the British success had not reached his remote outpost of His Majesty's Empire until 1818, which meant that the young clerk's salute was somewhat anticlimactic.

On 31 March 1853, the council appointed Tod to a two-member commission to oversee the construction of a school at an area that was known as "Minies Plain" which was some distance beyond the walls of the fort. With him on the commission was Robert Barr, the new school teacher. The council had determined that the size of the building would be 1,600 square feet with accommodation for boarding students. The charge for boarding children of island residents, whether colonist or Hudson's Bay employee, was to be 18 guineas a year.

The governor's attitude toward education showed the differences between Douglas and Tod in sharpest focus. Douglas's vision was that his tiny colony would be built upon a strong foundation of Christian values: the role of the school was not simply to educate, but to develop within the students a strict moral ethic. Tod, on the other hand, had become increasingly critical of organized religion and its role within the state. He made no secret of his belief that the church had no place in the classroom.

In 1853, a contentious liquor licence tax was passed by Tod and his fellow council members, finally overcoming the objections of Captain Cooper. Because the income from land sales was remitted to the Colonial Office, these licences were the only source of income for the colony and the need for funds was increasing: the few roads that existed became almost impassable during the heavy winter rains.

A further colonial expense was incurred when in December, at a salary of £100 a year, Douglas appointed his brother-in-law, David Cameron, as judge of the Colony's Supreme Court. Cameron had no legal training, and this case of blatant patronage further angered the independent colonists. Whatever Tod's personal opinions, however, as a council member he remained loyal to Douglas.

* * * * *

Few personal glimpses of Tod during his early retirement have survived, but one rare account was provided by James Robert Anderson, the son of Hudson's Bay explorer Alexander Caulfield Anderson. When he was nine, young James Robert was taken to Fort Victoria where he attended the school operated by Reverend Robert Staines and his wife Emma. On one spring day in 1851, Anderson and his classmates were given the day off, and he and several other boys spent their time exploring the open meadows around the fort, which were then laden with ripening berries. Enjoying the rare pleasure of a sunny afternoon, the boys allowed their imaginations to run free. To resemble more closely their Indian neighbours, Anderson and his friends painted their faces with the juice of wild fruit. After some time the boys found themselves at the Tod farm, where they stopped to pay a visit. Hospitably, Tod provided suitable refreshments and entertained the boys with selections on his violin. Tod was in the habit of keeping time by tapping his foot on the floor, and Anderson and his friends soon followed suit. It may have been that Tod interpreted the boys' behaviour as mockery, for his attitude toward his guests suddenly changed. Putting down his violin, Tod took out pens and paper and passed them out to the students. As Anderson recalled in his memoirs:

> In order to test our proficiency in calligraphy and orthography, he got each boy to write down separately the words, 'My face is painted.' These slips were duly sent to Mrs. Staines accompanied by some interesting and as we thought, rude remarks on our proficiency and by inference, the proficiency of our teachers. Then we ... were held up to ridicule and severely reprimanded, our spelling and our writing criticized and our personal appearance held to the derision of the girls. Personally, whilst my writing was somewhat inferior, in fact, bad, my spelling was good which I took occasion to point out. By way of compensation for our day's enjoyment we were given the task of writing out the sentence as stated several hundred times and kept in.[3]

The boys, who were obviously fond of the old trader, felt betrayed. However, Tod's target was probably not Anderson and his friends, but their teachers, the Staines.

Many Hudson's Bay officers believed that Staines was concerned more with fighting Douglas and the Company than with educating his charges. A continual prick in the side of the Hudson's Bay, Staines met a tragic end in 1854 when the barque *Duchess De Lorenzo*, on which he was a passenger, foundered off Cape Flattery. He had been on his way to England via San Francisco to deliver a petition to the British Government condemning Douglas's actions as governor.

Tod, who carried with him the memory of his own failed schooling in Scotland, bitterly resented the practice of wedding education with religion. He believed that the religious dogmas taught in church schools prevented the free expression of rational ideas within the classroom. Some years later, during the debate on British Columbia's entry into Confederation, Tod would count Canada's system of secular schools as one of the greatest advantages of union.

* * * * *

In 1853, New Caledonia and what remained of the Hudson's Bay territory north of the new border were reorganized into the Western Department. Unlike the old Columbia Department, its administration was entirely independent of the Northern Department. For Tod, though, happenings within the Company were increasingly remote, for much of his time was taken up with his growing family. By the summer of 1854, he was the father of five young children, some of whom were attending school. While Tod had no difficulty meeting the school fees, they were well beyond the means of most settlers and lower-ranking Company employees. By firmly controlling access to education, the Hudson's Bay perpetuated its control of the colony. It was no wonder that Tod and his fellow senior officers were called the "Family-Company-Compact," by less privileged members of Vancouver Island society.

In the summer of 1855, Emma, Tod's oldest daughter, was in England where she had probably gone to finish her education. Surprisingly, during this time, Emma did not visit her mother or her family. The reason may have been that she had never been told about Eliza's mental illness, for in her reminiscences Emma wrote that she was less than a year old when her mother died. Yet it seems strange that she would not have sought out other members of the Waugh family who could have provided information on Eliza. What seems more plausible is that she knew the truth about her mother and preferred to deny it. For Emma, who was now at a marriageable

Emma Tod. (COURTESY BCARS, 4075)

age, rumours about her mother's condition could have hindered matrimonial prospects.

Eliza's death from kidney failure at Guy's Hospital on 12 May 1857, prompted a letter to Tod from her sister, Jane Lloyd. The black-edged envelope, however, was not picked up — the only letter addressed to Tod via the Hudson's Bay to remain so. The reason may have been that its contents with its inevitable request for burial money were all too obvious. Jane Lloyd's letter provided a final glimpse into Eliza's troubled life, for as she wrote Tod:

> I regret very much I could not secure the Wedding ring, it had been taken away from her 4 months before she died and no one at the Hospital can render any information how it disappeared. It must have been stolen from her for you might take anything from her, but her ring was sacred [and] no one should touch it. ... She always asked after you at particular Periods of the Year. I think in October she always anticipated a Visit from you and her dear little Emma.[4]

Fortunately, Emma exhibited no signs of her mother's instability. In the early spring of 1856, Tod paid £60 for a cabin aboard the

Company ship *Princess Royal* from London to Victoria via Cape
Horn. On reaching Vancouver Island, Emma took up lodgings with
her father but these living arrangements proved unworkable. Emma
looked down on her mixed-blood kin, and she soon went to live at
the fort. Some years later Tod wrote, "in all cases where the
maternal affection had been wanting, or partially so in childhood, a
harshness had been imparted to the character in after life."[5]
Doubtless he had in mind his eldest daughter.

Emma's stay in the single quarters was short. On 30 September
1856, she married William Henry Newton at the newly constructed
First English Church in Victoria. Newton had arrived in Victoria in
1851 to act as assistant to Edward Edwards Langford, the manager
of the Puget's Sound Agricultural Company's farm at Colwood. The
wedding of Tod's eldest daughter was a simple affair, but the bridal
dress of light blue silk supported by a full crinoline was sufficiently
elegant to impress the guests. (Not until some years later did white
become the standard for bridal dresses.) The lack of an available
wedding ring prompted the post blacksmith to shape one from an
American gold coin. "I feel certain that no jeweller could have
produced a better piece of work," Emma recalled later.[6]

Afterward, the couple left by canoe for Metchosin where they
honeymooned, and on their return, they moved into the post's
married quarters. Six months later the Newtons were transferred to
the farm at Fort Langley, on the mainland, which was under the
command of Tod's old colleague Chief Trader James Murray Yale.
With the Fort George incident long past, Tod and Yale had become
close friends, and Emma and her new husband received special
kindness from the often irascible Yale. Although the post was usually
quiet, the arrival of the northern brigades in the spring broke the
monotony of the routine. Emma had brought a Collard piano from
England — the first on the mainland — and her playing entertained
the trail-weary travellers.

Tod lacked the temperament necessary to make a success of his
land, and even with the assistance of his son James his farm did not
flourish. "The poor old gentleman is not very enterprising," Douglas
had once noted.[7] Tod's short temper also caused difficulties with his
neighbours. According to the diary of Robert Melrose, a labourer on
the Craigflower Farm, Tod was charged in April of 1856 with cattle
theft. There may have been a reasonable explanation for this.
Because the Hudson's Bay's Cadboro Bay Farm adjoined his
property, Company cattle would have probably ranged onto Tod's

land. Tod may not have taken kindly to these Company interlopers on his land and his response can be readily imagined. Since there is no record of a trial, it would appear the matter was smoothed over and quickly forgotten.

Despite problems on his own farm, Tod purchased an additional 187 acres near Cedar Hill in August 1858 for his son James. James had married Flora MacAulay, daughter of Hudson's Bay farm employee Donald MacAulay, a year earlier, and the couple wished to begin a life of their own. The land given to him by his father was rugged, but James set to work immediately clearing the bush and preparing the ground. In the Victoria area, James's strength was legendary — he was said to be able to do the work of three men, and it was not long before he turned his property, Cedar Hill Farm, into one of the finest independent farms on Vancouver Island.

Although Tod was clearly not a farmer like his son, nor even his brother Sym, he had few wants, and desired only to produce enough for the needs of his family. Despite his earlier misgivings, Edward Ermatinger had placed his money wisely in the Bank of Montreal and other solid securities, and when Samuel Greenshields became Tod's agent these investments were left undisturbed. Tod might have continued on in the routine of retirement for the rest of his days had it not been for the discovery of gold on the Fraser River. As a result, Tod's familiar world was changed forever.

* * * * *

The British government had entertained modest hopes for the eventual success of the Vancouver Island colony, but few knowledgeable Britons would have predicted a glowing future for the Hudson's Bay territory on the mainland. Even by mid-century Britain seemed little concerned about its possessions west of the Rockies. *The Illustrated Atlas and Modern History of the World*, published in London in 1851, all but ignored the British territories west of Canada. On the Pacific, only the Queen Charlotte Islands were singled out for special note. This desolate spot, the atlas concluded, "is admirably suited to the formation of a penal settlement, being impossible to escape from."[8]

Ironically, the Hudson's Bay's first real inkling of the potential of the west occurred when small quantities of gold were received in trade from the Haida Indians of the Queen Charlotte Islands in 1850. Although the find attracted some miners, it was not until seven years later that American prospectors discovered significant amounts of the precious metal mixed with alluvium at Hill's Bar on the Fraser River. By the first months of 1858, word of the gold had reached California, and by the end of April the first shipload of prospectors reached Victoria. The little Vancouver Island community quickly became the entrepôt for the miners as well as their equipment and supplies. The sea route from San Francisco to Victoria was favoured by most travellers — the combination of rugged terrain and hostile Indians had made an overland trail north from California difficult, and the small ports that had sprung up on the American side of the border were less convenient.

The Fraser discovery was relatively small compared to the California find ten years earlier, but the changes gold brought to the island and mainland were nonetheless dramatic. Within months, the population of the town of Victoria had grown tenfold to more than 3,000 residents. In addition, as many as 30,000 miners passed through on their way to the Fraser diggings. Lots near the waterfront, which the Hudson's Bay had purchased for less than $300 American in 1852, now sold for as much as $3,000.

The rapid influx of Americans made it clear to Douglas that the days of Hudson's Bay rule over the mainland had come to a end, and that if the Crown did not move to take possession of what remained of the Columbia Department, the territory would be annexed by the United States. Thus, in early 1858, the governor of Vancouver Island overreached his authority and imposed a licence fee on prospectors heading to the mainland. Although Douglas was criticized by the Colonial Office for what was called an impetuous move, he had little choice. The Hudson's Bay was incapable of controlling the current situation and the Colonial Office was required to take action.

Originally, the mainland colony was to be called New Caledonia — a name that had been applied to much of the territory within the new boundaries since 1806 — but a French possession in the Pacific had prior claim to that name. British Columbia was a last-minute substitution, and on 2 August 1858, the act creating the new mainland colony was proclaimed. As well as retaining the governorship of Vancouver Island, Douglas was given charge of British Columbia. There was a condition to the appointment, however, for he was required to resign his Hudson's Bay commission. Douglas complied, albeit reluctantly, and was replaced as head of the Western Department by Alexander Grant Dallas, the husband of his second daughter, Jane. Like George Simpson, Dallas had not risen through Company ranks — he was a successful businessman who had been sent by the London Committee to Victoria to assist Douglas and to straighten out the affairs of the Hudson's Bay's subsidiary, the money-losing Puget's Sound Agricultural Company. After accomplishing this task, Dallas prepared to return to England with his young bride. The sudden turn of events on the mainland, however, forced the London Committee to draft him as the new head of the Western Department.

Before the full impact of the gold rush was felt on Vancouver Island, Tod chose to resign from the Legislative Council. The reason for his departure was never made clear. The minutes for 11 October 1858, noted curtly that Douglas "informed Council that he had received a commission from Mr. Tod resigning his office as member of Council."[9] There is no doubt, though, that Tod opposed the way Douglas had governed Vancouver Island. While no transcripts of the council meetings exist, it is not difficult to imagine Tod's outrage at the governor's 1854 initiative to use colonial tax money to support the construction of an Anglican church. To make his disagreement with Douglas public, however, would have been regarded by the governor as an act of betrayal. If he wished to retain Douglas's friendship, the only honourable course open to Tod would be to submit his resignation.

Chapter Twelve

DUST ALWAYS RETURNS TO DUST

Although Tod was now beyond middle age, his family continued to grow. Elizabeth, born in 1858, and Simeon in 1859 — the same year as his 65th birthday — were the last of the Tod children. Late fatherhood, however, could not hide the results of passing years. He was subject to hand tremors which irritated him greatly, for the shaking made letter writing difficult. As a result, Tod's list of correspondents had become smaller. He had earlier lost contact with old friends James Hargrave and Robert Seaborn Miles who had remained in the east. Further, since Tod's retirement many of his old comrades had died. Archibald McDonald, his longtime friend and correspondent, left the Columbia for Canada in 1844, three years after receiving his chief factorship. After using his leave, he officially retired in 1847. McDonald survived only another six years, dying on 15 January 1853. Frank Ermatinger was also dead; he had hung on to his career hoping for promotion to chief factor, but it never came. Embittered, Frank finally left the service in 1853 and died five years later. Most of Tod's superiors from the early days were also gone. John Stuart, the first Hudson's Bay superintendent of New Caledonia, retired to Scotland where he died in 1847. Peter Skene Ogden, explorer, adventurer and friend of the treacherous Samuel Black, died peacefully in his sleep at his home in Oregon City on 27 September 1854. He was 60 years old. The venerable Sir George Simpson outlived his former Nor'West enemies, Stuart and Ogden, but even he could not go on forever. Long in failing health, Simpson died after a stroke on 7 September 1860. Simpson's exact age has remained a mystery, for the governor chose never to reveal the year of his birth.

By 1860, almost all of Tod's contemporaries had left Hudson's Bay service. After a one-year furlough in Canada, newly retired James Murray Yale bought property that year at Colquitz, about four miles northeast of Fort Victoria. As he made plans for the construction of his house, a prospective builder arrived with a letter of recommendation from Tod. "I have the pleasure of introducing to your acquaintance Mr. R[ober]t Alford, a contractor, whom, should you employ to put up your house, I feel assured, from his good character, would do you justice," Tod had written.[1] Whether Yale took this recommendation or not is uncertain, but the old trader must have considered the note important for it survived among his papers. Yale's new house was a large, two-storey structure made bright by a large number of expensive windows. Tod, whose own house was made to look poorer by comparison, found the effect ostentatious.

James Murray Yale's many-windowed farmhouse. (COURTESY BCARS, 7681)

John Work never retired, but continued until his death as a member of the Board of Management for the Hudson's Bay's Western Department. As he laboured on, his health began to deteriorate rapidly. Work suffered from a weak heart and an eye condition that left him almost blind. "It is pittiful [sic]," Tod noted, "to see him still clinging to service, as if he would drag it along with him to the next world."[2]

In 1860, Tod was surprised to receive a letter from Edward Ermatinger who had not written him in 15 years. Ostensibly, the reason was that Edward's nephew, the son of Axie's brother Mark Burnham, was stopping in Victoria on his way to the Fraser River gold camps. Given the wild reputation of these lawless tent towns, the family had every reason for concern, but the deaths of his brother Frank and their mutual friend Archie McDonald had probably also contributed to Edward's desire to mend his broken relationship with Tod.

Tod eventually located Burnham in one of the Victoria hotels and invited him to stay until he left for the gold fields. The old trader used the three days of Burnham's visit to acquaint him with some of the difficulties facing him. Before he left, the young man was given a letter of introduction to Tod's daughter Emma, who was still living at Fort Langley. Tod's reply to Edward's letter was to gloss over the difficulties of 15 years earlier, and to instead recall the youthful pleasure and happiness the two old men had shared. "You have not forgot the amiable Lewisa?"[3] he wrote in an attempt to evoke ancient memories. The girl, daughter of a Swiss settler at Red River, had evidently stolen the young Edward's heart.

The present, though, was certainly less romantic. As always, Edward carried a heavy workload. In addition to occupying the presidency of the Bank of the County of Elgin, maintaining his mercantile concerns, and writing articles for a local newspaper, he found time to complete a book, *The Life of Colonel Talbot*, in 1859. The work was a biography of his hero, Thomas Talbot, who had been the force behind the settlement of much of what had become Elgin County. Edward, as always, had little patience with fellow citizens who did not share his political opinions, and his attacks on those whom he regarded as enemies of the late colonel were ruthless. Tod read a copy of the biography Edward had sent to James, and noted only that the work "greatly increased my respect and veneration for the memory of the illustrious deceased."[4]

Tod held Edward's talent for musical composition in much higher regard. He had given one of the pieces that Edward had written 40 years earlier to members of Victoria's Philharmonic Society who arranged it for their ensemble. When Tod attended their evening performances, the musicians treated him to their rendition of the piece. Their playing brought back a flood of old memories, Tod wrote Edward in 1861, with the result that "my whole soul seems to vibrate from Yourself to the music and vice versa."[5]

* * * * *

By 1859, the gold rush on the Fraser was almost over, but later strikes near the Quesnel River drew prospectors farther inland. While Victoria remained the hub of the economy, the newly constructed port of New Westminster on the lower Fraser River was becoming a serious commercial rival. Although officially separate colonies, Vancouver Island and British Columbia were both dependent on mainland gold. However, like the fur traders earlier, the miners faced the problem of developing a practical route by which to move people and resources beyond the Fraser Canyon. The Harrison-Lillooet route, first used by A. C. Anderson in 1846, had to be widened for the use of wagons. Work on the road was begun in 1858 and continued on until the early 1860s. The job was made difficult by the stream of traffic heading north and south, and at an estimated £85 per mile, the cost of construction was high. Still, in the midst of boom times, it seemed a small price to pay. For the wealthy Victoria wholesalers and retailers who were the colonial elite, it appeared as though their golden dream would go on forever.

While the boom had made some of his fur-trade friends extremely wealthy, Tod had not been a major speculator in Vancouver Island land. Early on, he had bought a few town lots, but the source of his greatest wealth was his 100-acre farm, which occupied a choice location. His affluence also rested on the increasing value of the Bank of Montreal bonds Edward had added to his portfolio years earlier. Tod took little pleasure from his new prosperity. "The prospect of wealth in my old age," Tod wrote Edward, "assuredly adds nothing to my happiness. It has really come unsought unexpectedly upon me."[6]

Ironically, as Tod prospered, his friend and one-time financial agent suffered a serious economic setback when the Bank of the County of Elgin was forced to close its doors. The reason was the sudden collapse of the great Canadian railway boom of the 1850s. Edward, like other bankers, had seen new railways as a sure generator of wealth, but the reality was far different. The London and Port Stanley Railway did not bring prosperity to St. Thomas, but instead reduced the once-thriving crossroads to little more than a whistle-stop on the rail line. In 1860, the heavy debt of the railway, together with ruinous competition from the established banks, forced Edward's institution over the brink. Although all the depositors and most of the stockholders were eventually paid off in full, the affair affected Edward deeply. His superficial self-confidence crumbled under the strain of his financial problems, and he was tipped once more toward the dark valley of despondency.

Tod's St. Thomas relatives probably kept him fully apprised of Ermatinger's financial difficulties, for time had not dulled the hard feelings that existed between Edward and Sym. Although by 1861, both of Tod's aged parents had died, his brothers and sisters still wrote him. Sym was now married with a small family and living in a log house he had built on Tod's property. Brother James was still a bachelor and living with his two spinster sisters, Margaret and Mary, in the original frame farmhouse. Elizabeth, Tod's youngest sister, had married a cousin of Alexander Caulfield Anderson, and the couple had taken up a place near St. Thomas.

It had been almost a quarter century since Tod had seen his brothers and sisters, and although they sent the occasional photograph, memories of them were fading. With the dream of his St. Thomas farm now long dead, Tod concentrated his energies on family and friends closer to home. The impending departure for Scotland of the Western Department head Alexander Grant Dallas and his wife Jane, prompted a flurry of activity in Victoria's Hudson's Bay community and Tod had been drafted to assist Dallas in organizing his farewell party. As one of his duties, Tod penned a brief invitation to his friend Yale:

Dear Yale -

Mr. Dallas has commissioned me to inform you that, being on the eve of leaving us, he is preparing to have a party in the Hall at the Company's old Fort, on Tuesday evening, and hopes to have the pleasure of your company, along with other friends, on that occasion. Do not, therefore, disappoint us.

Endeavour to be here at my house at four o'clock in the
afternoon, and we can go together.

Yours truly

Jno. Tod [7]

The abrupt tone was intended to pressure Yale to attend, for his
friend seemed uncomfortable even in the company of his old
comrades of the fur trade. Indeed, he had withdrawn so completely
that Tod questioned his ability to survive in Victoria society. "Yale is
perfectly temperate in all his habits," Tod had written Edward, "but
a long life of total seclusion from the haunts of civilized beings, has
... to a considerable extent, unfited [sic] him to cope successfully
with his change of circumstances."[8]

In the autumn of 1861, Tod was also concerned about another
friend, John Work, who was suffering a recurrence of the malaria he
had contracted at Fort Vancouver. While a few years earlier he
might have been able to overcome the malady, Work's general
health had been failing, and the frequent bouts of high fever
followed by chills were taking their toll. Tod was a constant visitor
at his friend's house and did his best to cheer him up, but day by day
Work's condition was worsening. On 20 December, Tod was at
Work's beside when he happened to mention the letter he was
writing to their mutual friend, Edward. The patient struggled to sit
up on his pillows and said, "Tell him that I shall never see him again
in this world."[9] Two days later Work was dead.

Work's passing three days before Christmas meant a sombre
holiday season for Tod. On 23 December he performed the
unpleasant duty of informing Edward. Tod enclosed a brief note
with a copy of the obituary: "I have just returned home from the
house of Mourning where lays the body of our departed friend
Work — the enclosed note will explain all," he scrawled in his shaky
hand. "Feeling so jaded & worn out from want of sleep these many
nights past I am quite unable to say more at this time."[10]

The funeral was held on the day after Christmas, with burial
taking place in the new Quadra Street Cemetery. In the following
months, the usually garrulous Tod remained by himself. Friends and
neighbours caught only brief glimpses of the old man as he rode to
or from the Work house. Only among Work's family, who, like
himself, grieved deeply, did Tod feel comfortable. Tod was not

alone in his sense of loss, for the chief factor had been a popular person. "The kindly disposition of the late Mr. Work and his open hearted character obtained for him the warmest respect and love of not only his immediate associates in the service but also of many others who had the opportunity of appreciating these good qualities," wrote A. C. Anderson.[11]

The death of Work worsened Edward's already despondent mood, and Tod found himself in the familiar role of emotional lifeline for his troubled friend. "For goodness sake cheer up, and do not always look on the dark side of things," Tod wrote in response to one of Edward's particularly gloomy letters.[12] For his friend, though, the road back from depression was travelled slowly.

Since Tod had resumed his correspondence with Edward, the contents of his letters had become increasingly concerned with religion. Over the years Tod had drifted further and further from his Calvinist origins — its view of God as a wrathful deity cutting down sinners like stocks of wheat he found absurd. Other religions fared little better. The notion of the Trinity, which was central to the Anglican idea of God, Tod regarded as no more than an idea borrowed from the Persian, Zarathustra, who taught 600 years before Christ, and he took particular exception to Roman Catholicism whose priests he considered held too much power over parishioners.

In 1864, the suicide of an itinerant young school teacher in a Victoria rooming house created a minor storm in the local press when it was revealed that prior to the inquest, the man's body had been left for several days uncovered on the floor of a storeroom. What incensed Tod, though, was that a Victoria minister had refused to allow the man a proper Christian burial. As he wrote Edward:

> Consecrated ground! What is that? What can it avail the departed? Can it be of any use even to the doctrine of resurrection? Decomposition levels all, and in any case, excepting the pickled Egyptian, dust always returns to dust.[13]

It is impossible to know when Tod first turned to spiritualism, but from middle age onward he seems to have been drawn in unorthodox directions. "I am sorry to say he [Tod] is much taken up with notions of Phrenology and Socialism which may yet cause bitter regret when it is too late," wrote a disgusted John Work to

Edward in 1846.[14] As a loyal Company officer, Work had found the new ideas Tod expounded dangerous. Even less open to radical notions was Edward. Although many of his letters to his friend were concerned with religious questions, Tod did not explicitly acknowledge his belief in spiritualism until 1870.

The modern spiritualist movement had begun in Hydesville, New York, when, during the winter of 1848, mysterious rapping noises were heard in the small cottage occupied by John and Margaret Fox. It soon became clear that the sounds occurred only in the presence of either of the two Fox children, Margaretta, 13, and Katherine, 11. Gradually, the notion that the dead could communicate through particularly gifted living persons became the foundation of the movement. Spiritualism grew with surprising speed, spurred on by the incredible carnage of the American Civil War. Many of the families who had lost fathers, brothers and sons on the bloody battlefields were unable to come to terms with their loss, and spiritualism seemed to offer a chance to prove that their separation was only temporary.

George Barnston, who had served with Tod in the Columbia, had been surprised by his old comrade's conversion to spiritualism. "I could never have imagined that spiritualism could have caught him as a votary," Barnston noted. "He was as much a matter of fact man as any one I ever knew."[15] Yet Tod's beliefs were not entirely out of character, for spiritualism appealed to the anarchism at the root of his long-standing antipathy toward authority. The movement had none of the rigid structure of the Christian churches — believers were free to accept or reject whatever they wished.

Although Tod continued to call himself a Christian, his beliefs were now far beyond the theological boundaries of the organized churches. Tod had come a long way from the little Scottish village of his childhood — a lifetime of reading had left him open to new ideas based on what he believed to be the supremacy of reason over dogma. He rarely accepted anything simply on faith, but was impressed by "proof" of life after death offered by mediums. Psychological investigations, he noted in a letter to Edward, "have at length resulted in the Self-evident facts of the Soul's immortality and the existence of the Spirit World."[16] His experiences were not entirely second hand, for he was a frequent attendant at seances.

By 1863, Tod had long given up attending church, but on 17 August he still had the need of a minister when he formalized his long-standing marriage to Sophia. The reason for Tod's sudden

Sophia Lolo Tod. (COURTESY BCARS, 3495)

wedding plans — he had been free to marry Sophia since Eliza's death in 1857 — was the pending union of Mary, his oldest daughter by Sophia, to John S. Bowker, an American. Mary's marriage took place on the morning of 24 May 1864, at Tod's house, which had recently been expanded with the addition of another wing. After the wedding the newlyweds moved to the San Juan Islands where Bowker ran sheep, but a few years later they returned to Vancouver Island. Bowker and his brother-in-law John, Jr. established a sheep ranch on Pender Island, and while living at Oak Bay, the two young men commuted to their ranch by sailboat. The elder Tod had considerable influence over his young son-in-law, who also became an advocate of spiritualism.

Tod's first child, James, did not share the bond that united his father with the younger children. Their separation during James's early years had left a gulf between them that was never entirely closed. Although their farms were only a few miles apart, James seems to have been an infrequent visitor to Oak Bay. Unlike Emma, James was on good terms with the children of his father's last marriage, and when he married Flora in 1857, his half-sister Mary was one of the witnesses. Although James prospered, he was never able to escape the shadow of his larger-than-life father. Given the easy temperament of the son, it is doubtful that this situation gave James much concern.

Tod's disdain for James's mother, Catherine Birston, also contributed to the distance between father and son. In 1863, James received a visit from Catherine, who arrived calling herself the Widow Tod. She soon offered her services as tender to the sick and dispenser of herbal remedies and quickly built up a local clientele. On one occasion, Catherine nearly poisoned one of her customers when she mistakenly gave him a toxic concoction made from deer antlers rather than the honey he had requested. The presence of Catherine may also have hastened Tod's marriage to Sophia, for although Victoria had traditionally tolerated fur-trade liaisons, the existence of two "unchurched" wives would undoubtedly have been the subject of much small-town gossip.

Catherine's nursing skills were probably called on to care for James's wife, Flora who was subject to periods of violent mental instability. The elder Tod attributed the cause to heredity, for Flora's mother had suffered similar episodes.* Although Tod had earlier suffered the anguish of his own wife's emotional illness, he seems to have had little sympathy with his son's plight, for James had been aware of the family history.

* * * * *

At the beginning of 1864, James Douglas finally stepped down as governor of Vancouver Island and British Columbia. Though he had successfully governed Britain's two Pacific colonies during difficult times, he was now regarded by the Colonial Office as yesterday's man. British Columbia and Vancouver Island would be presided over by career British colonial bureaucrats. Douglas's long career was not forgotten, however, for as a reward for his service he was given a knighthood.

As governor of Vancouver Island, the Colonial Office appointed Arthur Edward Kennedy. Kennedy was an administrator with extensive experience in the remote corners of the British Empire. On the mainland, Frederick Seymour was appointed to head the government of British Columbia. Like his island counterpart, Seymour was an experienced colonial administrator. Both men, however, would

---

* The real cause may have been that James's wife was nearly always pregnant. Between 1859 and 1881, Flora gave birth to 13 children.

become caught up in the rivalry between Victoria and New Westminster. As the gold-mining activity moved into the Cariboo, New Westminster had taken a larger share of shipping.

Douglas's support for the construction of a wagon road through the Fraser Canyon to the Cariboo had been unpopular with Victoria merchants, who realized that New Westminster would be the logical starting point for inland travel. As an alternative they proposed a road beginning at Bute Inlet and winding through the Coast Mountains. The moving force behind the project was Alfred Waddington, a prominent Victoria businessman. Waddington soon discovered that the construction of the Bute Inlet toll road would be difficult and expensive, for the passage along the canyon of the Homathko River had to be extended out from a sheer rock face. Further, the proposed route passed through the territory of the Chilcotin Indians. Unlike other tribes, the Chilcotins had resisted forming trading partnerships with the Europeans, and Hudson's Bay posts in their territory had been unprofitable. The route, though, had one major advantage over its Fraser Canyon rival — it bypassed New Westminster entirely. For that reason, Waddington and his Victoria business associates wanted to press on.

As the construction crew pushed ahead, they seemed amazingly blind to the native mood, and treated the proud Chilcotins, who were aware that the route would bring settlers into their territory, with characteristic European disdain. With one or two exceptions, the men were unarmed, and did not even bother to place a night watch at their camp. Only a small spark was needed to touch off open conflict, and on 29 April 1864, when Tim Smith, one of the crew who operated a ferry across the Homathko River, refused the Chilcotins' demand for food, he was shot. The Indians helped themselves to the stores and destroyed the barge that the construction crew used as a ferry, and before the alarm could be raised, Chilcotin Chief Klatsassin and his followers murdered more than a dozen of Waddington's men.

When word of the tragedy reached Victoria, the town was in an uproar; the residents collected arms and ammunition to outfit a Chilcotin expedition to put down the uprising. To his surprise, Tod was suddenly the centre of attention as the leading Victoria citizens, officers of the British navy stationed at Esquimalt, and even Governor Kennedy himself, sought his advice on how to deal with the Indians. "To one and all of these gentleman," Tod wrote Edward, "it seems altogether incomprehensible, how the Company's officers, in former times, always few in number ... should Yet have been able to Keep its numerous and lawless tribes of Savages in such complete subjection as they generally did."[17] What Tod failed to appreciate, however, was that this was a new era, and there was a marked difference between the way the Hudson's Bay and later colonial governments viewed the natives. For the Company, the Indians had played a necessary role in the exploitation of furs. For the later colonial governments, who were interested only in exploiting the abundant mineral, lumber, and agricultural resources of the new land, the Indians were only an obstacle.

On 15 August, after a few skirmishes, Chief Klatsassin and seven other ringleaders of the uprising surrendered to Gold Commissioner William George Cox, leader of the expedition. The terms, as Klatsassin believed, were that his life and those of his companions would be spared, but less than two months later he and five other Chilcotin prisoners felt the hangman's rope. A point frequently made by Tod was that, despite its shortcomings, the Hudson's Bay Company knew the meaning of honour. This could not be said for the later colonial administrations.

Ironically, the Bute Inlet trail, which had been the flashpoint of the conflict, was never built. Only in the minds of Victoria merchants, who were desperate to retain control of inland commerce, had it been a practical alternative to the Fraser Canyon route. In the end, the dense rainforest closed in to erase all traces of Waddington's folly.

* * * * *

As Tod approached his 70th birthday in October 1864, his family included eight grandchildren — Emma and James each had four children. The passing of the years had increased his worry over the relatives still living on his land in St. Thomas. Brothers James and Sym, as well as his two unmarried sisters, would have no legal right to their houses or land following his death. He had given them accommodation and the use of the land, but had no confidence that the arrangement would be continued by his heirs. To remedy the matter he had written his brothers requesting a full legal description of his property. Not surprisingly, the brothers seem to have viewed Tod's request with suspicion, and when he received no word from St. Thomas, he sent a letter to Edward asking that he stress the importance of the information. Tod made his fears concerning their fate clear:

John Tod in old age. This newspaper photograph was probably taken when he was young, and retouched to make him look older. (COURTESY BCARS, HP3762)

My object in making the request is, that, having made up my mind to let them both have a life interest in the property, I mean to insert a clause to that effect in my will ... otherwise my daughter, Mrs. Newton, after I'm dead and gone, may possibly attempt to litigate the affair, and give them both [James and Sym] some trouble, which, if possible, I would avoid. Her ardent and dominant spirit joined to selfish ambition, will never allow her to rest satisfied with anything less than the lions share of this worlds goods.[18]

Tod's practice of referring to Emma as "Mrs. Newton" underlined the alienation between father and daughter. This stood in contrast to his love for his second daughter, Mary, on whom he had come to depend. Before her marriage she had taken her father's dictation to relieve his shaky hand, but now he had to manage as best he could by himself. Her departure was a loss he keenly felt.

By 1865, the heady days of the gold rush were over, and the residents of Vancouver Island and the mainland faced a severe economic depression. Making the situation worse, falling revenues combined with the heavy debt of road construction to the gold fields brought the mainland colony perilously close to bankruptcy. To decrease administrative costs as well as increase the colonial tax base, the two colonies were united in the summer of 1866 under mainland Governor Seymour. Neither colony welcomed the union. The mainlanders saw Vancouver Island as nothing more than a drain on their own resource-rich economy, while the residents of Victoria and the coal-mining community of Nanaimo farther up island, wished no part of the mainland's heavier debt load. In a letter to Edward that December, Tod expressed feelings of frustration and anger:

Affairs here appear to be growing worse every day. The Colonial office, so noted for its official blunders ... has lately deprived V[ancouver] I[sland] of its popular institutions, and imposed on its inhabitants a form of Gov[ernmen]t than which nothing could be more unjust or oppressive. Taxation is ruinously extravagant, and altogether unconstitutionally imposed, and the people, in consequence flying from the country as fast as the Steamers can take them.[19]

The surface gold that could be worked easily by independent miners had been all but exhausted. It was now time for large mining syndicates that could afford the expensive mining equipment to obtain the precious mineral locked deep below the surface. Such techniques required little labour, and the size of the interior gold camps shrank. With less demand for their goods, Victoria merchants fell increasingly on hard times. Like the island city, New Westminster experienced a considerable loss of population, but adding to the latter's difficulties, Governor Seymour in 1867 had chosen Victoria as the capital of the united colony.

Although he continually grumbled about the high cost of goods, exorbitant taxes, and the incompetence of Governor Seymour, Tod did not regret settling on Vancouver Island. "If, as it has been said of the ancient Greeks," he had written in 1865, "that the natural beauties of their country had a tendency to develop their ideal faculties; then it follows that our descendents [sic] in the next generation or so, ought to be a nation of poets."[20]

In 1865, Tod wrote Edward that he had taken a leisurely tour along some of the new British Columbia highways leading inland, but an accident on a road more familiar was almost his undoing. The day after his return home, he was in a wagon driven by a local resident, a young man much addicted to speed. When the vehicle hit a rock on the road, it suddenly overturned. Although his companion landed on the road unhurt, Tod was thrown about ten feet into a small gully, injuring his right shoulder, neck, and head. He was in much pain, but the old man stubbornly refused to see a doctor, instead treating himself with cold compresses made from well water. Given his age, it was not surprising that his recovery was slow — even five months later he had not fully healed — but the years he had spent in Indian country had toughened Tod's spare body.

In the winter of 1868, James Murray Yale suffered a stroke which left him partially paralysed. The old fur trader's two daughters seemed to care little about their suffering father. "There he lays in his big house," Tod wrote Edward, "... alone without attendance of any Kind."[21] During the next few months, Tod spent much of his time at Yale's bedside where he saw to his friend's comfort. Yale's condition eventually improved, but he never recovered completely. Tod noted that he seemed to slip back into his fur-trade persona — an autocrat ruling his isolated empire with a fist of iron. Now, the boundaries of the trader's domain had shrunk to the walls of his bedroom and the orders he gave to family members were often ignored.

Although nine years younger than Tod, Sir James Douglas, too, was beginning to show the effects of advancing years. In 1870, Tod wrote Edward that "Friend Douglas has of late become very unsteady of step, shaky of the hand, and dim of eye, but as he gets older, seems more and more engrossed with the affairs of this world notwithstanding his ample means, he is as eager and grasping after money as ever, and am told, at times Seized with gloomy apprehensions of dying a beggar at last."[22]

Tod, though, remained remarkably healthy. The tremors which made writing difficult continued to bother him, as did the common aches and pains of old age, but considering his years such complaints could only be regarded as minor. For everyone interested in the secret of his robustness, Tod readily offered his prescription: "light food and little of it."[23]

In the late summer of 1868 when he was 73, Tod was well enough to undertake a rigorous tour along the Cariboo Road. What he found greatly surprised him, and on his return he wrote Edward:

You could hardly fail being astonished, I should think, were You to witness the changes together with the numerous substantial improvements, the lapse of a few years has wrought on the face of that recently rugged and inhospitable Country. All along the banks of the Fraser may now be Seen, in striking contrast to that of former times, thriving little villages, well stocked farms, tastefully ornamented cottages, inhabited generally, by a young, hardy and interprising [sic] race.[24]

Many of the settlers living in the Cariboo were the mixed-blood children of Hudson's Bay men and Indian women, a people whom Tod believed would eventually completely displace the existing native cultures.

Although most of the Europeans who had come in search of gold had left, a few remained in 1869 to wrest a living in a depressed economy. To stay in British Columbia, however, required an abiding faith in the future, for the present was difficult. Tod, like many other residents of the colony, was dissatisfied with the colonial administration — the debt load for roads to the gold fields had to be borne by a shrinking tax base. As far as the Colonial Office was concerned, British Columbia had become a burden on Britain. The obvious alternative to the situation was union with the new nation of Canada, but as Tod observed in December 1869, "the most influential portion of the Community are decidedly against it."[25]

The sudden death of Governor Seymour earlier that year had allowed the British government to appoint a successor with strong Confederation sentiments. He was Anthony Musgrave, the former governor of Newfoundland, who set about stitching British Columbia to the Canadian quilt. In the summer of 1870, B. C. sent a three-member delegation to Ottawa to discuss Confederation with the Canadian government. Although the retirement of the huge colonial debt ranked high in the minds of the delegates, the construction of an intercontinental railway across the new nation was the primary demand. To the surprise of the three British Columbians, the Canadians readily acceded to their terms. The agreement did much to change the minds of many of those who opposed Confederation, so that by February 1871, Tod could write:

Affairs here begin to brighten and in fact have already assumed a much more cheerful aspect than these many Years past. An act passed the Legislative Council a short time ago in favour of Union with the Dominion Gov[ernmen]t of Canada & Confederation is now looked forward to as the grand panacea for all the evils we have been heir to for some time past.[26]

Tod personally favoured Confederation, for the only viable alternative was annexation by the United States, a course unacceptable to him. Despite his liking for his American son-in-law, John Bowker, Tod's distrust of the nation to the south was ingrained.

On 20 July 1871, British Columbia shed its status as a British colony and became the sixth province in the Dominion of Canada. It had been almost 50 years since Tod had first crossed the Rocky Mountains with Chief Factor John Stuart. The great Hudson's Bay empire of which he had been a part was now no more than a ghost of its glorious past. In 1869, the Company's historic rights to Rupert's Land had been surrendered to the Canadian government for £300,000. While the Company retained its fur-trade concessions within the territory, it was subject to the laws of Canada. In the west, the Hudson's Bay was now no longer master of its domain.

* * * * *

In the spring of 1871, James Murray Yale suffered another stroke. Already weakened, the old man hung on until 7 May, when he died quietly. Soon after his friend's passing, Tod tried again to put his own house in order. After some haggling, Tod finally sold Sym the land he and his brother James had worked for 30 years. The remainder of Tod's St. Thomas property — the lot where his two unmarried sisters lived — was sold to Edward, but with the provision that Mary and Margaret have life tenancy to the house, use of their small garden plot, and pasture for a cow, as well as a small cash allowance. James, who was now finally married and had taken a house in St. Thomas, received payment from Sym for his share of the property. For Tod, the terms of the deal were important; he did not wish to incur the animosity of his relatives, but neither could he bring himself to present the land as a gift. Why Edward had become a principal in what was essentially a family arrangement is not clear, but the sale of the house and land meant that the original Tod farm was now legally subdivided. Sym's holding was one of the smallest farms in the area. Still, after years of uncertain tenancy, legal possession of the land he farmed must have been satisfying.

With the conclusion of the deal, family ties were not enough for Tod to maintain contact with his St. Thomas relatives. The news contained in the letters from his brothers and sisters seemed trifling and inconsequential, and he found it increasingly difficult to find the energy to answer them. Even letters between Tod and Edward had become infrequent until, in 1874, they stopped altogether.

By October 1874, when Tod celebrated his 80th birthday, he was suffering the results of advancing years. The previous year he had had a severe attack of what was probably kidney stones, and although he eventually recovered, he spent months in agony. The frailty of his body only contributed to his feeling of isolation from the world around him. The men who had shared the hardships of the trade west of the Rockies were almost all gone and the deaths of Edward in 1876 and James Douglas the following year broke his last solid link with his Hudson's Bay past. Of his generation of fur-trade officers, John Tod was the last survivor.

As a living artifact of early British Columbia history, Tod enjoyed a special status within his community. On Sunday afternoons, young people from town would often ride to the Tod farm where the old man would entertain them with stories of his adventures in the west. For the benefit of this attentive audience, he frequently exaggerated his exploits. In one case — an often-told Fort Kamloops story — he claimed to have forced Chief Nicola and his band of warriors to back down by threatening to blow up the Indians, as well as himself, with a keg of gunpowder he held in front of him. The bluff worked, and the chief backed down. The truth was something else, though, for Tod appears to have borrowed the tale from trader Archibald McKinlay, who had been in command of Fort Nez Percés.

When historian Hubert Howe Bancroft visited Victoria in 1878, he was clearly entertained by Tod the showman, but that same year, when the old man came to write down his adventures for the historian, the accounts he included were less fanciful. While Tod liked to tell a good story, he was also reluctant to claim these varnished truths as history. He did include what was probably his best-known story, the Fort Kamloops gunpowder incident, perhaps because for the proud old trader to admit the tale was a fabrication would have been to lose face, and Tod did not like to acknowledge his shortcomings.

On 27 April 1881, Tod and Sophia faced the loss of their son, William. The cause of death is not certain, although William had been sick for some time. For Tod in the twilight of his life, William's death must have seemed doubly tragic, for his son was not yet 30 years old. The funeral was held at Tod's house, with the coffin adorned with garlands of spring flowers. William's school friends, mostly the sons of Hudson's Bay officers, acted as pallbearers, and friends and neighbours came to offer sympathy to Tod and Sophia.

The following year, Tod had a new will prepared by his lawyer, Thornton Fell. It dispersed his property among Sophia and his surviving children. Mary received most of her father's assets with instructions to care for Sophia, while the other children and grandchildren received smaller cash amounts. Of his St. Thomas relatives, only his niece Jane, the daughter of his sister, Elizabeth Todd Anderson (who now lived in Victoria), was mentioned. One of the greatest beneficiaries of the will was Tod's youngest daughter Elizabeth, who had married a Victoria stove dealer, James Smith Drummond, several years earlier. For whatever reason, Tod had taken a violent dislike to his son-in-law, and to prevent Drummond from appropriating the money, he put Elizabeth's share of his estate in trust, with the interest to be paid to his daughter alone. If she predeceased her husband, Tod directed that the money should be held in trust for her children. For good measure, Tod inserted a clause in his will that all bequests to his daughters, "be for their respective use independently of their respective present or future husbands."[27]

Emma, whose first husband had died and who was now in a second marriage, received no bequest, but her four daughters by Newton were given $500 each. Tod may have believed this fair, since Emma had had the benefit of a good education at his expense, but it seems likely that she would not have been pleased. Also absent from the list of beneficiaries was his son James who was prosperous in his own right.

Not surprisingly, since Tod eschewed the pomp and splendour of orthodox Christian rituals, he directed that, "my body be buried wherever I happen to die and that my funeral be as simple and inexpensive as possible, and further that no clergyman or minister of any religious denomination shall read or hold any of their forms of burial service over my remains."[28]

Death, the result of prostate cancer that had spread to his bladder, finally came on Thursday afternoon, 31 August 1882, less than two months before his 88th birthday. In the end, Tod's final wishes were all but ignored. On 3 September, his body was taken from St. Joseph's Hospital to the home of his despised son-in-law, James Smith Drummond, on Rae Street where a funeral was conducted by a Methodist minister, R. H. Smith. Curiously, during the service the minister acknowledged Tod's unusual religious views — notions that had long placed the old man at odds with the established churches — as a mere peccadillo. Tod, who had worn his nonconformity as a badge of pride, would not have been pleased with his religious rehabilitation after death.

That Tod had been one of Victoria's most prominent citizens was not forgotten. Among the pallbearers were Chief Factor Roderick Finlayson, who had recently served as mayor of Victoria, and Chief Justice Sir Matthew Baillie Begbie. At two PM, Tod's body began its short journey from Rae Street to the Ross Bay Cemetery. The procession was large, for during his more than 30 years in Victoria, the old man had made many friends. Twenty-eight buggies adorned in black crepe fell into solemn procession behind the hearse.

* * * * *

Sophia and many of her children did not long survive Tod. She died on 9 September 1883, a year after her husband. Elizabeth, Tod's youngest daughter died in 1884, victim of a particularly virulent form of consumption. She was only in her mid-30s. Because of the provisions in Tod's will, Elizabeth's inheritance was held in trust for her only child. In 1889, Alexander, who also contracted consumption, followed his brother and sister to an early grave. Mary Tod Bowker, Tod's oldest daughter by Sophia, lived beyond her 70th year, passing away in California shortly before the beginning of the First World War.

Emma and James, the children of earlier marriages, were both long lived. Emma died in 1928 at 92 years of age, while 86-year-old James succumbed in 1904. Even in death, the slow, plodding James was overpowered by his famed parent. Almost half the obituary that appeared in the Victoria *Daily Colonist* was devoted not to James, but to the exploits of his father.

In the late 1880s, much of Tod's original Oak Bay estate was subdivided, and in the early 1890s, Tod House became the residence of Fred Pauline, a sitting member of the provincial legislature.

In keeping with his final request, no headstone was erected above Tod's grave. He is recalled, though, by a number of British Columbia place names, including Tod Inlet, on the west side of the Saanich Peninsula. Probably the most appropriate monument to him is Mount Tod, a rugged peak rising a few miles northeast of the city of Kamloops. It is not difficult to imagine it as the embodiment of the old trader himself, standing a little apart from his comrades and looking ever northward toward that inhospitable stepmother, New Caledonia.

Tod House, a watercolour painting by L. Lebrun, 1915. (COURTESY BCARS, PDP02736)

ENDNOTES

INTRODUCTION

1. Gilbert Malcolm Sproat, "Career of a Scotch Boy," ed. Madge Wolfenden, *British Columbia Historical Quarterly* 18, nos. 3 and 4 (1954), p. 134.
2. Hubert Howe Bancroft, *The History of British Columbia, 1792-1887*, vol. 32, The Works of Hubert Howe Bancroft (San Francisco, 1887), p. 139.
3. Thomas Douglas (Earl of Selkirk), *Observations on the Present State of the Highlands of Scotland with a View to the Consequences of Emigration* (1805; New York: Johnson Reprint), p. 8.
4. Chester Martin, Introduction to George Simpson, *Journal of the Occurrences in the Athabasca Department by George Simpson, 1820, and 1821, and Report*, ed. E. E. Rich (Toronto: Champlain Society, 1938), p. xviii.
5. E. E. Rich, *The Fur Traders and the Northwest to 1857* (Toronto: McLelland and Stewart, 1967), pp. 233-34.

CHAPTER ONE
THE NE'ER-DAE-WELL IS BACK

1. Cited in James Scotland, *The History of Scottish Education*, vol. 2 (London: University of London Press, 1969), p. 174.
2. Angus MacVicar, *Salt in My Porridge* (Glasgow: Fontana/Collins, 1971), p. 12.

3. Gilbert Malcolm Sproat, "Career of a Scotch Boy," ed. Madge Wolfenden, *British Columbia Historical Quarterly* 18, nos. 3 and 4 (1954), p. 136.
4. *Ibid.*
5. Arthur S. Morton, *A History of the Canadian West to 1870-71*, 2nd ed., ed. Lewis G. Thomas (1939; Toronto: University of Toronto Press, 1973), p. 540.
6. John Tod, History of New Caledonia and the Northwest Coast by John Tod, 1878, National Archives of Canada, Ottawa, p. 1.
7. Colin Robertson, Letter to Selkirk, 1 January 1817, Selkirk Papers, p. 3037.
8. James Swain, Sr., report on the death of James Wilson dated 23 April 1812, B239/b/82 fo. 33d, Hudson's Bay Company Archives, Provincial Archives of Manitoba, Winnipeg.
9. John Tod, History of New Caledonia, p. 39.
10. Francis Ermatinger, "Letter to Edward Ermatinger," 22 July 1823, letter 1 of *Fur Trade Letters of Francis Ermatinger*, ed. Lois Halliday McDonald (Glendale, California: Arthur H. Clark, 1980), p. 49.

CHAPTER TWO
THE HEROES OF THE OPPOSITION

1. Hubert Howe Bancroft, *The History of the Northwest Coast, 1800-1846*, vol. 2 (San Francisco, 1884), p. 139.
2. John Tod, History of New Caledonia and the Northwest Coast by John Tod, 1878, National Archives of Canada, Ottawa, p. 26.
3. *Ibid.*
4. *Ibid.*, p. 27.
5. *Ibid.*
6. *Ibid.*, p. 30.
7. *Ibid.*, pp. 28-29.
8. *Ibid.*, p. 29.

CHAPTER THREE
THE VOYAGE WAS A TERRIBLE ONE

1. John McLean, *Notes of a Twenty-five Year Service in the Hudson's Bay Territory*, ed. W. S. Wallace (Toronto: Champlain Society, 1932), p. 389.
2. Gilbert Malcolm Sproat, "Career of a Scotch Boy," ed. Madge Wolfenden, *British Columbia Historical Quarterly* 18, nos. 3 and 4 (1954), p. 158.
3. John Tod, History of New Caledonia and the Northwest Coast by John Tod, 1878, National Archives of Canada, Ottawa, p. 41.
4. George Simpson, "The Character Book of George Simpson," *Hudson's Bay Miscellany, 1670-1870*, (Winnipeg: Hudson's Bay Record Society, 1975), p. 230.

5. *Ibid.*
6. John Tod, letter to Edward Ermatinger, 27 February 1826, Ermatinger Papers, British Columbia Archives and Records Service, Victoria.
7. George Simpson, "To A. Colvile," 8 September 1823, *Fur Trade and Empire: George Simpson's Journal*, ed. Frederick Merk (Cambridge: Harvard University, 1931), Appendix A, p. 203.
8. John Tod, History of New Caledonia, p. 41.
9. McLeod Lake Post Journal, 16 August 1823, Hudson's Bay Archives, B. 119/a/1.
10. *Ibid.*, 3 September 1823.
11. *Ibid.*, 30 September 1823.
12. *Ibid.*, 14 October 1823.
13. *Ibid.*, 24 October 1823.
14. *Ibid.*, 26 October 1823.

CHAPTER FOUR
THAT INHOSPITABLE STEPMOTHER, NEW CALEDONIA

1. John Tod, History of New Caledonia and the Northwest Coast by John Tod, 1878, National Archives of Canada, Ottawa, p. 16.
2. *Ibid.*, p. 19.
3. John Stuart, letter to the Governor and chief factors, 30 October 1823, letter 7 of Fort McLeod Correspondence Book, B.119/b/1, Hudson's Bay Company Archives, Provincial Archives of Manitoba, Winnipeg.
4. John Stuart, letter to John Tod, 16 February 1824, letter 125 of Fort McLeod Correspondence Book, B.119/b/1, Hudson's Bay Company Archives, Provincial Archives of Manitoba, Winnipeg.
5. *Ibid.*
6. John Tod, letter to John Stuart, 1 March 1824, letter 126 of Fort McLeod Correspondence Book, B.119/b/1, Hudson's Bay Company Archives, Provincial Archives of Manitoba, Winnipeg.
7. John Tod, letter to John Stuart, 24 April 1824, letter 127 of Fort McLeod Correspondence Book, B.119/b/1, Hudson's Bay Company Archives, Provincial Archives of Manitoba, Winnipeg.
8. John Stuart, letter to John Tod, 25 April 1824, letter 128 of Fort McLeod Correspondence Book, B.119/b/1, Hudson's Bay Company Archives, Provincial Archives of Manitoba, Winnipeg.
9. *Ibid.*
10. John McLean, *Notes of a Twenty-five Year Service in the Hudson's Bay Territory*, ed. W. S. Wallace (Toronto: Champlain Society, 1932), p. 144.
11. George Simpson, *Part of a Dispatch from George Simpson Esq. Governor of Rupert's Land to the Governor and Committee of the Hudson's Bay Company, London*, ed. E. E. Rich (Toronto: Champlain Society, 1947), p. 17.
12. William McGillivray, "Report of Fort Alexandria Western Caledonia Columbia District Outfit 1827," in Simpson, *Part of a Dispatch*, Appendix A, p. 210.

13. *Ibid.*
14. John Tod, History of New Caledonia and the Northwest Coast by John Tod, 1878, National Archives of Canada, Ottawa, pp. 29-30.
15. Cited in A. G. Morice, *The History of the Northern Interior of British Columbia* (1904; Smithers B. C.: Interior Stationery, 1978), p. 178.
16. John Tod, letter to Edward Ermatinger, 27 February 1826, Ermatinger Papers, British Columbia Archives and Records Service, Victoria.
17. *Ibid.*
18. John Tod, letter to Edward Ermatinger, 27 February 1826, Ermatinger Papers.
19. John Tod, letter to Edward Ermatinger, 14 February 1829, Ermatinger Papers.
20. Simpson, p. 16.
21. John Tod, letter to Edward Ermatinger, 27 February 1826, Ermatinger Papers.
22. *Ibid.*
23. *Minutes of Council Northern Department of Rupert Land, 1821-32*, ed. R. Harvey Fleming (Toronto: Champlain Society, 1940), p. 107.
24. Quoted in Simpson, p. 27n.
25. *Ibid*, p. 18.
26. John Tod, letter to Edward Ermatinger, 16 February 1829, Ermatinger Papers.
27. John Tod, letter to Edward Ermatinger, 10 April 1831, Ermatinger Papers.
28. Archibald McDonald, *Peace River: A Canoe Voyage from Hudson's Bay to the Pacific*, ed. Malcolm McLeod (1971; Edmonton: Hurtig), pp. 24-25.
29. *Ibid.*, p. 27.
30. *Ibid.*, p. 28.
31. Cited in B.A. McKelvie, *Tales of Conflict* (Vancouver: The Daily Province Press, 1949), p. 30.
32. William Connolly, "To George Simpson Esqr.," 27 February 1829 in Simpson, *Part of a Dispatch*, Appendix A, pp. 243-44.
33. Cited in A. G. Morice, *The History of the Northern Interior of British Columbia*, p. 118. Morice incorrectly attributes the source of the quote to Hudson's Bay trader William Todd.
34. John Tod, letter to Edward Ermatinger, 14 February 1829, Ermatinger Papers.
35. John Tod, letter to Edward Ermatinger, 18 February 1830, Ermatinger Papers.

CHAPTER FIVE
JUST CAUSE TO COMPLAIN

1. John Tod, letter to Edward Ermatinger, 14 February 1829, Ermatinger Papers, British Columbia Archives and Records Service, Victoria.

2. Francis Ermatinger, "Letter to Edward Ermatinger," 16 February 1831, letter 15 of *Fur Trade Letters of Francis Ermatinger*, ed. Lois Halliday McDonald (Glendale, California: Arthur H. Clark, 1980), p. 81.
3. John Tod, letter to Edward Ermatinger, 16 February 1829, Ermatinger Papers.
4. John Tod, History of New Caledonia and the Northwest Coast by John Tod, 1878, National Archives of Canada, Ottawa, p. 52.
5. *Ibid.*, pp. 23-24.
6. John Tod, letter to Edward Ermatinger, 18 February 1830, Ermatinger Papers.
7. *Ibid.*
8. *Ibid.*
9. John Tod, letter to Edward Ermatinger, 10 April 1831, Ermatinger Papers.
10. *Ibid.*, p. 46.
11. John Tod, letter to Edward Ermatinger, 27 February 1826, Ermatinger Papers.
12. John Tod, History of New Caledonia, p. 48.
13. *Ibid.*
14. *Ibid.*, 49.
15. John Tod, letter to Edward Ermatinger, 18 February 1830, Ermatinger Papers.
16. John Tod, letter to Edward Ermatinger, 10 April 1831, Ermatinger Papers.
17. *Ibid.*
18. Edward Ermatinger, Journal of Travels in Upper Canada, 1830, National Archives of Canada, MG 19 A2.
19. John Tod, letter to Edward Ermatinger, 10 April 1831, Ermatinger Papers.
20. Francis Ermatinger, "Letter to Edward Ermatinger," 24 March 1832, letter 17 of *Fur Trade Letters of Francis Ermatinger*, p. 157.
21. *Ibid.*, p. 160.
22. Cited in McDonald ed., *Fur Trade Letters*, p. 128-29.
23. John Tod, letter to Edward Ermatinger, 23 August 1832, Ermatinger Papers.
24. George Simpson, "The Character Book of George Simpson," *Hudson's Bay Miscellany, 1670-1870* (Winnipeg: Hudson's Bay Record Society, 1975), pp. 229-30.
25. John Tod, letter to Edward Ermatinger, 23 August 1832, Ermatinger Papers.

CHAPTER SIX
SHE IS SUBJECT TO A MENTAL AFFLICTION

1. Cited in Alexander Simpson, *The Life and Times of Thomas Simpson* (London, 1845), p. 83.

2. Francis Ermatinger, "Letter to Edward Ermatinger," 16 February 1831, letter 15 of *Fur Trade Letters of Francis Ermatinger*, ed. Lois Halliday McDonald (Glendale, California: Arthur H. Clark, 1980), p. 137.

3. John McLoughlin, "To George Simpson Esqr.," 16 March 1831, in *The Letters of John McLoughlin from Fort Vancouver to the Governor and Committee, 1825-38*, ed. E. E. Rich (Toronto: Champlain Society, 1941), Appendix A, p. 227.

4. John Tod, letter to Edward Ermatinger, 10 April 1831, Ermatinger Papers, British Columbia Archives and Records Service, Victoria.

5. *Ibid.*

6. George Simpson, letter to John Tod, 4 June 1835, Provincial Archives of Manitoba, Winnipeg.

7. Members of the Northern Council, letter to the Governor and Committee, June 18, 1835, Provincial Archives of Manitoba, Winnipeg, enclosure.

8. George Simpson, letter to John Tod, 12 July 1837, Provincial Archives of Manitoba, Winnipeg.

9. John Tod, letter to Edward Ermatinger, 29 June 1836, Ermatinger Papers.

10. *Ibid.*

11. William Sinclair, letter to Edward Ermatinger, 1 August 1835, Ermatinger Papers.

12. John Tod, letter to Edward Ermatinger, 29 June 1836, Ermatinger Papers.

13. Cited in George Bryce, *MacKenzie, Selkirk, Simpson* (Toronto, 1910), pp. 268-69.

14. John Tod, letter to Edward Ermatinger, 15 July 1837, Ermatinger Papers.

15. John Tod, History of New Caledonia and the Northwest Coast by John Tod, 1878, National Archives of Canada, Ottawa, p. 33.

16. John Tod, will filed with the Hudson's Bay Company, 27 November 1837, Provincial Archives of Manitoba, Winnipeg.

CHAPTER SEVEN
ONE OF THE MOST APPALLING CALAMITIES

1. John Tod, letter to Edward Ermatinger, 12 July 1838, Ermatinger Papers, British Columbia Archives and Records Service, Victoria.

2. Francis Ermatinger, "Letter to Edward Ermatinger," 11 March 1836, letter 21 of *Fur Trade Letters of Francis Ermatinger*, ed. Lois Halliday McDonald (Glendale, California: Arthur H. Clark, 1980), p. 186.

3. John Tod, letter to Edward Ermatinger, 24 April 1838, Ermatinger Papers.

4. *Ibid.*

5. John Tod, letter to Edward Ermatinger, 12 July 1838, Ermatinger Papers.

6. Carl Landerholm, ed. *Notices and Voyages of the Famed Quebec Mission to the Pacific Northwest* (Portland: Oregon Historical Society, 1956), pp. 3-4.

7. George Simpson, *Fur Trade and Empire: George Simpson's Journal, 1824-25*, ed. Frederick Merk (Cambridge: Harvard University Press, 1931), p. 34.

8. Archibald McDonald, letter to Edward Ermatinger, 1 Februrary 1839, Ermatinger Papers.

9. John Tod, letter to Edward Ermatinger, 28 February 1838, Ermatinger Papers, BCARS. Tod's notation of this date appears to be in error. It makes sense if it were written as 28 February 1839.

10. John Tod, letter to Edward Ermatinger, 1 March 1841, Ermatinger Papers.

11. Quoted in James Robert Anderson, Notes and Comments on Early Days and Events in British Columbia, Washington and Oregon, 1925, BCARS, Victoria, p. 163.

12. John Tod, letter to Edward Ermatinger, 28 February 1838, Ermatinger Papers. Tod's notation of this date appears to be in error. It makes sense if it were written as 28 February 1839.

13. James Douglas, "To the Governor, Deputy Governor and Commitee," 18 July 1838, in *The Letters of John McLoughlin from Fort Vancouver to the Governor and Committee, 1825-1838*, ed. E. E. Rich (Toronto: Champlain Society, 1941), Appendix A, p. 264-65.

14. James Douglas, "To the Governor, Deputy Governor and Committee," 14 October 1839, in *The Letters of John McLoughlin from Fort Vancouver to the Governor and Committee, 1839-44*, ed. E. E. Rich (Toronto: Champlain Society, 1943), Appendix A, p. 221.

15. *Ibid*, p. 231.

16. John Tod, letter to Edward Ermatinger, February 1840, Ermatinger Papers.

17. *Ibid*.

18. John Tod, letter to Edward Ermatinger, 1 March 1841, Ermatinger Papers.

19. John Tod, letter to Edward Ermatinger, 19 May 1838, Ermatinger Papers.

20. Letitia Waugh, letter to the Governor and Committee, 24 February 1838, Provincial Archives of Manitoba, Winnipeg.

21. John Tod, "To James Hargrave," 15 March 1843, letter 163 of *The Hargrave Correspondence*, 1821-1843 ed. G. P. de T. Glazebrook (Toronto: Champlain Society, 1938), p. 372.

22. John Tod, letter to Donald Ross, 10 February 1840, Donald Ross Papers, BCARS, Victoria.

23. John Tod, History of New Caledonia, p. 6.

24. Landerholm, *Notices and Voyages of the Famed Quebec Mission*, p. 18.

25. John Work, letter to Edward Ermatinger, 15 February 1841,

Ermatinger Papers, BCARS.
26. John Tod, letter to Edward Ermatinger, February 1840, Ermatinger Papers.
27. *Ibid.*

CHAPTER EIGHT
HE MERITED DEATH AT OUR HANDS

1. John Tod, letter to Edward Ermatinger, February 1840, Ermatinger Papers, British Columbia Archives and Records Service, Victoria.
2. John Tod, letter to Edward Ermatinger, 1 March 1841, Ermatinger Papers.
3. *Ibid.*
4. *Ibid.*
5. John Tod, History of New Caledonia and the Northwest Coast by John Tod, 1878, National Archives of Canada, Ottawa, p. 10.
6. Fort Thompson Journal, 12 August 1841, BCARS, Victoria.
7. *Ibid.*, 19 August 1841.
8. *Ibid.*, 27 August 1841.
9. *Ibid.*, 6 September 1841.
10. *Ibid.*, 10 September 1841.
11. *Ibid.*, 9 September 1841.
12. *Ibid.*, 12 September 1841.
13. *Ibid.*, 22 September 1841.
14. *Ibid.*, 5 October 1841.
15. Cited in Samuel Black, *Black's Rocky Mountain Journal, 1824* (London: Hudson's Bay Record Society, 1955), Appendix, p. 232.

CHAPTER NINE
I DO NOT WISH TO INCUR THEIR CONTEMPT

1. John Tod, "To James Hargrave," March 1842, letter 143 of *The Hargrave Correspondence, 1821-1843,* ed. G. P. de T. Glazebrook (Toronto: Champlain Society, 1938), p. 372.
2. John Tod, letter to Edward Ermatinger, 1 March 1841, Ermatinger Papers, British Columbia Archives and Records Service, Victoria.
3. John Tod, letter to Edward Ermatinger, 10 March 1842, Ermatinger Papers.
4. *Ibid.*
5. John Tod, letter to Edward Ermatinger, 1 March 1841, Ermatinger Papers.
6. John Tod, letter to Edward Ermatinger, 10 March 1845, Ermatinger Papers.
7. John Tod, "To James Hargrave," March 1842, letter 143 of *The Hargrave Correspondence*, p. 371.

8. John Tod, letter to Edward Ermatinger, 10 March 1842, Ermatinger Papers.

9. *Ibid.*

10. *Ibid.*

11. George Simpson, "To the Governor, Deputy Governor and Committee," 5 January 1843 in *The Letters of John McLoughlin from Fort Vancouver to the Governor and Committee, 1839-44*, ed. E. E. Rich (Toronto: Champlain Society, 1943), Appendix A, pp. 351-52.

12. Fort Thompson Journal, 13 August 1842, BCARS, Victoria.

13. John Tod, letter to Edward Ermatinger, 1 September 1842, Ermatinger Papers.

14. *Ibid.*

15. *Ibid.*

16. *Ibid.*

17. John Tod, letter to George Simpson, 18 February 1842, Hudson's Bay Archives, Provincial Archives of Manitoba, Winnipeg.

18. George Simpson, letter to Benjamin Harrison, 28 June 1843, Provincial Archives of Manitoba, Winnipeg.

19. John Tod, letter to George Simpson, 20 March 1846, Hudson's Bay Archives, Provincial Archives of Manitoba, Winnipeg.

20. John Tod, letter to Edward Ermatinger, 20 March 1843, Ermatinger Papers.

21. *Ibid.*

22. *Ibid.*

23. John Tod, letter to Edward Ermatinger, 1 September 1842, Ermatinger Papers.

24. John Tod, letter to Edward Ermatinger, 20 March 1843, Ermatinger Papers.

25. John Tod, letter to Edward Ermatinger, 10 March 1845, Ermatinger Papers.

26. John Tod, letter to Edward Ermatinger, 20 March 1843, Ermatinger Papers.

27. *Ibid.*

28. *Ibid.*

29. *Ibid.*

30. John Tod, letter to Edward Ermatinger, March 1844, Ermatinger Papers.

31. Francis Ermatinger, "Letter to Edward Ermatinger," 4 April 1844, letter 35 of *Fur Trade Letters of Francis Ermatinger*, ed. Lois Halliday McDonald (Glendale, California: Arthur H. Clark, 1980), p. 262.

32. John Tod, letter to Edward Ermatinger, 21 March 1844, Ermatinger Papers.

33. *Ibid.*

34. *Ibid.*

35. *Ibid.*

36. John Tod, letter to Edward Ermatinger, March 1844, Ermatinger Papers.
37. Robert Miles, letter to Edward Ermatinger, 30 August 1844, Ermatinger Papers.
38. John Tod, letter to Edward Ermatinger, 20 March 1846, Ermatinger Papers.

CHAPTER TEN
A PERFECT EDEN

1. John Tod, History of New Caledonia and the Northwest Coast by John Tod, 1878, National Archives of Canada, Ottawa, p. 50.
2. John McLoughlin, "To the Governor, Depy. Govr. and Comittee.," 19 July 1845, in *The Letters of John McLoughlin from Fort Vancouver to the Governor and Committee, 1844-46*, ed. E. E. Rich (Toronto: Champlain Society, 1944), p. 91.
3. John Tod, History of New Caledonia, p. 62.
4. John Tod, letter to Edward Ermatinger, 10 March 1845, Ermatinger Papers, British Columbia Archives and Records Service, Victoria.
5. Cited in Samuel Black, *Black's Rocky Mountain Journal, 1824* (London: Hudson's Bay Record Society, 1955), Appendix, p. 235.
6. John Tod, History of New Caledonia, p. 49-50.
7. John Tod, letter to George Simpson, 3 March 1850, Simpson's Inward Correspondence, January-March 1850, Provincial Archives of Manitoba, Winnipeg.
8. *Ibid.*
9. *Ibid.*
10. George Simpson, letter to John Tod, 20 June 1850, Simpson's Correspondence Book, No. 14, Provincial Archives of Manitoba, Winnipeg.
11. James Douglas, letter to A. C. Anderson, March 1850, quoted in Richard Mackie, "The Colonization of Vancouver Island," *BC Studies*, 96 (winter 1992-93), p. 34.
12. James Douglas, "To James Hargrave," 15 March 1843, letter 161 of *The Hargrave Correspondence, 1821-1843*, ed. G. P. de T. Glazebrook (Toronto: Champlain Society, 1938), p. 420.
13. John Tod, letter to George Simpson, 29 January 1851, Simpson's Inward Correspondence, January-March 1851, Hudson's Bay Archives, Provincial Archives of Manitoba, Winnipeg.
14. Quoted in Corday MacKay, "Victoria's Oldest House," *The Beaver*, Summer 1948, pp. 38-39.

CHAPTER ELEVEN
MY FACE IS PAINTED

1. *Journals of the Colonial Legislature of the Colonies of Vancouver Island and British Columbia*, vol. 1, ed. James E. Hendrickson (Victoria: British Columbia Archives, 1980), p. 8.

2. James Douglas, letter to A. Barclay, 15 March 1854, British Columbia Archives and Records Service, Victoria, quoted in G. Hollis Slater, "Rev. Robert Staines: Pioneer Priest, Pedagogue and Political Agitator," *British Columbia Historical Quarterly*, vol. 14, no. 4, p. 211.
3. James Robert Anderson, Notes and Comments on Early Days and Events in British Columbia, Washington and Oregon,1925, BCARS. Typed copy of manuscript.
4. Jane Lloyd, undelivered letter to John Tod, n.d., Provincial Archives of Manitoba, Winnipeg.
5. John Tod, letter to Edward Ermatinger, 20 April 1862, Ermatinger Papers, BCARS.
6. N. de Bertrand Lugrin, *Pioneer Women of Vancouver Island, 1843-1866* (Victoria: Women's Canada Club), 1928, p.36.
7. Quoted in Anderson, *ibid.*
8. *The Illustrated Atlas and Modern History of the World* (London, 1851), p.153; rpt. as *The Illustrated Atlas of the Nineteenth Century World* (London: Bracken Books), 1989.
9. *Journals of the Colonial Legislature, ibid.*, p. 20.

CHAPTER TWELVE
DUST ALWAYS RETURNS TO DUST

1. John Tod, letter to James Murray Yale, 4 April 1861, Yale Family Manuscripts, British Columbia Archives and Records Service, Victoria.
2. John Tod, letter to Edward Ermatinger, 21 July 1861, Ermatinger Papers, BCARS.
3. *Ibid.*
4. John Tod, letter to James Murray Yale, 1 September 1861, Yale Family Manuscripts.
5. John Tod, letter to Edward Ermatinger, 4 April 1861, Ermatinger Papers.
6. John Tod, letter to Edward Ermatinger, 21 February 1864, Ermatinger Papers.
7. John Tod, letter to James Murray Yale, n.d., Yale Family Manuscripts.
8. John Tod, letter to Edward Ermatinger, 16 December 1866, Ermatinger Papers.
9. John Tod, letter to Edward Ermatinger, 20 December 1861, Ermatinger Papers.
10. John Tod, letter to Edward Ermatinger, 23 December 1861, Ermatinger Papers.
11. A. C. Anderson, The History of the Northwest Coast,1821-1836. Typed copy of manuscript. Original in the Bancroft Collection, University California, Berkeley.
12. John Tod, letter to Edward Ermatinger, 20 April 1862, Ermatinger Papers.
13. John Tod, letter to Edward Ermatinger, 18 March 1864, Ermatinger Papers.

14. John Work, letter to Edward Ermatinger, 10 January 1846, Ermatinger Papers.
15. Quoted in James Robert Anderson, Notes and Comments on Early Days and Events in British Columbia, Washington and Oregon, 1925, BCARS, Victoria, p. 163.
16. John Tod, letter to Edward Ermatinger, 22 March 1870, Ermatinger Papers.
17. John Tod, letter to Edward Ermatinger, 1 June 1864, Ermatinger Papers.
18. *Ibid.*
19. John Tod, letter to Edward Ermatinger, 16 December 1866, Ermatinger Papers.
20. John Tod, letter to Edward Ermatinger, 21 July 1865, Ermatinger Papers.
21. John Tod, letter to Edward Ermatinger, 14 January 1868, Ermatinger Papers.
22. John Tod, letter to Edward Ermatinger, 22 March 1870, Ermatinger Papers.
23. John Tod, letter to Edward Ermatinger, 1 September 1869, Ermatinger Papers.
24. John Tod, letter to Edward Ermatinger, 12 November 1868, Ermatinger Papers.
25. John Tod, letter to Edward Ermatinger, 24 December 1869, Ermatinger Papers.
26. John Tod, letter to Edward Ermatinger, 10 February 1871, Ermatinger Papers.
27. John Tod, will of 25 July 1882, BCARS. E/A/T 56.9.
28. *Ibid.*

BIBLIOGRAPHY

PRIMARY SOURCES

UNPUBLISHED

Victoria, British Columbia: British Columbia Archives and Records Service.
  A. C. Anderson Papers.
  J. R. Anderson Papers.
  Edward Ermatinger Papers.
  Donald Ross Papers.
  Journal of John McLeod, Senior Chief Trader, Hudson's Bay Company.
  Thompson River Journal, 1841-42.
  John Tod Papers.
  Yale Family Collection.
  Individual letters, reports, and related documents cited in endnotes.

Winnipeg, Manitoba: Hudson's Bay Archives, Manitoba Archives.
  Fort McLeod Correspondence Book, 1823-24.
  McLeod Lake Post Journal, 1823.
  Selkirk Papers.
  Individual letters, reports, and related documents cited in endnotes.

Ottawa, Ontario: National Archives of Canada.
  Census Records, 1871, 1881.
  Ermatinger Family Papers.
  Tod, John. History of New Caledonia and the Northwest Coast by John
    Tod, 1878. Typed copy of the ms. Original in Bancroft Library,
    University of California, Berkeley.

PUBLISHED

Newspapers:

Victoria *Daily Colonist*
Victoria *Daily Standard*
Victoria *Daily Times*
St. Thomas *Standard*

Books and Journals:

Black, Samuel. *Black's Rocky Mountain Journal, 1824.* Ed. E. E. Rich. London: Hudson's Bay Record Society, 1955.
Bowsfield, Hartwell, ed. *Fort Victoria Letters, 1846-1851.* Introduction by Margaret A. Ormsby. Winnipeg: Hudson's Bay Record Society, 1979.
Bushby, Arthur Thomas. "The Journal of Arthur Thomas Bushby, 1858-1859." Ed. D. Blakey Smith. *British Columbia Historical Quarterly* 21, nos. 1-4 (1858).
Douglas, Thomas (Earl of Selkirk). *Observations on the Present State of the Highlands of Scotland with a View to the Consequences of Emigration.* 1805; rpt. New York: Johnson Reprint, 1969.
Ermatinger, Francis. *The Fur Trade Letters of Francis Ermatinger: Written to his Brother Edward During His Service in the Hudson's Bay Company.* Ed. Lois Halliday McDonald. Glendale, California: Arthur H. Clark, 1980.
Farrar, Victor J., ed. "The Nisqually Journal." *The Washington Historical Quarterly* 10-12 (1919-1921).
Fleming, R. Harvey, ed. *Minutes of Council Northern Department of Rupert Land, 1821-32.* Introduction by H. A. Innis. London: Hudson's Bay Record Society, 1940.
Fraser, Simon. *The Letters and Journals of Simon Fraser, 1806-1808.* Ed. W. Kaye Lamb. Toronto: Macmillan, 1960.
Hargrave, James. *The Hargrave Correspondence, 1821-1843.* Ed G. P. de T. Glazebrook. Toronto: The Champlain Society, 1938.
Hargrave, Letitia. *The Letters of Letitia Hargrave.* Ed. Margaret Arnett McLeod. Toronto: The Champlain Society, 1947.
Harmon, Daniel Williams. *Sixteen Years in Indian Country: The Journal of Daniel Williams Harmon.* Ed. W. Kaye Lamb. Toronto: Macmillan, 1957.
Helmcken, John Sebastian. *Reminiscences.* Ed. D. Blakey Smith. Vancouver: University of British Columbia Press, 1975.
Hendrickson, James E., ed. *Journals of the Colonial Legislatures of the Colonies of Vancouver Island and British Columbia.* Vol. 1. Victoria: British Columbia Archives, 1980.
Landerholm, Carl, ed. *Notices and Voyages of the Famed Quebec Mission to the Pacific Northwest.* Portland: Oregon Historical Society, 1956.

McDonald, Archibald. *Peace River: A Canoe Voyage from Hudson's Bay to the Pacific by Sir George Simpson.* Ed. Malcolm McLeod, 1872; rpt. Edmonton: Hurtig, 1971.

McLean, John. *Notes of a Twenty-five Year Service in the Hudson's Bay Territory.* Ed. W. S. Wallace. Toronto: The Champlain Society, 1932.

McLoughlin, John. *Letters of Dr. John McLoughlin Written at Fort Vancouver, 1829-1832.* Ed. Burt Brown Barker. Portland: Binfords & Mort, 1948.

—————. *The Letters of John McLoughlin from Fort Vancouver to the Governor and Committee, 1825-38.* Ed. E. E. Rich. Introduction by W. Kaye Lamb. Toronto: The Champlain Society, 1941.

—————. *The Letters of John McLoughlin from Fort Vancouver to the Governor and Committee, 1839-44.* Ed. E. E. Rich. Introduction by W. Kaye Lamb. Toronto: The Champlain Society, 1943.

—————. *The Letters of John McLoughlin from Fort Vancouver to the Governor and Committee, 1844-46.* Ed. E. E. Rich. Introduction by W. Kaye Lamb. Toronto: The Champlain Society, 1944.

Melrose, Robert. "The Diary of Robert Melrose." Ed. W. Kaye Lamb. *British Columbia Historical Quarterly* 7, no. 4 (1943).

Simpson, George. *Fur Trade and Empire: George Simpson's Journal 1824-25.* Ed. Frederick Merk. Cambridge Mass.: Harvard University Press, 1931.

—————. *Part of a Dispatch from George Simpson Esq., Governor of Rupert's Land, to the Governor and Committee of the Hudson's Bay Company, London, March 1, 1829.* Ed. E. E. Rich. Introduction by Stewart Wallace. Toronto: The Champlain Society, 1947.

—————. "The Character Book of George Simpson." *Hudson's Bay Miscellany, 1670-1870.* Ed. Glyndwr Williams. Winnipeg: Hudson's Bay Record Society, 1975.

—————. *Journal of the Occurrences in the Athabasca Department by George Simpson, 1820, and 1821, and Report.* Ed. E. E. Rich. Introduction by Chester Martin. Toronto: The Champlain Society, 1938.

SECONDARY SOURCES

Akrigg, G. V. P. and Helen B. Akrigg. *British Columbia Chronicle, 1778-1846.* Vancouver: Discovery Press, 1975.

—————. *British Columbia Chronicle, 1847-1871.* Vancouver: Discovery Press, 1977.

Balf, Mary. *Kamloops: A History of the District to 1914.* Kamloops, British Columbia: Kamloops Museum, 1955.

Bancroft, Hubert Howe. *The History of British Columbia, 1792-1887.* Vol. 32. San Francisco, 1887.

—————. *The History of the Northwest Coast, 1800-1846.* Vol. 2. San Francisco, 1884.

Binns, Archie. *Peter Skene Ogden: Fur Trader*. Portland, Oregon: Binfords & Mort, 1967.

Brandon, Ruth. *The Spiritualists: The Passion for the Occult in the Nineteenth and Twentieth Centuries*. London: Weidenfeld and Nicholson, 1983.

Brown, George D. and W. Kaye Lamb. "Captain St. Paul of Kamloops." *British Columbia Historical Quarterly* 3, no. 2 (1939).

Brown, Jennifer S. H. *Strangers in Blood: Fur Trade Families in Indian Country*. Vancouver: University of British Columbia Press, 1978.

Bryce, George. *MacKenzie, Selkirk, Simpson*. Toronto, 1910.

Bumsted, J. M. *The People's Clearance: Highland Emigration to British North America*. Winnipeg: University of Manitoba Press, 1982.

Campbell, R. H. *Scotland Since 1707: The Rise of an Industrial Society*. 1965; rpt. Edinburgh: John Donald, 1985.

Chalmers, John W. *The Fur Trade Governor, 1820-1860*. Edmonton: The Institute of Applied Art, 1960.

Cole, Jean Murray. *Exiles in the Wilderness: The Biography of Chief Factor Archibald McDonald, 1790-1853*. Toronto: Burns and MacEachern, 1979.

Dee, Henry Drummond. "An Irishman in the Fur Trade." *British Columbia Historical Quarterly* 7 no. 4 (1943).

Davidson, Gordon Charles. *The North West Company*. Berkeley: University of California Press, 1918.

Decker, Jody F. "Scurvy at York." *The Beaver* (February/March, 1989).

Devine, T. M. *The Great Highland Famine: Hunger, Emigration and the Scottish Highlands in the Nineteenth Century*. Edinburgh: John Donald, 1988.

Favrholdt, Kenneth. *Kamloops: An Illustrated History*. Burlington, Ontario: Windsor Publishing, 1989.

Fisher, Robin. *Contact and Conflict: Indian-European Relations in British Columbia, 1774-1890*. Vancouver: University of British Columbia Press, 1977.

Francis, Daniel. *Battle for the West: Fur Traders and the Birth of Western Canada*. Edmonton: Hurtig, 1982.

————. *The Imaginary Indian in Canadian Culture*. Vancouver: Arsenal Pulp Press, 1992.

Galbraith, John S. "The Early History of the Puget's Sound Agricultural Company, 1838-43." *Oregon Historical Quarterly* 55 (March to December, 1954).

————. *The Hudson's Bay Company as an Imperial Factor, 1821-1869*. Toronto: University of Toronto Press, 1967.

————. "The Little Emperor." *The Beaver* (Spring, 1960).

————. *The Little Emperor: Governor Simpson of the Hudson's Bay Company*. Toronto: Macmillan, 1976.

Girard, Charlotte S. M. "Some Further Notes on the Douglas Family." *BC*

Studies, no. 72 (Winter, 1986).

Hall, David John. *Economic Development in Elgin Country, 1850-1880.* Petrolia, Ontario: Western District Publishing Company, 1972.

Hussey, John A. " 'Unpretending' but not 'Indecent': Living Quarters at Mid-19th Century Hudson's Bay Posts." *The Beaver* (Spring, 1975).

Innis, Harold A. *The Fur Trade in Canada.* 1930; revised 1956 and rpt. Toronto: University of Toronto Press, 1970.

Ireland, Willard E. "Captain Walter Colquhoun Grant: Vancouver Island's First Independent Settler." *British Columbia Historical Quarterly* 17, nos. 1 and 2 (1953).

Jenness, Diamond. *The Indians of Canada.* Seventh edition 1932; rpt. Toronto: University of Toronto, 1977.

Johnson, F. Henry. "John Tod." *The Beaver* (Spring, 1948).

Karamanski, Theodore J. *The Fur Trade and Exploration: Opening of the Far Northwest, 1821-1852.* Vancouver: University of British Columbia Press, 1983.

Leitch, John S. "Through the Canyon." *The Beaver* (Spring, 1963).

Lillard, Charles. *Seven Shillings a Year: The History of Vancouver Island.* Ganges, B. C.: Horsdal & Schubart, 1986.

Lugrin, N. de Bertrand. *Pioneer Women of Vancouver Island, 1843-1866.* Victoria: Women's Canada Club, 1928.

MacKay, Corday. "The Pacific Coast Fur Trade." *The Beaver* (Summer, 1955).

———. "Victoria's Oldest House." *The Beaver* (Summer, 1948).

MacKay, D. *The Honourable Company: A History of the Hudson's Bay Company.* Toronto: McClelland and Stewart, 1936.

Mackie, Richard. "The Colonization of Vancouver Island, 1849-1858." *BC Studies*, no. 96 (Winter, 1992)

McKelvie, B. A. "New Caledonia Conflict," *Tales of Conflict.* Vancouver: The Vancouver Daily Province Press, 1949.

McKervill, Hugh W. *The Salmon People: The Story of Canada's West Coast Salmon Industry.* Sidney, BC: Gray's Publishing, 1967.

MacVicar, Angus. *Salt in My Porridge.* Glasgow: Fontana/Collins, 1971.

Middleton, Jesse Edgar. *The Province of Ontario: A History, 1615-1927.* Vol. 3. Toronto: Dominion Publishing, 1927.

Morice, A. G. *The History of the Northern Interior of British Columbia Formerly New Caledonia.* Toronto, 1904; rpt. Smithers, B. C.: Interior Stationery, 1978.

Morton, Arthur S. *A History of the Canadian West to 1870-71.* 2nd. edition. Ed. Lewis G. Thomas. 1939; rpt. Toronto: University of Toronto Press, 1973.

———. *Sir George Simpson: Overseas Governor of the Hudson's Bay Company, a Pen Picture of a Man of Action.* Portland: Oregon Historical Society, 1944.

Murray, Keith A. "The Role of the Hudson's Bay Company in Pacific

Northwest History." *Pacific Northwest Quarterly* 52, no. 1 (1961).

Murray, Peter. *Homesteads and Snug Harbours: The Gulf Islands*. Ganges. B. C: Horsdal & Schubart, 1991.

Newman, Peter C. *Caesars of the Wilderness*. Toronto: Viking-Penguin, 1987.

Ormsby, Margaret A. *British Columbia: A History*. Toronto: Macmillan, 1958.

Patterson, R. M. "Peace River Passage." *The Beaver* (Winter, 1956).

————. "The Trail to the Big Bend." *The Beaver* (Spring, 1960).

Pethick, Derek. *James Douglas: Servant of Two Empires*. Vancouver: Mitchell Press, 1969.

————. *Victoria: The Fort*. Vancouver: Mitchell Press, 1969.

Prebble, John. *The Highland Clearances*. London: Secker and Warburg, 1963.

Reksten, Terry. *More English than the English: A Very Social History of Victoria*. Victoria: Orca, 1986.

Rich, E. E. *The Fur Traders and the Northwest to 1857*. Toronto: McLelland and Stewart, 1967.

————. "The Fur Traders, Their Diet and Drugs." *The Beaver* (Summer, 1976).

————. "The Indian Traders." *The Beaver* (Winter, 1970).

————. *The History of the Hudson's Bay Company, 1670-1870*. Vol. 2. London: Hudson's Bay Record Society, 1959.

Robertson, Colin. *Colin Robertson's Correspondence Book, September 1817 to September 1822*. Ed. E. E. Rich. Toronto: The Champlain Society, 1939.

Sage, Walter N. "New Caledonia: The Siberia of the Fur Trade." *The Beaver* (Summer, 1956).

Scotland, James. *The History of Scottish Education*. Vol. 2. London: University of London Press, 1969.

Simpson, Alexander. *The Life and Times of Thomas Simpson*. London: 1845.

Slater, G. Hollis. "Reverend Robert Staines: Pioneer Priest, Pedagogue and Political Agitator." *British Columbia Historical Quarterly* 14, no. 4 (1950).

Sproat, Gilbert M. "The Career of a Scotch Boy." Ed. Madge Wolfenden. *British Columbia Historical Quarterly* 19, nos. 3 and 4 (1954).

Spry, Irene M. "Routes Through the Rockies." *The Beaver* (Autumn, 1963).

Stark, Stuart. *Oak Bay's Heritage: More than Just Bricks and Boards*. Victoria: Heritage Trust, 1982.

Stevenson, J. A. "Disaster in the Dalles." *The Beaver* (September, 1942).

Timbs, John. *Curiosities of London: Exhibiting the Most Rare and Remarkable Objects of Interest in the Metropolis*. London: 1867.

Voorhis, Ernest, comp. *Historic Trading Posts of the French Regime and the English Trading Companies*. Ottawa: National Development Bureau, Department of the Interior, 1930.

Wheatley, H. B. *London Past and Present: A Dictionary of its History and Traditions*. London: 1891.
Woodcock, George. *British Columbia: A History of the Province*. Vancouver: Douglas & McIntyre, 1990.

MISCELLANEOUS SOURCES

British Columbia, Division of Vital Statistics, Ministry of Health, John Tod: Certificate of Death.
Old Cemetery Committee, Victoria. John Tod: Plot Registration.
Stark, Stuart. Tod House Historic Site Investigation. Unpublished report to the Heritage Conservation Branch, Ministry of Small Business, Tourism and Culture, Province of British Columbia, 25 March 1992.

INDEX